America and the World since 1945

D0282116

STUDIES IN CONTEMPORARY HISTORY

Series Editors: T. G. Fraser and J. O. Springhall

PUBLISHED

THE ARAB-ISRAELI CONFLICT
T. G. Fraser

AMERICA AND THE WORLD SINCE 1945
T. G. Fraser and Donette Murray

THE ULSTER QUESTION SINCE 1945
James Loughlin

THE RISE AND FALL OF THE SOVIET EMPIRE, SECOND EDITION
Raymond Pearson

THE CIVIL RIGHTS MOVEMENT:
Struggle and Resistance
William T. Martin Riches

THE UNITED NATIONS AND INTERNATIONAL POLITICS
Stephen Ryan

JAPAN SINCE 1945
Dennis B. Smith

EUROPEAN DECOLONIZATION SINCE 1945
John Springhall

Studies in Contemporary History
Series Standing Order
ISBN 978-0-333-71706-6 hardcover
ISBN 978-0-333-69351-3 paperback
(*outside North America only*)

You can receive future titles in this series as they are published by placing a standing order. Please contact your bookseller or, in the case of difficulty, write to us at the address below with your name and address, the title of the series and the ISBN quoted above.

Customer Services Department, Macmillan Distribution Ltd
Houndsmill, Basingstoke, Hampshire RG21 6XS, England

AMERICA AND THE WORLD
SINCE 1945

T. G. FRASER AND DONETTE MURRAY

First published 2002 by
PALGRAVE MACMILLAN
Houndmills, Basingstoke, Hampshire RG21 6XS and
175 Fifth Avenue, New York, N.Y. 10010
Companies and representatives throughout the world

PALGRAVE MACMILLAN is the global academic imprint of the Palgrave
Macmillan division of St. Martin's Press, LLC and of Palgrave Macmillan Ltd.
Macmillan® is a registered trademark in the United States, United Kingdom
and other countries. Palgrave is a registered trademark in the European
Union and other countries.

ISBN 978-0-333-75432-0   ISBN 978-1-4039-0727-1 (eBook)
DOI 10.1007/978-1-4039-0727-1

This book is printed on paper suitable for recycling and
made from fully managed and sustained forest sources.

A catalogue record for this book is available
from the British Library.

A catalogue record for this book is available
from the Library of Congress .

9   8   7   6   5   4   3   2   1
10 09 08 07 06 05 04 03 02

CONTENTS

Contents

Contents

Contents

Contents

SERIES EDITORS' PREFACE

There are those, politicians among them, who feel that historians should not teach or write about contemporary events and people – many of whom are still living – because of the difficulty of treating such matters with historical perspective, that it is right to draw some distinction between the study of history and the study of current affairs. Proponents of this view seem to be unaware of the concept of contemporary history to which this series is devoted, that the history of the recent past can and should be written with a degree of objectivity. As memories of the Second World War recede, it is surely time to place in perspective the postwar history that has shaped all our lives, whether we were born in the 1940s or the 1970s.

Many countries – Britain, the United States and Germany among them – allow access to their public records under a thirty-year rule, opening up much of the postware period to archival research. For more recent events, diaries, memoirs, and the investigations of newspapers and television, confirm the view of the famous historian Sir Lewis Namier that all secrets are in print provided you know where to look for them. Contemporary historians also have the opportunity, denied to historians of earlier periods, of interviewing participants in the events they are analysing. The problem facing the contemporary historian is, if anything, the embarrassment of riches.

In any case, the nature and extent of world changes since the late 1980s have clearly signalled the need for concise discussion of major themes in post-1945 history. For many of us the difficult thing to grasp is how dramatically the world has changed over recent years: the end of the Cold War and of Soviet hegemony over eastern Europe; the collapse of the Soviet Union and Russian communism; the unification of Germany; the peace of integration in the European Union; the disintegration of Yugoslavia; political and economic turbulence in South East Asia; communist China's reconciliation with consumer capitalism; the faltering economic progress of Japan. Writing in a structured and cogent way about these seismic changes is what makes contemporary history so challenging and we hope that the end result will convey some of this excitement and interest to our readers.

The general objective of this series, written by members of the School of History and International Affairs of the University of Ulster, is to offer concise and up-to-date treatments of postwar themes considered of historical and political significance and to stimulate critical thought about the theoretical assumptions and conceptual apparatus underlying interpretations of the topics under discussion. The series should bring some of the central themes and problems confronting students and teachers of recent history, politics, and international affairs, into sharper focus than the textbook writer alone could provide. The blend required to write contemporary history which is both readable and easily understood but also accurate and scholarly is not easy to achieve, but we hope that this series will prove worthwhile for both students and teachers interested in world affairs since 1945.

University of Ulster at Coleraine T. G. FRASER
J. O. SPRINGHALL

ACKNOWLEDGEMENTS

The authors gratefully acknowledge a number of debts they have acquired in the course of this collaboration. Alan Sharp and Keith Jeffery were unfailingly supportive at all stages of the project, as was the joint series editor, John Springhall. Colleagues in the School of History and International Affairs, Steve Ickringill, Ray Pearson and Dennis Smith, read and commented on individual chapters and answered queries on their areas of expertise. Special thanks go to our research assistant, Christer Grenabo, for his work on the Clinton administration. Gillian Coward and William Norris freely gave advice on the technical aspects. Our heartfelt thanks go to the library staff of the University of Ulster for responding to our unending requests for assistance. Terka Acton of Palgrave Macmillan waited patiently as we juggled the book against the other demands of academic life. Above all, our thanks must go to Joanne Taggart, whose patience and sharp eye for detail contributed so much to the preparation of the final text.

LIST OF ABBREVIATIONS

ABM	antiballistic missile
AEC	(USA) Atomic Energy Commission
AIPAC	American Israel Public Affairs Committee
ALCM	air-launched cruise missile
APEC	Asia-Pacific Economic Community
AWACS	Airborne Warning and Control System
CCP	Chinese Communist Party
CIA	Central Intelligence Agency
CIS	Commonwealth of Independent States
COMECON	Council for Mutual Economic Assistance
CSCE	Conference on Security and Cooperation in Europe
DefCon	Defense Condition
EDC	European Defence Community
ERP	European Recovery Program (Marshall Plan)
EU	European Union
GATT	General Agreement on Tariffs and Trade
GNP	gross national product
GOP	(USA) Grand Old Party (the Republican Party)
ICBM	intercontinental ballistic missile
IFOR	International Implementation Force
IMF	International Monetary Fund
INF	intermediate-range nuclear forces
IRBM	intermediate-range ballistic missile
KFOR	Kosovo Peacekeeping Force
KLA	Kosovo Liberation Army
KMT	Kuomintang (Chinese Nationalist Party)

List of Abbreviations

MAD	mutual assured destruction
MIRV	multiple independently targeted re-entry vehicle
MNF	most favored nation
MRBM	medium-range ballistic missile
NAFTA	North American Free Trade Agreement
NASA	National Aeronautics and Space Administration
NATO	North Atlantic Treaty Organization
NLF	National Liberation Front
NPT	Non-Proliferation Treaty
NSA	National Security Agency
NSAM	National Security Action Memo
NSC	National Security Council
OAPEC	Organization of Arab Petroleum-Exporting Countries
OAS	Organization of American States
OPEC	Organization of Petroleum-Exporting Countries
OSCE	Organization for Security and Cooperation in Europe
OSS	Office of Strategic Services
PDD	Presidential Decision Directive
PFP	Partnership for Peace
PLO	Palestine Liberation Organization
SACEUR	Supreme Allied Commander Europe
SALT	Strategic Arms Limitation Talks/Treaty
SCAP	Supreme Command(er) Allied Powers
SDI	Strategic Defense Initiative
SEATO	South-east Asia Treaty Organization
SFRC	Senate Foreign Relations Committee
SIOP	Single Integrated Operations Plan
SLBM	submarine-launched ballistic missile
START	Strategic Arms Reduction Talks/Treaty
TEA	Trade Expansion Act
TOW	tube-launched optically tracked wire-guided (anti-tank missile)

List of Abbreviations

UAR	United Arab Republic
UN	United Nations
UNEF	United Nations Emergency Force
UNSCOP	United Nations Special Committee on Palestine
USSR	Union of Soviet Socialist Republics
VC	Vietcong
WMD	weapons of mass destruction
WTO	World Trade Organization

CHRONOLOGY

1945

Yalta Conference (4–11 Feb.). Truman becomes president on death of Roosevelt (12 Apr.). Victory in Europe (8 May). Potsdam Conference (15 July–1 Aug.). Atomic bomb exploded over Hiroshima (6 Aug.). Peace with Japan (15 Aug.).

1946

Kennan's 'Long Telegram' (22 Feb.). Churchill's Fulton speech (5 Mar.).

1947

'Truman Doctrine' announced to Congress (12 Mar.). Announcement of ERP by General Marshall (6 June). Publication of 'X' article (July). Soviet rejection of Marshall Plan (2 July). National Security Act creates Department of Defense, NSC and CIA (26 July). Inter-American Treaty of Reciprocal Assistance (2 Sept.). Cominform established (Sept.). UN partition resolution on Palestine (29 Nov.).

1948

Communist takeover of Czechoslovakia (27 Feb.). Start of Berlin blockade (24 June). Yugoslavia's expulsion from Cominform (28 June).

1949

Truman inaugurated (20 Jan.). North Atlantic Treaty
signed (May). End of Berlin blockade (4 Apr.). Soviets test
atomic bomb (Sept.). People's Republic of China
proclaimed (1 Oct.).

1950

Truman authorises production of thermonuclear weapons
(31 Jan.). NSC 68 (14 Apr.). Start of Korean War (25 June).
Chinese troops attack in Korea (Nov.).

1951

San Francisco peace treaty with Japan (8 Sept.).

1953

Eisenhower inaugurated (20 Jan.). Death of Stalin (5 Mar.).
Armistice Agreement ending Korean War signed at
Panmunjon (26 July). Explosion of first Soviet hydrogen
bomb (8 Aug.). CIA-backed coup in Iran removes Prime
Minister Mossadegh (19–20 Aug.). Eisenhower's Atoms for
Peace initiative launched (8 Dec.).

1954

Policy of 'Massive Retaliation' inaugurated (15 Jan.). French
surrender at Dien Bien Phu (7 May). Senator Joseph
McCarthy makes new accusations about Communists in
government (2 June). CIA-backed coup deposes Guatemalan
President Arbenz (18 June). Geneva Accords signed in Paris
partitioning Vietnam at the 17th parallel (21 July). Collapse
of EDC Treaty (30 Aug.). Chinese shell Quemoy, launching
first Taiwan Straits crisis (3 Sept.). SEATO signed (8 Sept.).
US Senate condemns Senator McCarthy (2 Dec.).

1955

West Germany joins NATO (8 May). Formation of Warsaw Pact (14 May). Soviet and western foreign ministers sign Austrian State Treaty (15 May). Geneva summit between Eisenhower, Khrushchev, Eden and Faure (18–24 July).

1956

Nasser nationalises Suez Canal company (26 July). Israel invades Egypt; Suez Crisis begins (29 Oct.). Britain and France bomb Egypt; Eisenhower condemns Allies' actions (31 Oct.). Hungary withdraws from Warsaw Pact and declares neutrality; Soviets begin military action (1–2 Nov.). Red Army invades Budapest (4 Nov.). Eisenhower defeats Adlai Stevenson in US election; Britain and France accept ceasefire in Middle East (6 Nov.).

1957

Eisenhower doctrine for Middle East announced (5 Jan.). Soviets launch first earth-orbiting satellite, Sputnik (4 Oct.).

1958

Nuclear test-ban talks begin in Geneva and continue sporadically until 1963 (1 July). US marines sent to Lebanon to support government of President Chamoun (15 July). Second Taiwan Straits crisis (6 Aug.–6 Oct.). Moratorium on tests announced by US and USSR (31 Oct.). Berlin crisis develops as Khrushchev threatens to sign separate peace with East Germany (10 Nov.).

1959

Fidel Castro deposes Batista and takes power in Cuba (2 Jan.). John Foster Dulles resigns; dies on 24 May (15 Apr.).

1960

Gary Francis Powers shot down (1 May). Paris Summit begins (14 May). Summit abandoned (16 May). John F. Kennedy defeats Nixon in presidential election (8 Nov.). Vietnamese National Liberation Front formed (20 Dec.).

1961

Khrushchev's 'Wars of National Liberation' speech (6 Jan.). Kennedy inaugurated (20 Jan.). Peace Corps established (1 Mar.). Alliance for Progress launched (13 Mar.). Bay of Pigs invasion (17–20 Apr.). Vienna Summit (3–4 June). East German police begin closing off East Berlin (13 Aug.). Construction of Berlin Wall begins (19 Aug.).

1962

Declaration and Protocol on Neutrality in Laos signed (23 July). U-2 spy plane photographs missiles in Cuba (14 Oct.). Cuban Missile Crisis begins (16 Oct.). Khrushchev agrees to withdraw missiles in exchange for American non-invasion pledge and removal of Jupiter missiles in Turkey (28 Oct.). Cuban Missile Crisis officially over (20 Nov.). Nassau meeting between Kennedy and Macmillan; Britain gets Polaris deal to extend life of her independent nuclear deterrent force (18–21 Dec.).

1963

Kennedy's 'peace speech' given at the American University, Washington, DC (10 June). Buddhist crisis in South Vietnam (June). Kennedy's 'Ich bin ein Berliner' speech in Berlin (26 June). Partial Nuclear Test-Ban Treaty signed in Moscow (5 Aug.). President Diem assassinated (1 Nov.). Kennedy assassinated in Dallas, Texas. LBJ sworn in as 36th president of USA (22 Nov.).

1964

USS Maddox attacked in Gulf of Tonkin (2 Aug.). Alleged second attack takes place (4 Aug.). US retaliatory bombing strikes targets in North Vietnam (5 Aug.). South-east Asian (Gulf of Tonkin) Resolution passed (7 Aug.). LBJ wins landslide victory, defeating Barry Goldwater (3 Nov.).

1965

LBJ inaugurated; announces 'Great Society' for US (20 Jan.). Attack on Pleiku airbase in South Vietnam (7 Feb.). Operation Rolling Thunder begins (2 Mar.). US marines land at Da Nang (8 Mar.). Coup in Dominican Republic; Dominican crisis begins (24 Apr.). US marines arrive in Dominica (30 Apr.). LBJ announces increases of troops in Vietnam to 125,000 (28 July).

1966

SFRC hearings begin (Jan.). Pro-US General Suharto deposes Indonesian President Sukarno (11–12 Mar.).

1967

Six-Day War (5–10 June). Glassboro mini-summit between LBJ and Kosygin (23–25 June). UN passes Resolution 242 (22 Nov.).

1968

Tet offensive (30 Jan.–25 Feb.). LBJ announces intention not to seek re-election and bombing halt (31 Mar.). Martin Luther King assassinated (4 Apr.). Robert Kennedy assassinated (5 June). Non-Proliferation Treaty signed by US and USSR; SALT announced (1 July). Czechoslovakian uprising (20 Aug.). LBJ announces total bombing halt (1 Nov.).

Nixon wins presidential election, beating Hubert
Humphrey (5 Nov.). 'Brezhnev Doctrine' enunciated
(12 Nov.).

1969

Nixon inaugurated (20 Jan.). Nixon authorises secret
bombing of Cambodia (16 Mar.). Nixon informs President
Thieu of 'Vietnamisation' of the war (8 June).
Announcement of 'Nixon Doctrine' (25 July).

1970

American–South Vietnamese invasion of Cambodia
(30 Apr.–30 June).

1971

South Vietnamese invasion of Laos (8 Feb.).

1972

Nixon in China (21 Feb.). Nixon in Moscow; SALT agreements with Soviet Union signed (20 May). Watergate
burglars arrested (18 June). Bombing of Hanoi and
Haiphong (14–29 Dec.).

1973

Nixon's second inauguration (20 Jan.). Paris agreements
on ending Vietnam War (23 Jan.). Kissinger becomes
Secretary of State (22 Aug.). Egypt and Syria attack Israel
(6 Oct.). Security Council Resolution 338 on ending the
war (22 Oct.).

1974

First Sinai disengagement agreement (18 Jan.).
Israeli–Syrian disengagement agreement (31 May). Nixon

resigns; replaced by Ford (8 Aug.). Vladivostok Summit
between Ford and Brezhnev (23 Nov.).

1975

Communists capture Cambodian capital (17 Apr.). Fall of
Saigon (30 Apr.). Communists capture Laotian capital
(23 Aug.). Helsinki conference (30 July–1 Aug.). Second
Sinai disengagement agreement (1 Sept.).

1977

Carter inaugurated (20 Jan.). Panama Canal treaties
(10 Aug.).

1978

Camp David summit on Middle East (5–17 Sept.). Carter
announces normalisation of relations with China (15 Dec.).

1979

Shah of Iran goes into exile (15 Jan.). Ayatollah Khomeini
returns to Tehran (1 Feb.). Carter brokers Egyptian–Israeli
peace treaty (26 Mar.). SALT II agreement concluded at
Vienna Summit (15–18 June). Seizure of American embassy
in Tehran (4 Nov.). Soviets invade Afghanistan (27 Dec.).

1980

Failure of Iran rescue mission (24 Apr.).

1981

Reagan inaugurated (20 Jan.).

1982

Israeli invasion of Lebanon (6 June). Multinational force
deployed in Beirut (21 Aug.). Reagan peace plan for Middle

East (1 Sept.). Sabra and Shatila massacres (16 Sept.).
Reagan announces Multinational Force II (20 Sept.).

1983

Reagan's 'evil empire' speech (8 Mar.). Reagan announces
SDI (23 Mar.). Flight KAL 007 shot down (1 Sept.). Suicide
bombers attack American and French bases in Beirut (23
Oct.). American intervention in Grenada (25 Oct.).

1985

Reagan's second inauguration (20 Jan.). Gorbachev
assumes Soviet leadership (11 Mar.). Reagan–Gorbachev
summit at Geneva (19–21 Nov.).

1986

American air raids on Libya (14 Apr.). Reagan–Gorbachev
summit at Reykjavik (11–12 Oct.). Iran-Contra affair
revealed (3–25 Nov.).

1987

Reagan and Gorbachev sign INF treaty (8 Dec.).

1988

Gorbachev announces withdrawal from Afghanistan (8
Feb.). Reagan–Gorbachev summit in Moscow (29 May).

1989

Bush inaugurated (20 Jan.). Tiananmen Square massacre (3
June). Opening of Hungarian border (10 Sept.). Gorbachev
repudiates Brezhnev Doctrine (25 Oct.). Fall of Berlin Wall
(9 Nov.). American intervention in Panama (20 Dec.).

1990

Iraqi invasion of Kuwait (2 Aug.).

1991

Operation Desert Storm (24 Feb.). Unsuccessful coup
against Gorbachev (19 Aug.). Resignation of Gorbachev;
end of Soviet Union (25 Dec.).

1993

Clinton inaugurated (20 Jan.). US fires cruise missiles at
Baghdad in retaliation for alleged plot to assassinate Bush
(27 June). Oslo Accords signed in Washington (13 Sept.).
Clinton orders additional troops to Somalia after 18
soldiers die in Mogadishu (30 Oct.). Congress passes
NAFTA (20 Nov.).

1994

Clinton announces PFP (10 Jan.). Genocide begins in
Rwanda and continues until late July (7 Apr.). Clinton
warns Junta in Haiti to leave, allowing return of ousted
President Aristide (15 Sept.). North Korea and US sign
Agreed Framework requiring Pyongyang to freeze its
nuclear development programme (21 Oct.). Senate
approves sweeping global tariff-cutting trade pact, creating
WTO (1 Dec.).

1995

Clinton uses emergency authority to lend Mexico up to $20
billion to stave off imminent bankruptcy (31 Jan.). Serbs
begin to attack and ethnically cleanse UN safe haven of
Srebrenica (6 July). NATO forces begin two-week bombing
campaign – Operation Deliberate Force – against Bosnian

Serbs after the shelling of a marketplace in Sarajevo (30 Aug.). Israeli Prime Minister Rabin assassinated (4 Nov.). Dayton Accords signed by the presidents of three Balkan states, ending three years of war in Bosnia (21 Nov.).

1996

Clinton wins presidential election, beating Bob Dole (5 Nov.).

1997

Clinton's second inauguration (20 Jan.). Russian–NATO Founding Act signed in Paris (27 May).

1998

Good Friday Agreement in Northern Ireland (10 Apr.). US launches cruise missiles at sites in Afghanistan and Sudan following the bombing of its embassies in Kenya and Tanzania (20 Aug.). Israel and Palestine reach modest agreement at Wye River Conference (23 Oct.). Operation Desert Fox begins (17 Dec.).

1999

Hungary, Czech Republic and Hungary join NATO (12 Mar.). Operation Allied Force begins: lasts 78 days (24 Mar.).

2000

Civil unrest grows in Israel (Sept.). Clinton visits Vietnam (19 Nov.).

2001

George W. Bush inaugurated (20 Jan.). Terrorists attack the Pentagon and destroy twin towers of World Trade Center, New York (11 Sept.).

INTRODUCTION

We are going to win this war and we are going to win the peace that follows.

Franklin D. Roosevelt, 9 December 1941

Victory over Japan saw the United States touch a zenith of power without equal in world history. The most obvious symbols of that power were the atomic bombs which had devastated the cities of Hiroshima and Nagasaki and hastened the Japanese surrender. But by every other yardstick American military and economic strength in the summer of 1945 was awesome, both in scale and for the effectiveness with which it had been mobilised. There were 12,123,455 men and women in uniform compared with 458,363 in 1940. They were deployed on a global scale across two widely separated theatres of war; 68 army divisions contributed to the defeat of Germany, while in Asia and the Pacific a further 22 army and 6 marine divisions fought against Japan. Even before the use of atomic weapons, American strategic bombing had ruined Japan's cities, and, with their British allies, brought similar destruction to Germany. In naval terms, the fast carrier force and submarine fleet had projected American offensive power across the Pacific. No armed forces had ever been as well equipped and supplied. Behind this military strength lay the world's most powerful and dynamic economy, which had seen the country's GNP more than double in the course of the war, enabling the United States to give vital economic and financial assistance to her British, Soviet, French and Chinese allies. The country had come through the conflict largely untouched. While some 400,000 members of the armed forces had been killed, American civilians had been spared

1

the experience of their European and Asian counterparts. No American city had been fought over like Stalingrad, Warsaw, Caen, Florence, Budapest, Breslau or Berlin. No American city had been subjected to saturation bombing. Instead, industrial cities from Seattle to Detroit were poised to push the country to even greater economic prosperity as millions of young servicemen returned to take up the threads of family life.

Poignantly, the man who had directed this unprecedented war effort, Franklin D. Roosevelt, died on 12 April 1945. As a veteran of the Wilson administration, he knew that the United States could not afford to repeat the errors made in the aftermath of the previous war, above all that there could be no retreat into a sterile isolation. To that end he set out to win the confidence of Josef Stalin, whose continued partnership he knew to be vital to the stability of the post-war world. There is evidence to suggest that he succeeded in doing this, not least through his courage in travelling to Yalta in February 1945. Posthumously denounced by Republicans for having surrendered eastern Europe to Stalin at Yalta, Roosevelt knew, as did British premier Winston Churchill, that the Red Army's victories had made Russia the arbiter of the region's fate. He was also well aware of Stalin's need for future security. The best the two western leaders could achieve was try to abate the nature of Soviet control by securing Stalin's commitment to 'free and unfettered elections' in Poland, a pledge which should be seen in the context of expectations of post-war collaboration. Even before the defeat of Germany, American and British dismay over Stalin's obvious unwillingness to abide by the Yalta pledge over Poland saw the wartime alliance begin to fray. Roosevelt's vision of a post-war world was one in which peace would be guaranteed by an international organisation, with the United States, the Soviet Union, the United Kingdom and China taking the leading parts. This was the driving force behind the creation of the United Nations organisation (UN) at the San Francisco Conference, from 25 April to

26 June 1945. His insistence on China was based on his belief that the Allies should not be seen to be waging a white man's war and that a strong China was essential to the future stability of Asia. This perception also helped inform his anti-colonialism. While he did not go so far as to advocate the dismantling of the European empires, Roosevelt did believe that where possible colonial territories, especially those liberated from the Japanese, should be placed under a system of trusteeship, pending independence. He also wished to open up the imperial systems, indeed as much of the world as possible, to international trade. While Americans saw this as averting the trade tensions of the inter-war period which had contributed to the Great Depression, Europeans inevitably saw it as a mask for American economic penetration.

Roosevelt's vision of the post-war world was a positive, and not ignoble, one, but there is inevitably another side to be considered. Roosevelt held an intensely personal view of politics. His methods of government were notoriously haphazard and, to his critics, secretive. Foreign policy he held to be his preserve. His long-serving Secretary of State, Cordell Hull, was the executor of presidential politics. Hull's successor, Edward J. Stettinius, was a makeweight. Famously, Roosevelt barely confided in his third Vice-President, Harry S. Truman, whom he scarcely knew. Truman, in the cliché only a heartbeat from the presidency, was not even told of the development of the atomic bomb. In foreign affairs Roosevelt relied on his ability to charm others, including Stalin, to his way of thinking. His view on China was questionable. Having built up the Chinese Nationalist President, Chiang Kai-shek, as one of the principal Allied leaders, he then had to set aside well-documented advice from his officials in the country that Chiang's government was venal and incompetent. Finally, he was all too human in refusing to contemplate his own mortality. Bravely undertaking a fourth term in office to secure post-war peace, his appearance shocked those who saw him at Yalta, not least his friend

Churchill. At 63 he was was not an old man, but the strain of the war had told on a constitution weakened by disease. It is pointless to speculate as to how American–Soviet relations would have developed had he lived, since he was not tested by Stalin's actions. Even so, his death could not have come at a more critical moment in American, and world, history.

Far from working out to Roosevelt's hopes, the post-war world was characterised by acute international tension, the Cold War, which saw much of the world polarised into two armed camps, which through time developed the capacity, though fortunately not the desire, to destroy each other. When that conflict ended with the collapse of communism and the Soviet system in 1989–91, the United States was once again left in a position of unparalled economic and military power, possibly even more pronounced than in 1945. The suddenness of what happened presented American policy-makers with unique problems of adjustment, just as interesting, if less immediately dangerous, as those which had gone before. The legatee of America's success in the Cold War was another Democrat, Bill Clinton, who had to attempt the challenging task of redefining his country's relationship with the rest of the world.

The Cold War both dominated, and distorted, America's international relations. Throughout the period 1945–2002 there were problems of structural inequality, economic deprivation, abuses of human rights, endemic disease, and regional and ethnic conflict, all areas where America could have shown a lead – and often did, but generally through the prism of Cold War perceptions and priorities. It is not surprising, since jealousy is a natural human emotion, that American actions were often seen as patronising, and that the caricature of the 'ugly American' became part of saloon-bar wisdom. That few Americans held passports and that their newspapers and television stations concentrated upon local rather than international matters could be seen as reflecting an incurious and unsophisticated view of the world. Anyone who has read the documents in the *Foreign*

Relations of the United States, or the memoirs of those who helped form foreign policy throughout these years, would at times refute such a view. American policy-makers were as prone to lapse as anyone. Where judgement failed, as over Vietnam, the consequences were desperate. Where it did not, as in the Cuban missile crisis, there was cause to be grateful, if only just. More often than not, policies driven by self-interest had far-reaching global consequences.

This study takes as its focus how foreign policy emerged and developed in the post-war presidencies. This is not meant to suggest that the underlying issues reflected the presidential cycle, still less that the world outside the United States did so. All these men came with their distinctive agendas, each, it may safely be assumed, hoping to make his mark. The Constitution says little about the conduct of foreign policy, seemingly charging the president with not much more than the power to appoint and receive ambassadors, subject to the advice and consent of congress, and to make treaties, subject to the approval of two-thirds of the senators. But these powers, with the checks and balances set out, are generally accepted as giving the president the responsibility of conducting the nation's diplomacy, reinforced by his or her role as commander-in-chief of the armed forces. It is, of course, what is left unsaid, and hence implied, in the Constitution that has enabled chief executives to assert presidential power (Spanier and Uslaner, 1975). In the period covered in this book, when the possibility of nuclear attack left little scope for consultation, presidential power and responsibility in the area of foreign affairs inevitably grew. The president's finger was, indeed, on the nuclear trigger. 'The decision to launch the weapons', Reagan recorded, 'was mine alone to make', adding that he might have only six or eight minutes to make it (Reagan, 1990). All these men were faced with dangers unimaginable a few years before. Of the presidents analysed, only the last two grew up with the reality of nuclear warfare; all the others had to make the adjustment from the apparent certainties of a simpler era when Americans could rest behind their two oceans and stable borders. As he pointed out in his inaugural, Kennedy was the first president to be born in the twentieth century; Truman and Eisenhower, who between them ushered in the thermonuclear age, had their formative years in the nineteenth. In that sense, whatever their frailties, the presidents from Harry S. Truman to George W. Bush are a unique group of individuals, matched only by their counterparts in Moscow. The buck, as the sign on Truman's desk famously observed, did rest with them.

But if each presidency brought its own agenda, presidents and their teams reflected the prevailing ideological concerns of their fellow countrymen and women. Throughout the period after 1945, however much society might agonise over racial issues, reassess attitudes towards gender and argue over the extent of government intervention, there was a keenly felt identification with core values which underlay assumptions about foreign policy. The outside world was not an abstraction; it was where America sought to project her ideology in a variety of ways (Lucas, 1999). Although often dismissed as instantly forgettable, presidential inaugurals provide useful snapshots of how presidents, and their speechwriters, set out these values. As Clinton said in 1993, they were trying to 'define what it means to be an American', or, as Carter hoped in 1997, to affirm 'our belief in an undiminished, ever-expanding American dream'.

At the heart of that dream lay the conviction that the country stood for liberty and democracy, religion and material success. Thus, in the century's last inauguration in 1997, Clinton could claim that America had 'saved the world from tyranny in two world wars and a long Cold War; and time and again, reached out across the globe to millions who, like us, longed for the blessings of liberty'. Most new incumbents linked that freedom with religion, whether the Quaker Nixon 'sustained by our faith in God who created us', the Protestant Reagan who believed that 'God intended us to be free', or the Catholic Kennedy who charged his audience to

6

'go forth to lead the land we love, asking His blessing and His help, but knowing that here on earth God's work must truly be our own'. Freedom also went hand in hand with the fruits of individual enterprise. What for Clinton in 1997 was 'the world's mightiest economic power' was portrayed by Eisenhower 40 years earlier as a country where the 'air rings with the song of our industry – rolling mills and blast furnaces, dynamos, dams, and assembly lines – the chorus of America the bountiful'.

Such an America could not but stand in the starkest ideological contrast to the Soviet Union with a command economy, state atheism and dictatorship of the proletariat through the Communist Party. It fell to Truman in 1949 to put this at its baldest when he claimed that the Soviet regime 'adheres to a false philosophy which purports to offer freedom, security, and greater opportunity to mankind. Misled by this philosophy, many peoples have sacrificed their liberties only to learn to their sorrow that deceit and mockery, poverty and tyranny, are their reward. That false philosophy is communism.' This was the ideological chasm which in 1961 led Kennedy famously to declaim that America would 'pay any price, bear any burden, meet any hardship, support any friend, oppose any foe, in order to assure the survival and success of liberty'.

These core American values were basic to the articulation of a foreign policy dedicated to the pursuit of national interest. In that regard, America was no different to any other state, but the reality of American power after 1945 meant that the impact of these values on the peoples across the world was profound. In Europe the peace was kept, but at what cost in other parts of the world?

1

TRUMAN AND THE COMING
OF THE COLD WAR

> We have learned to be citizens of the world, members of the human
> community. We have learned the simple truth, as Emerson said, that
> 'The only way to have a friend is to be one.' We can gain no lasting
> peace if we approach it with suspicion and mistrust or with fear.
>   Franklin D. Roosevelt, Inaugural, 20 January 1945

Contrary to Roosevelt's hopes, suspicion, mistrust and fear
would come to be defining characteristics of American
foreign policy for the next four decades. His successor, Harry
S. Truman, betrayed few of the attributes which would in
time reveal him as the most substantial president of the post-
war era. Little, it seemed, connected him to his predecessor
beyond a common devotion to the politics of the Democratic
Party. While Roosevelt was educated at Groton and Harvard,
Truman had never attended college. The young Roosevelt
travelled widely in Europe; Truman's only experience of the
outside world was as an artillery officer in France during the
previous war. Truman's entire experience was of domestic
politics, his skill in the Senate being precisely what had
recommended him to Roosevelt as a running-mate in 1944.
No president in American history, faced as he was with the
task of ending the war and reconstructing the post-war world,
had a more daunting challenge, made no lighter by the fact
that he had not been elected to the job. But if he was igno-
rant of the nuances of international politics, he had all the
strength of character of someone who had risen through his

own efforts. Conscious of the prerogative of his office, he had the ability to take decisions. While he liked to express his disdain for the 'striped-pants' boys of the State Department, he was willing to take their advice and was not afraid to put strong men in positions of power. His choice of Secretary of State, James F. Byrnes, was not to prove a great success, but fortunately Byrnes appointed as his Under-Secretary Dean Acheson. A lawyer who had come into public service under Roosevelt, Acheson had ended the war as Assistant Secretary of State. His influence on foreign policy was to be profound (Isaacson & Thomas, 1986). Like Roosevelt, Truman had become a convinced internationalist, conscious that the United States should not repeat the isolationist errors of the 1920s.

The European Vacuum

If Truman had doubted the need for active participation in the affairs of Europe, this was dispelled on 17 July 1945 when he toured the ruins of Berlin. What was becoming increasingly clear to the president and his advisers was that the war had left an unprecedented vacuum in international affairs. In Europe, Italy and France had ceased to be powers of major rank. The legacies of fascism and occupation had left poisonous tensions in their societies, a principal symptom of which was the strength of their communist parties. Given the honourable role of these parties in resisting fascism this was not surprising, but the fear of these two countries 'going communist' was increasingly to exercise American policy-makers. Even more destructive in the long run was France's desire to restore something of her battered esteem by reimposing imperial control in Indo-China, an act of folly. Opposed to any return to French imperialism was the Vietminh, led by the steely revolutionary Ho Chi Minh, who was determined to seize the chance for an independent Marxist Vietnam. The result was a new thirty years' war in which the Vietnamese were to defeat first the French and then the Americans. The relative positions of the other two major European powers, Germany and Britain, could not have stood in sharper contrast. Germany, as Truman saw, was prostrate as a result of Allied bombing and the ferocity of the Red Army's final assault. Every German city of any size or consequence was in ruins, communications severed and the infrastructure of modern life destroyed. As a result of Allied decisions over boundaries, and the hatreds generated by the years of occupation, over eleven million refugees from Poland, Czechoslovakia and other parts of eastern Europe had to be accommodated. The country itself was under the military occupation of the four victorious Allied powers, as was Berlin. German policies in occupied Europe, and in particular those of extermination against Jews, gypsies and others, meant that the country was defeated morally as well as militarily. The power whose economic and military strength had been at the heart of European affairs from the 1870s had, for the foreseeable future, ceased to count. Its rehabilitation would come about in a way which no one had foreseen.

Britain, it seemed, could not have been more different. If Germany was discredited, Britain was widely respected for her refusal to compromise with Hitler in 1940. American leaders believed Britain would continue to take a leading role in areas of traditional influence. The Soviets did not see the British and Americans as an inevitable partnership (Jensen, 1993). The reality was very different, since her efforts in two world wars had exhausted Britain economically and financially. Moreover, the rise of colonial nationalism was undermining the empire. As early as December 1940, the British had informed an initially sceptical Roosevelt of their inability to finance the war effort. The result was the initiation of the Lend-Lease scheme through which essential supplies reached Britain and, later, the Soviet Union. While its possible extension had been discussed by Roosevelt and Churchill in September 1944, inadequate thought had been given to the need for some kind of transition. Hence, on VE Day Truman signed an order ending Lend-Lease except for what would be needed for the war against Japan. Ships already en route to Europe were ordered to turn back. Then, on 15 August, VJ Day, the scheme was formally ended. To the Soviet government, the decision was seen as exposing American bad faith, but to the British, by far the largest recipients of Lend-Lease, the consequences were potentially catastrophic. It is hard to see the American action as other than excessively legalistic, driven by domestic considerations in ignorance of the effects on the two wartime allies (Truman, 1955; Gaddis, 1972; Hamby, 1995).

In the circumstances, the Labour government of Clement Attlee which took office in July 1945 had no alternative but to apply to Washington for a loan to stave off bankruptcy. Not all legislators were inclined to grant it, not least because of the socialist measures of the Attlee government. But it went before congress on 30 January 1946 with Truman's backing and after six months' debate a loan of $3,750 million was approved in the summer. The loan was instructive at various levels. The need for it exposed the depth of Europe's economic plight and hence pointed the way to a more extensive American attempt to reconstruct the continent. Secondly, it became clear that congressional support for the loan reflected an increasing concern over the growing division in Europe. Attlee's Britain was a friend which had to be propped up. Even so, this did not yet extend to other fields, notably atomic research. Although the United States was undoubtedly the prime mover in the Manhattan Project which had produced the atomic bombs, the British had made important contributions. As part of a wider debate about the control of atomic weapons, the McMahon Act in the summer of 1946 ended collaboration with the British. It was clear that in the immediate post-war period the British could not take the Americans for granted. Influential Britons sought to counter this with the concept, or myth, of a 'Special Relationship'. While the 'Special Relationship' was always much more a British than an American concept, it did have elements of reality. For the decade or so after 1945 there was an ease of intercourse amongst the men who had worked together for the defeat of Hitler, even though this did not work to Britain's advantage in 1956. English was a common bond, not least in the armed forces. Even after the war's end there was a substantial British military presence in the Pentagon. Above all, the 'Special Relationship' existed in the unique collaboration between the intelligence services of the two countries, which meant that there were no secrets between Washington and London. In time, Britain became America's most dependable ally. The essential point to remember was that Roosevelt had assumed that Britain would continue to be a more or less equal partner, and that, in the words of the diplomat Charles Bohlen, 'one of most astounding features of the war and immediate post-war period was that literally no one in the American government foresaw the extent and rapidity of the decline of British power' (Bohlen, 1969).

The Americas

If Europe was rapidly becoming the central area of concern to the United States, central and southern America were well-established ones, dating from the collapse of the Spanish empire in the early nineteenth century. From the time of the Monroe Doctrine of 1823, the United States had warned the European powers away from the western hemisphere. The practical result of this was that large parts, particularly of central America, became an extension of the United States' capitalist system, with powerful companies flourishing with the support of local elites. The result, for the mass of the population, were some of the poorest living standards in the world. But the region was also judged essential to American security, with the Panama Canal the most obvious symbol. Off the Florida coast was Cuba, her politics dominated since 1940 by the corrupt Fulgencio Batista, her economy dependent on American sugar companies, her security seemingly overshadowed by the American naval base at Guantanamo. Cuba can almost be taken as an exemplar of America's relationship with her southern neighbours. Once the Cold War had started, the United States became locked into support for impeccably anti-communist right-wing dictatorships whose attitudes to human rights could rarely have stood the light of day. It was not the least paradoxical aspect of America's attitude to the world after 1945 that she condoned, and supported, regimes in the western hemisphere whose treatment of their people differed only in emphasis from the communist governments of eastern Europe. At least the latter aspired, in their own fashion, to some form of social justice, as their medical and educational provisions testified.

The United States and her Soviet Ally

Unquestionably, the Soviet Union dominated America's world-view. There could have been no greater contrast than the position of the two countries in 1945. Hitler's war in the east had been one of extermination. As the Red Army retreated in 1941 and 1942, Stalin's policy was one of 'scorched earth'; then, as the Germans withdrew in 1943 and 1944 they, too, destroyed everything in their reach. In the course of this struggle, it was the Red Army which defeated the Wehrmacht, two thirds of which was engaged on the eastern front. The Soviet Union suffered devastation and casualties quite unlike those of any other combatant. Not less than 20 million Soviet citizens died, and the loss has been put as high as 27 million. Some 70,000 villages had been destroyed, major cities were shells, 32,000 factories had been blown up, and an estimated 30 per cent of the country's wealth had been lost (Volkogonov, 1991). Any attempt to chart the subsequent course of east–west tensions must acknowledge such facts.

As long as Hitler was alive the three Allied powers could focus on his destruction, allowing them to put to one side potential areas for future conflict, but even before the war's end two issues had brought tension to the surface. On the Soviet side this focused on the failure of the Anglo-Americans to mount the invasion of north-west Europe before the summer of 1944, thus leaving to the Red Army the main burden of the war. Their suspicion was that they were being left to take enormous casualties in order to weaken their position in the post-war world. The invasion of France, so the suspicion went, had only been undertaken after the German army had been beaten in the east. For their part, the Americans and British were appalled at Stalin's seemingly cynical refusal to aid the Warsaw Uprising in August 1944, seeing it as his opportunity to destroy the position of the non-communist Poles of the Home Army. Although it was the SS who killed some 300,000 Poles and destroyed 80 per cent of the city, the fact that the Red Army was sitting on its outskirts was an uncomfortable one. In fairness to Stalin, it has been pointed out that there was still a substantial German armoured force before the city. But a bad taste was left, especially when Home Army generals were then taken to Moscow, tried and imprisoned for collaboration with the Germans (Burleigh, 2000).

As the result of the Red Army's sacrifices, the summer of 1945 saw its soldiers in Berlin, Vienna, Budapest, Warsaw and Bucharest, all the historic capitals of central and eastern Europe. Stalin was determined to use his victory to ensure that his country would never again be in the position of fighting off foreign, especially German, armies from the suburbs of Moscow and Leningrad. To that end, his mind focused both on Germany and her invasion route to Russia, Poland. Although both Roosevelt and Churchill had acknowledged Stalin's needs in these two countries, the realities of Soviet policy as it unfolded went to the heart of post-war tension. Poland, the ostensible reason for Britain going to war in 1939, was basic to Anglo-American concerns.

Within days of taking up office, Truman became convinced that Stalin was not honouring his Yalta commitments. On 23 April, he taxed Soviet Foreign Minister V. M. Molotov with this in a stark exchange which left the latter protesting that he had never been spoken to like that before (Isaacson & Thomas, 1986). The following day Stalin replied in no uncertain manner, pointing out that Poland was as essential to Russian security as were Belgium and Greece to that of Great Britain. The Soviet government, he observed, had not been consulted on the form of government for these two countries, nor had it expected to be. A government 'friendly toward the Soviet Union' was 'demanded by the blood of the Soviet people abundantly shed on the fields of Poland in the name of the liberation of Poland' (Truman, 1956). The warning shot could not have been clearer. Days later, American and Soviet troops were embracing on the Elbe, but any surge of emotion did not last. The two sides found they did not much like each other. No doubt language was a barrier.

Truman at Potsdam

Truman explored these, and other, issues at length with Stalin at the Potsdam Conference held between 17 July and 1 August 1945, the only direct encounter between the leaders of the post-war world. Churchill represented Britain until the results of the general election meant that he was replaced by Attlee and his Foreign Secretary, Ernest Bevin, though there was no change of policy by the Labour government. Bevin proved to be a doughty anti-communist whose views were listened to with increasing respect in Washington (Miscamble, 1992). In retrospect, Potsdam can be seen as a transitional phase in east–west relations, though that was not so apparent at the time. The war in Europe might be over, but the Japanese were still resisting tenaciously and the Soviet Union was, as a result of commitments given at Yalta, preparing join the Americans and British. The situation in Europe was still in flux. Although his armies dominated much of the continent, Stalin's control was far from complete and his ultimate purposes opaque. What was revealed at Potsdam was his Realpolitik, especially over the Polish and German borders.

In a sense, Potsdam merely confirmed what had already been established in the course of the war. As the result of wartime agreements, Germany had been divided into American, British, French and Soviet zones of occupation. The four occupying powers also had zones in Berlin, which lay deep inside the Soviet sphere, with the three western countries having rights of access. Stalin had also ensured that the Soviet border would be advanced substantially to the west at Poland's expense, and that the Poles would be compensated by parts of eastern Germany. It was not until Potsdam that the full implications of shifting Poland some 150 miles to the west began to be teased out, not least the human dimensions of expelling millions of people from regions they and their ancestors had inhabited for centuries. Stalin had already been conceded the historic city of Koenigsberg. Practically destroyed and of no great use as a port, he seems to have wanted to come out of the war with a piece of German territory. The rest of east Prussia and the territory to the east of the River Oder went to the Poles. The transfer to Poland of the great industrial region of Silesia was seen by Stalin as weakening Germany's future potential for war, but other areas were more contentious. In discussions at Tehran and Yalta, Roosevelt and Churchill had thought in terms of the Polish–German border being along the eastern Neisse. At Yalta, Stalin, candidly admitting that the Poles were taking their revenge on the Germans, pressed the Polish claims to the city of Stettin, west of the mouth of the Oder and long the Baltic port for Berlin, and, more significantly, to a border running along the western Neisse. The latter gave the Poles all of Silesia, including the great city of Breslau, Stalin's tactic being to bind Poland to the Soviet

Union against the day when Germans would wish to regain their lost territories. The best Truman and the British could do was acquiesce in the transfer of these German territories on a temporary basis until there was a full peace settlement. Eleven and a half million Germans were in the process of being expelled, none too gently, from their homes, 2,280,000 dying in the process (Burleigh, 2000). Their fate had to be set against the needs of continuing cooperation, but Stalin had shown just how ruthless he was where vital Soviet interests in eastern Europe were concerned.

Even so, it would be wrong to suggest that Truman left Potsdam in any sense cast down. A number of substantive issues had been worked through, arrangements for Soviet entry into the war against Japan had been confirmed, and he had established some kind of relationship with Stalin, or so he claimed. Moreover, on 18 July he received confirmation of the successful detonation of the atomic bomb, the use of which promised to bring an early end to the Japanese war, as it did within the month. Stalin's seeming indifference to the news of a new American weapon is generally put down to his knowledge of its existence through his spies (Hamby, 1995). In general, Truman was glad to return home, where there were pressing domestic issues.

East–West Relations in Transition

While tensions in Europe were central to the deterioration in American–Soviet relations over the winter of 1945–46, other irritants were at work, though the extent to which they were causes or symptoms of such tensions is less clear. Even before the end of the war, the Soviet leaders had been looking to the Americans for financial help to rebuild their shattered country. In August 1945, they submitted a request for $1,000 million in credits from the Export–Import Bank, but influential voices, not least in the Moscow embassy, were counselling against this. The following month, a congressional delegation recommended that the aid be conditional on free elections in eastern Europe and fulfilment of Yalta obligations (Kennan, 1967; Gaddis, 1972). This probably did not surprise Stalin very much, since it was pretty much what was expected of the capitalist system. So, too, was the projection of American power through the expansion of overseas bases. The lesson of the Second World War was that the North American continent needed a defence perimeter far out in the Atlantic and Pacific oceans. The Americans themselves had demonstrated how massive force could be used across 6,000 miles of the Pacific to the Japanese home islands. The result was a string of American bases from the Azores in the Atlantic to the Marianas in the Pacific (Leffler and Painter, 1994). Viewed from the Soviet perspective, this was not a defence perimeter, but proof of the Americans' offensive intent and desire for world dominance, which could only be achieved through a war against them (Jensen, 1993).

Crucially, the winter of 1945–46 saw the incremental consolidation of Soviet control in central and eastern Europe. The need for such an approach was demonstrated in the Hungarian general election of November 1945 in which the communist share of the vote was 17 per cent. Total communist control of Hungary was to take some four years, but from the start was aided by the party's insistence on retaining the Interior Ministry and the security police. In Poland, too, control of the security services proved to be a trump card (Crampton, 1994). By the beginning of 1946 it was already becoming clear that hopes for a post-war consensus based upon collaboration between Washington and Moscow were fast fading. Contacts between the two had been increasingly tetchy since September 1945 when there were bad-tempered exchanges between Secretary of State James Byrnes and Molotov, whose negotiating techniques were to become the bane of American diplomats' lives. At subsequent meetings in Moscow in December involving Stalin, Molotov and Bevin, Byrnes tried to inject some new momentum into east–west relations, and seemed to think that he had (Byrnes, 1947). But his diplomatic style was attracting powerful enemies. State Department officials believed that he was neglecting professional advice, but, more importantly, Truman was coming to the conclusion that Byrnes, his rival for the 1944 vice-presidential nomination, needed to be brought to heel. On 5 January 1946, he seems to have rebuked Byrnes for keeping him insufficiently abreast of key developments. More significant than his assertion of presidential authority were the revelations of his thinking on the state of American–Soviet relations. Castigating Stalin's actions at Potsdam over the German–Polish border as a 'high-handed outrage', he listed the various challenges which had developed since the end of the war with Japan, concluding that unless 'Russia is faced with an iron fist and strong language another war is in the making'. His graphic phrase, 'I'm tired of babying the Soviets', revealed just how far he had travelled from the spirit of wartime collaboration (Truman, 1955; Hamby, 1995). In addition, Americans, both official and unofficial, were looking to the recent past for lessons they should avoid. Inevitably, they turned to Neville Chamberlain and his policy of appeasement which had culminated in the Munich agreement of 1938. As the winter of 1945–46 developed, the words 'Chamberlain', 'Munich' and 'appeasement' were increasingly heard (Gaddis, 1972). That Chamberlain's actions should have been seen in the context of 1938 does not seem to have been of interest.

George Kennan and the 'Long Telegram'

The evidence, then, suggests that Truman and his advisers were ready for the kind of intellectual demolition of current Soviet policies which they were about to receive from the Moscow embassy. Its author, George F. Kennan, Counselor at the Moscow embassy, was already a veteran analyst of Soviet affairs. While acknowledging the Soviet leader's cruelty,

Kennan appreciated that Stalin was one of the most remarkable figures of his time. Moreover, he was convinced that Stalin was not an adventurer like Hitler, but a skilled tactician, a talent which made him no less dangerous. In mid-February 1946, Kennan received a request from Washington to provide an explanation of current Soviet policies. Two things triggered this. The first was Soviet obstructionism over the World Bank and the International Monetary Fund (IMF), which the Americans were counting on to provide post-war stability. The second was a major election speech delivered by Stalin on 9 February in which he appeared to pour cold water on the idea of a peaceful international order. In an echo of 1930s Germany, he announced that consumer goods would have to take second place to the needs of rearmament (Acheson, 1969). It was just the opportunity for which Kennan had been waiting.

His response, the 'Long Telegram', sent on 22 February, was a prolonged critique of Soviet actions in which he sought to blow away what he felt were the comfortable myths of wartime collaboration. The document pointed to the clear ideological gulf between capitalist America and the communist Soviet Union. The latter believed that the contradictions within capitalism would produce wars, and that capitalists would prefer this to be against the Soviet Union. Soviet vulnerability was compounded by the Russian legacy of striving to survive in agricultural plains under threat from nomads. From this thesis, Kennan argued that the Soviet Union would direct its policies towards building up the country's military and industrial strength, pursue self-sufficiency for the areas it controlled rather than international economic cooperation, and only use the United Nations for its own ends rather than as a mechanism for mutual interest. Kennan warned that the Soviet Union was 'committed fanatically to the belief that with the US there can be no modus vivendi', and that it would work to destroy 'our traditional way of life'. But he did suggest a counter-strategy. Arguing that, unlike Hitler's Germany, Soviet foreign policy was not adventuristic; 'it can easily withdraw

– and usually does – when strong resistance is encountered at any point. Thus, if the adversary has sufficient force and makes clear his readiness to use it, he rarely has to do so.' Although he did not use the word, what he was signalling was that any further advance of Soviet power should be contained. Any military dimension was, at best, oblique.

Kennan's analysis has been described as the most influential dispatch ever sent to Washington by an American diplomat, but its impact on policy was incremental. Crucially, it turned a spotlight on its author. In September, he returned to Washington to the National War College where he was able both to propagate and refine his views (Kennan, 1967; Clifford, 1991; Miscamble, 1992; Jensen, 1993).

The 'Iron Curtain'

Stalin's February speech signalled that the rhetoric was changing, nowhere more dramatically so than in Truman's home state of Missouri on 5 March 1946. The occasion has gone down in history as Churchill's 'Iron Curtain' speech, in which he depicted the historic region 'from Stettin in the Baltic to Trieste in the Adriatic' falling under Soviet influence. Truman had invited the former premier, arguably the most celebrated individual in the western world, to speak at Westminster College in Fulton. With all the verbal skills for which he was renowned, Churchill seized the occasion to publicise his views on the Soviet domination of eastern Europe and the need for Anglo-American cooperation to oppose it. There is no doubt that Churchill's speech, delivered in Truman's presence, helped focus for the public mind just how far things had deteriorated since the great victory of the previous summer. Truman made sure of clear water between the administration and Churchill's rhetoric, not least because he was still uncertain which course to take. But he had been there, aware of what would be said (Gaddis, 1972; Clifford, 1991; Hamby, 1995).

Soviet Retreat: Iran

Kennan and Churchill notwithstanding, relations with the Soviet Union were not yet black and white. The spring of 1946 saw the easing of one of area of friction. The place at issue, Iran, was far from the growing focus of tension in Europe, but was nonetheless both of strategic importance and of traditional Russian interest. Since 1942, Iran had been jointly occupied by British and Soviet troops, and in May 1945 the Shah requested that they leave. In September, Bevin and Molotov agreed on a full evacuation of their forces by 2 March 1946. It appeared, however, that the Red Army was using its presence in northern Iran to encourage a separatist movement in Azerbaijan, and was in little hurry to depart. American pressure was exerted through support for the Iranians in the United Nations Security Council and a stiff diplomatic note, as a result of which Soviet troops left by May. If the affair seemed to confirm the Kennan thesis that the Soviet Union would back away from confrontation if faced with firm resolve, it is also certain that the Soviets were angered by what had happened and that it did nothing to ease relations (Chace, 1998). It might also have suggested that Stalin was more flexible than people thought.

The 'Truman Doctrine'

For much of 1946, Truman's main concerns were largely domestic. Congressional elections in November would be the Democratic Party's first major test under his leadership. He was involved in a bitter dispute with organised labour, a major electoral prop of the Democrats, and had to sack his Secretary of Commerce, Henry Wallace, his predecessor as Vice-President and the remaining link with Roosevelt's New Deal. The cause of their quarrel was Wallace's publicly-expressed belief that the United States had no business interfering in the affairs of eastern Europe. Despite these preoccupations, in July he turned to his Special Counsel, Clark Clifford, for an appreciation of the state of relations with Moscow. It was not altogether an obvious choice. Clifford, a trusted aide, was a lawyer untrained in international affairs. His report, compiled with George Elsey, reached the president on 24 September. Their analysis did not differ from that of Kennan, but it did go a stage further in several significant respects which anticipated future policies. One was to suggest a vigorous information programme to counter Soviet propaganda. The second was to offer economic support to countries which felt threatened by the Soviet Union. Finally, the Clifford–Elsey Report advocated that if Soviet cooperation could not be secured, then the United States should combine with Britain and other western countries as a distinct entity. The implications were so far-reaching that Truman ordered all the report's copies locked in the White House (Clifford, 1991).

Domestically, the elections of November 1946 were a disaster for the Democrats, losing control of both houses, but this was not entirely a misfortune for Truman. It meant that he had to reach out to the Republicans, especially the new chairman of the Senate Foreign Relations Committee, Senator Arthur Vandenberg. Vandenberg proved to be a crucial ally in the months to come, ensuring bipartisan support for the far-reaching decisions taken by the administration (Hamby, 1995). In January 1947, Byrnes was replaced as Secretary of State by General George C. Marshall, one of the most distinguished public servants of his generation. The combination of Marshall and Dean Acheson as Under-Secretary proved ideal. They were soon to be tested by the implosion of their wartime ally. By February 1947, Britain's economic plight was such that the government was forced to a number of historic decisions, which put paid to any American illusions that she was still a power of world rank (Bohlen, 1969). The first was to grant independence to India, while a decision on Palestine was handed to the United Nations. Crucially, on 21 February Washington was informed that British aid to Greece and Turkey, key to the security of the eastern Mediterranean, would cease in six weeks and asked to take over the burden. Greece, in particular, was already a subject of considerable concern since she had been bitterly split between right and left since liberation and it seemed a distinct possibility that withdrawal of western aid would lead to a communist victory. Turkey's case was less obvious, resting essentially on her strategic position on the straits and Soviet border. On 27 February, Truman, Marshall and Acheson met key congressional leaders. Marshall and Acheson argued that Soviet success in either country would threaten other parts of Europe and the Middle East (Hamby, 1995; McCauley, 1995).

Truman knew that in asking for $400 million in aid to Greece and Turkey he was pointing in a new direction and that he had to take congressional opinion with him. His speech before a joint session of Congress on 12 March 1947 has become known as the 'Truman Doctrine', not a term Truman liked. In it he drew a clear distinction between the western and communist systems, the former 'distinguished by free institutions, representative government, free elections, guarantees of individual liberty, freedom of speech and religion, and freedom from political expression', the latter relying 'upon terror and oppression, a controlled press and radio, fixed elections, and the suppression of personal freedoms'. Since the choice between the two systems was not always a free one, he proclaimed 'that it must be the policy of the United States to support free peoples who are resisting attempted subjugation by armed minorities or by outside pressures'. He reassured his listeners that such aid should be mainly economic and financial, but notably failed to say what would be done should these fail. Opposition came from both left-wing supporters of Henry Wallace and isolationist Republicans, but congressional opinion was overwhelmingly behind the president, the proposed assistance to Greece and Turkey passing the Senate by 67 votes to 23, and the House by 287 to 107 (Feis, 1970; Acheson, 1969). Worries were expressed by Marshall that Truman's tone was too anti-communist. Kennan was concerned that the aid package to Greece and Turkey had been cloaked in dangerously universalist language. Would the undertakings announced by Truman apply in every case where there was a perceived communist threat? This was a dilemma which would eat at policy-makers over the next two decades (Bohlen, 1969; Kennan, 1967).

The Marshall Plan

With his military background, Marshall saw the need for some kind of planning mechanism, and inevitably his eye fell on Kennan. In May, the Policy Planning Staff began work under Kennan's directorship (Miscamble, 1992), and one of his first tasks was to address the problem of rehabilitating Europe. In April, Marshall travelled to Europe to attend a conference in Moscow, saw for himself the continuing extent of devastation, and on his return charged the Policy Planning Staff with drafting a plan to deal with the problem. The following month, Marshall's diagnosis was confirmed by Under-Secretary of State for Economic Affairs, William L. Clayton, who set out the potentially disastrous consequences to the American economy should Europe collapse completely. As Kennan and Clayton prepared their recommendations, Acheson was charged by Truman with a major foreign policy speech which would prepare the ground. Acheson outlined the exhaustion of Europe and Asia brought about by the war. As a result, they would need some $16 billion dollars of American exports, but could only provide imports to the United States to pay for half of this. The result would be bankruptcy. The remedy, he suggested, was new finance provided by the United States. When they reported, both Kennan and Clayton confirmed the need for substantial American aid. Kennan's paper, presented on 23 May, focused on the need for the Europeans to formulate a programme, on the critical importance of reconstructing the German economy, and the need to include the whole of Europe, though Kennan did not believe the Soviets would take part. Clayton reiterated the extent to which the European economy had collapsed. It would be necessary, he argued, for the United States to provide Europe with $6–$7 billion-worth of goods each year for three years, chiefly coal, food, cotton, tobacco and shipping. This formed the essence of the historic speech Marshall made at Harvard on 6 June. Emphasising that American policy was not directed against any country or doctrine but 'against hunger, poverty, desperation and chaos', he outlined a programme which would revive the world economy. The initiative, he said, should come from the Europeans. The European Recovery Program (ERP), or Marshall Plan as it inevitably became known, was an initiative of the first importance (Acheson, 1969; Miscamble, 1992).

Marshall left it to Bevin to lead the European response, together with French Foreign Minister Georges Bidault. The two men convened a conference in Paris in late June which Molotov agreed to attend. The American condition for aid to the Soviet Union was that all the east European countries be allowed to take part as well; if not, then the plan would be implemented for western Europe. Stalin initially dithered. He had, after all, looked for American aid only two years before. What seems to have convinced him to oppose the plan was the belief, reinforced by the Truman Doctrine, that the United States, Britain and Germany would form a revived capitalist system, contrary to earlier Soviet expectations (Volkogonov, 1991; Gaddis, 1997). It was a decisive moment in post-war history. Announcing that the programme would be an interference in the affairs of sovereign nations, Molotov left the conference on 2 July. The Soviet government then insisted that the states of eastern Europe, including Czechoslovakia which still clung on to a democratic government, refuse Marshall aid. More than the Truman Doctrine, the Marshall Plan marked America's leadership of what was becoming known as the 'free world'. Although it has been argued that the European economy was not quite as prostrate as Marshall and Clayton had thought, nevertheless the programme was instrumental both in the revitalisation of western Europe and in the creation of a western economic system built around the power of American finance and industry. Between 1948 and 1952 $12,992 million of Marshall Aid went to western Europe. Just as significant were the consequences for the Soviet Union and the states of eastern Europe. By putting themselves outside the ERP they were effectively declaring a state of siege which was to last over four decades. In January 1949, this was formalised with the establishment of the Council for Mutual Economic Assistance, or COMECON, which coordinated trade between the Soviet Union and eastern Europe. Such was the dynamic of the American economy, once it was joined by the sophisticated economies of western Europe, and later Japan, it was a competition that the Soviet system could not win. During the Cold War, especially during the febrile 1950s or at the height of the arms race, it was not always possible to perceive this reality.

The 'X' Article and Containment

Just as the Soviets were drawing their skirts back from the Marshall Plan, the American public was becoming increasingly focused on the realities of east–west tension. This came about, almost by accident it would appear, through the publication in July 1947 in the journal *Foreign Affairs* of an article 'The Sources of Soviet Conduct' by 'X'. Its author was Kennan. It said nothing that he had not been arguing in private, but since its authorship soon became a matter of public speculation, it was seen as an expression of official thinking and, as such, was widely publicised in popular journals such as *Life* and *Reader's Digest*. By early 1947, Kennan had been refining the arguments he had put forward in the

'Long Telegram'. In a paper on 24 January, he argued that the expansion of the Soviet Union should be 'contained' by counter-pressure. This was soon followed by a further paper on 'The Psychological Background of Soviet Foreign Policy', which became the 'X' article. In combating Soviet aims, Kennan argued for 'a policy of firm containment, designed to confront the Russians with unalterable counter-force at every point where they show signs of encroaching upon the interests of a peaceful and stable world'. Later, conceding that his language had been ambiguous, Kennan argued that what he had meant was political rather than military containment. Even so, 'containment' of the Soviet Union came to be elevated into a doctrine, to its author's later embarrassment. What the article provided at the time was a public rationale for what was already under way. The idea it set out underpinned what had been done over Greece and Turkey, and arguably Iran the previous year. The article was never intended to be some kind of master plan for American policy, and should not be seen as such, whatever the later ramifications of containment. Kennan's own reservations over the Truman Doctrine have already been noted (Kennan, 1951; Kennan, 1967; Miscamble, 1992).

By the summer of 1947, the main features of the Cold War were becoming apparent. The term itself was given wide currency by the influential journalist Walter Lippman in a strongly-argued riposte to the 'X' article, entitled *The Cold War: A Study in U.S. Foreign Policy*. In Germany, any lingering pretence at a four-power occupation had gone. Democratic politics had been revived by Kurt Schumacher of the Social Democratic Party and Konrad Adenauer of the Christian Democratic Union, both untainted by any Nazi past and determinedly anti-communist. In elections throughout the city of Berlin in August 1946, the communist Socialist Unity Party could only take 19.8 per cent of the vote to 48.7 per cent for the Social Democrats, a result which encouraged Stalin to concentrate on consolidating his position in the Soviet zone. In January 1947, the division of Germany was taken a stage further when the Americans and British merged their occupation zones as Bizonia. Then, in response to the Marshall Plan, the Soviets announced the formation of the Cominform, or Communist Information Bureau, a successor to the old Comintern, which had been abolished in 1943. At its opening meeting in Warsaw in September 1947, attended by Italian and French communists as well as those from eastern Europe, Andrei Zhdanov, the party's principal ideologist thought to be a particular favourite of Stalin, denounced the Americans for forming an anti-communist bloc. Zhdanov died mysteriously the following year, but his 'Two-Camp Doctrine', which divided the world into an imperialist camp, led by an expansionist United States, and an anti-imperialist camp, became Soviet orthodoxy, which other east European communists would learn to ignore at their peril. It also emphasised the ideological dimension to the Cold War (Volkogonov, 1991).

The shape of America's direction in international affairs was becoming apparent in two other key developments. The first had its origins in the armed forces' need to modernise their increasingly obsolescent stock of Second World War equipment and bitter inter-service rivalry over how to do it. The National Security Act, passed into law on 26 July 1947, created a 'comprehensive program for the future security of the United States'. The three services were brought together under the National Military Establishment, soon renamed the Department of Defense, under its own Secretary, the first being James Forrestal. It is a sobering reminder of the pressures of these times that Forrestal, a tough and brilliant Irish-American, jumped to his death in 1949, weeks after leaving office (Millis, 1951). A new body, the National Security Council (NSC), was established to advise the president in assessing and appraising the 'objectives, commitments and risks of the United States in relation to our actual and potential military power'. In time, presidents would come to recognize that, based as it was in the White House, the NSC could be used as a personal instrument of foreign policy.

One of the NSC's initial functions was to oversee the work of another new creation, the Central Intelligence Agency (CIA). Post-war American intelligence had got off to a curiously shaky start; even during the war it had not been as well developed as its British counterpart, especially in the crucial area of signals intelligence. By 1947, the need for an effective agency was clear. Progress was muddied by the nature of the relationship between the gathering and evaluation of intelligence and covert action. The CIA did not become independent of the NSC until 1949, and these two functions were brought together under its umbrella the following year. Like its British sister the Secret Intelligence Service, the CIA could not resist trying to take the war to the enemy, encouraged by the apparent success of aid to the Italian Christian Democrats in the 1948 elections. Covert operations were subsequently mounted in support of anti-communist groups in Albania, Poland, the Baltic states and the Ukraine, with uniformly tragic results. Intelligence gathering and evaluation were more prosaic, but did yield information invaluable to the formation of foreign policy. Invisible to the public eye was the highly-secret National Security Agency (NSA), which Truman authorised in 1952, which over the years employed increasingly sophisticated equipment in signals intelligence. While it would be going too far to say that the Cold War was fought by the rival intelligence agencies, their successes and failures materially affected its course (Andrew, 1996; Aldrich, 2001).

Concerns for security were further reflected on 2 September 1947, when the United States joined 18 Latin American countries in signing the Inter-American Treaty of Reciprocal Assistance in Rio de Janeiro. Truman marked its importance by travelling to Rio on the battleship *Missouri*, the platform for the Japanese surrender. The substantive point was that the treaty provided for joint action in the event of an attack on any of the signatories, the formula adopted for the North Atlantic Treaty two years later. This concern with Latin America was not reflected in the amount of aid Washington was willing, or able, to provide, the western hemisphere lagging well behind Europe. The fear that socio-economic instability would invite communist expansion did not, it seems, extend south of the Rio Grande.

The years 1945–47 proved critical for the future direction of American foreign policy. Hopes that some kind of world order could be pursued through a continuation of wartime collaboration expressed through the United Nations proved to be wide of the mark. While it is too simplistic to see the wartime alliance as the temporary convergence of the powers which Hitler attacked, pious hopes for its continuance in some form proved insufficient. Both the United States and the Soviet Union became enmeshed in the affairs of an exhausted continent. Their differing perceptions of national interest, reinforced by diametrically different ideological and economic systems, ensured that by the autumn of 1947 the Cold War between them had begun, even if its issues had yet to crystallise.

2

TRUMAN AND THE CRYSTALLISATION OF THE COLD WAR

> Events have brought our American democracy to new influence and new responsibilities. They will test our courage, our devotion to duty, and our concept of liberty. But I say to all men, what we have achieved in liberty, we will surpass in greater liberty. Steadfast in our faith in the Almighty, we will advance toward a world where man's freedom is secure.
>
> Harry S. Truman, Inaugural, 20 January 1949

The 'Fall' of China

The sharp deterioration in east–west relations in Europe in the course of 1947 did not mean that the Truman administration was free from pressing considerations elsewhere. Roosevelt's hopes that China would assume a major role in the post-war world foundered on the bitter hostility between Chiang Kai-shek's Kuomintang (KMT) and Mao Tse-tung's Chinese Communist Party (CCP), which the war against Japan had barely concealed. In November 1945, Patrick Hurley, Roosevelt's choice as ambassador to China, resigned, castigating the administration for its lack of a clear policy and accusing American diplomats of favouring the communist side. Hurley, whose ignorance of Chinese affairs was legendary, was replaced by the wiser head of General Marshall. But even Marshall, with all his qualities, spent 1946 in a vain quest for a solution to the country's divisions. The two factions could not be reconciled, while Chiang's government and army did everything they could to lose the resulting civil war. Chiang presided over a corrupt party and an incompetent and venal military. His government had largely avoided conflict with Japan, preferring to hoard American military supplies for the forthcoming war with the communists. In consequence, in the summer of 1945 the KMT had 39 American-equipped divisions which Chiang assumed would bring him victory over his rivals. This ignored the fact that these troops were almost entirely lacking in battle experience. Above all, the KMT alienated the peasantry, the key element in the Chinese population. By contrast, the CCP guerrillas had fought the Japanese, were largely honest, and had the sense to win over the peasantry by land reform. American diplomats in China would later suffer for their knowledge of these realities.

The decisive battle of Hwai-Hai began in central China on 7 November 1948. When it ended on 12 January 1949, the KMT armies had lost half a million men (Clubb, 1964). The Director of the United States Military Advisory Group, General David Barr, sombrely reported to Washington on 16 November that the KMT's military position had deteriorated so badly that only active American military intervention could help them. Castigating the KMT as 'the world's worst leadership', he strongly advised against such a step. In any event, there was neither the popular will nor adequate military resources in the United States to undertake such a far-reaching commitment. In the circumstances, the civil war drew to an inevitable conclusion. Chiang's capital of Nanking was taken on 22 April, followed by the great trading city of Shanghai on 27 May. With the surrender of the last major KMT army on 19 September, the civil war was effectively over. On 1 October 1949, Mao proclaimed the People's Republic of China, and by the end of the year Chiang had evacuated the remnants of his army and administration to the island of Taiwan. It was one of the most significant events of the post-war period. That a quarter of the world's population had become communist electrified an American public, which could now see, or thought they saw, a communist empire extending from the Elbe to the South China Sea. There were inevitable questions about how the 'loss' of China had come about. Republicans who had followed a bipartisan line over Europe seized the opportunity to make political capital out of what happened in China. The consequences for domestic and foreign policies were to be profound (Acheson, 1969).

The Independence of the Philippines and the Reconstruction of Japan

Elsewhere in Asia American policy was taking a different path. Prior to 1941, attention had largely focused on the Philippines, the straggling archipelago in the South-west Pacific acquired from Spain in 1898. In 1935, the Roosevelt administration granted the islands internal self-government with a view to full independence ten years later. This timetable was brutally interrupted by the Japanese conquest and occupation in 1942. It became a matter of honour, immortalised in General Douglas MacArthur's phrase 'I shall return', that the islands be liberated. On 1 February 1945, MacArthur redeemed his pledge by entering Manila. Independence quickly followed. On 4 July 1946, the Philippines became an independent republic. Even so, American economic and military interests remained strong, to many Filipinos excessively so. The naval base at Subic Bay and air base at Clark Field on Luzon Island were major assets in the Cold War, and they were only ceded to the Philippines in 1992 after somewhat bad-tempered negotiations.

As long as the assumption persisted that China would be one of the major props of post-war foreign policy, attitudes towards Japan remained somewhat detached. Responsibility for the defeated country lay with the Supreme Commander Allied Powers (SCAP), General MacArthur, who had accepted her surrender aboard the USS *Missouri* in Tokyo Bay. The term 'allied' was honoured in the breach, Soviet and British hopes of active participation being ignored, politely in the case of the latter. Largely independent of Washington, at least in the initial stages, MacArthur exerted an authority any imperial proconsul would have envied, his actions never wholly divorced from his hopes of gaining the Republican nomination for the presidency. SCAP's purpose was to remove the sources of Japanese militarism and reconstitute the country on liberal-democratic principles. To ease their task, the monarchy was retained and both government and bureaucracy quickly restored. The imminent threat of famine was eased by a massive programme of American aid. But by 1948, with the onset of the Cold War and growing fears over the turn of events in China, perspectives on Japan were changing. While no one, MacArthur included, advocated rearmament, the Japanese islands, especially Okinawa in the Ryukyus, were being thought of as essential base areas for American forces. A revitalised Japan was increasingly seen as the buttress of American power, even as her first line of defence, in the western Pacific. The Cold War was spawning another front, the potential of which would become apparent before very long. Little thought had been given to the future of the Japanese colony of Korea until after the explosions at Hiroshima and Nagasaki. A quick decision was taken that the country be divided into American and Soviet spheres of influence at the 38th parallel. In August–September 1945, it seems that neither country regarded Korea as much of a priority, nor, on any scale of world problems, should it have been (Lowe, 1997).

Palestine

Palestine was the one clear irritant in Anglo-American relations. Britain held the country under mandate from the United Nations. The Arab majority were demanding that the country become independent as a unitary state, while the

Jews wished all or part of it to become a Jewish homeland. Roosevelt was torn between the keen support for Zionism in the American Jewish community and the importance to the Allied war effort of the oil resources of the Arab Middle East. In May 1943, he assured Ibn Saud of Saudi Arabia that there would be no decision on Palestine without 'full consultation with both Arabs and Jews'. After meeting the Saudi ruler on his return from Yalta, Roosevelt wrote to the effect that he 'would do nothing to assist the Jews against the Arabs and would make no move hostile to the Arab people' (Fraser, 1989). Apart from anything else, the meeting acknowledged the growing importance of the Saudi kingdom, with its vast oil reserves.

As the reality of Hitler's extermination policies was exposed, American public sympathy swung behind the creation of a Jewish state in Palestine . Truman's response was to send Earl Harrison to Europe to find out how the Jewish survivors saw their future. Harrison reported that the only solution was emigration to Palestine, recommending that 100,000 immigration certificates be granted. Truman put this request to an unresponsive British government. On 13 November 1945, the question became less urgent with the appointment of the Anglo-American Committee of Inquiry, which set to work over the winter months. The president's hopes that it would come up with an acceptable solution proved false. In formulating a way forward, he was being pulled in two very different directions, something he greatly resented. On one flank was the State Department, including Acheson, Kennan and the main Middle East specialist, Loy W. Henderson, strongly supportive of the Arab position. Set against them were influential members of Truman's staff, Clifford, who believed that the 'Jews were entitled to have their own country', and David Niles, a romantic Zionist who felt deeply over the fate of the survivors of the extermination camps. Truman certainly shared the latter sentiment, but was also pulled by the organised lobbying power of the American Zionist Emergency Council.

It was not until 4 October 1946 that Truman came out in favour of a Jewish state through the mechanism of the partition of Palestine. At this stage the United States was simply a bystander, but once the British referred Palestine to the United Nations in February 1947 this changed. Once the United Nations Special Committee on Palestine (UNSCOP) reported in September 1947 that Britain's mandate be ended and that the country be partitioned into Arab and Jewish states, the United States would have to define her policy. On 10 October 1947, it was announced that the United States would support the partition plan. But the matter was far from straightforward. Two critical votes had to pass. The first, as the United Nations' members voted as the Ad Hoc Committee on the Palestinian Question, did so on 25 November 1947 by the margin of 25 votes to 13, with 17 abstentions and 2 absentees. Had this tally been repeated in the General Assembly four days later, the partition resolution would have failed, since a two-thirds majority was required. Truman issued orders for the vote to be secured. Pressure was exerted at various levels on such key states as the Philippines, Haiti and Liberia. When the roll was called on 29 November, the partition resolution passed by 33 votes to 13, with 10 abstentions. It was one of Truman's most personal foreign policy interventions, though not one that he had enjoyed making. The vote was historic, since it opened the way to the creation of the Jewish state.

But in Palestine itself the Arab majority bitterly rejected the plan and the British announced that they would thwart any attempt by the United Nations to implement it. A bitter civil war broke out between Arabs and Jews. By late January 1948, the situation in the country was such that the State Department began a campaign to reverse American policy. On 21 February, they presented Truman with a recommendation that if the United Nations Security Council could not secure implementation of the partition plan, then the United States should move to support some form of trusteeship. Truman agreed this in principle, but insisted that any speech which indicated a move away from partition should first come to him for consideration. On 19 March, to the president's fury, Warren Austin announced in the Security Council that the United States wanted temporary trusteeship. Behind Truman's discomfort was an assurance he had given the veteran Zionist leader Chaim Weizmann the previous day that the United States still supported partition. With statehood almost within reach, Zionist lobbying on Truman reached a pitch. Concentrating everyone's minds was what would happen when the British mandate formally ended on 14 May. Clifford argued that as the Jewish leadership in Palestine had made partition an accomplished fact, it would be to the advantage both of the United States and the Democratic Party to recognise the Jewish state when it was proclaimed. Truman's desire to announce this at a press conference on 13 May was thwarted by a thunderous rebuke from Marshall. By the 14th, Marshall had been persuaded, however reluctantly, to acquiesce in Truman's policy. At six o'clock Washington time on 14 May, David Ben-Gurion proclaimed the existence of the State of Israel. Eleven minutes later, the United States announced her *de facto* recognition, the first country to do so. The following day, the first Arab–Israeli war began. When it ended in January 1949, Israel had secured her independence, while some 750,000 Palestinians were refugees. The Arab–Israeli conflict would absorb the attention of policy-makers for the next 50 years, confounding most of them (Fraser, 1989; Clifford, 1991).

Crises in Europe: Prague, Berlin and Belgrade

These significant events in China, Japan and the Middle East were a counterpoint to what was going on in Europe, confirming the global nature of America's involvement in foreign affairs. In 1948–49, however, it was still Europe which lay at the heart of Washington's concerns. In late February 1948, two events conspired to illustrate how dangerous the division of the continent was becoming. On 23 February, the United States, Britain, France, Belgium, the Netherlands and Luxembourg met in London to consider the future of Germany. It was clear that, bitter legacies of distrust notwithstanding, events were leading to the creation of a west German state out of the three western zones. Then, on 27 February, dramatic events took place in Czechoslovakia which seemed confirmation of Stalin's intention to dominate central Europe, though it was not quite as straightforward as that. Since liberation, the country had maintained its independence. With some 38 per cent of the popular vote, the communist Klement Gottwald presided over a coalition government. The veteran, and highly popular democrat, Edvard Benes, was President, and the internationally respected Jan Masaryk, son of the state's founding father, was foreign minister. In February 1948, increasing communist control of the police provoked a confrontation with the non-communist members of the government. The latter resigned, seeking to challenge the communists at the polls. Instead, Benes allowed Gottwald to form a communist-dominated government, which wasted no time in securing unfettered control. A few days later, Masaryk was found dead beneath his office window; whether his death was caused by murder or suicide was never found out. Although these events in Prague were less than a planned communist coup, it is clear that Benes was being influenced by the prospect of Soviet intervention. The communist takeover of Czechoslovakia removed any lingering doubts in congress about the need to become involved in west European security.

Despite the seemingly relentless erosion of east–west relations, there had so far been no direct confrontation between Washington and Moscow, but this was not long in coming. For some time it had been apparent that the logical culmination of western policy in Germany would be the coming together of the three zones of occupation, not least because such an important element in the political and economic life of Europe could not indefinitely be held in limbo. That such a policy would stir up Soviet fears of German revanchism was inevitable. In February 1948, the western powers decided to introduce a common currency in their zones. On 24 June 1948, Stalin reacted to this by cutting off the western allies' land communications to their occupation zones in Berlin. This was followed by the severance of all supplies, including electricity, to west Berlin, effectively imposing a blockade of the city. Raising as it did the prospect of the ultimate starvation of two and a quarter million Berliners, this presented the Americans with a number of uneasy options. To withdraw from the city was quickly dismissed; so, too, was the option of forcing supplies through by land. The course adopted, an airlift of supplies by the American and British air forces, surprised its authors and confounded the Soviets by its effectiveness. Stalin did not challenge the airlift, despite the striking way in which it was undermining Soviet prestige. Truman reinforced the message of western resolve by sending to British air bases, on the suggestion of Ernest Bevin, a force of B-29 bombers. These had the range to attack the Soviet Union with atomic bombs, though these particular planes had not been adapted to carry them, something which Stalin almost certainly knew from his British agents (Eisenberg, 1996; Gaddis, 1997). Certain lessons may be drawn from this gesture. The first was a signal that in the absence of substantial ground forces in Europe, the only means of stopping a possible Soviet attack was the threat of atomic warfare, something which was to be at the heart of east–west relations for the next four decades. The second was that the United States was prepared to sustain her commitment, both to her former enemy, Germany, and to her former ally, Britain, proof, if such were still needed, that there was to be no return to isolationism. Through their restraint, Truman and Stalin had shown a desire to avoid the step to armed conflict. By the time the Berlin Airlift ended, in May 1949, some 2.3 million tons of supplies had been flown into the city.

American policy had passed a major test (Millis, 1951; Hamby, 1995).

As the crisis over Berlin developed, Stalin had to face problems on another front, Yugoslavia. In contrast to other parts of eastern Europe, the communist partisans, led by Josip Broz Tito, had largely liberated themselves, with some assistance from the British, but virtually none from the Soviets. As a result, Tito increasingly bridled at Stalin's assumptions of hegemony over the region, while the Soviet leader could not afford to acquiesce in Yugoslav defiance. The result, on 28 June 1948, was Yugoslavia's expulsion from the Cominform. Contrary to expectation, Tito survived this, though the word 'Titoism' soon acquired a sinister significance. From 1948 until Stalin's death in 1953, a succession of leading communists in eastern Europe, accused of 'Titoism', were arrested, imprisoned, tortured and executed. Stalin had reverted to the methods of terror he had exercised against his own people before 1941, a lesson which was not lost in western Europe or the United States (Crampton, 1994).

The End of Isolation: The NATO Alliance

These critical events in Prague and Berlin brought into focus ideas which had been maturing on each side of the Atlantic for some kind of collective defence. Truman chose the occasion, on 17 March 1948, when Britain, France, Belgium, the Netherlands and Luxembourg signed a mutual defence pact, to make a major speech before a joint session of Congress. Signalling his approval, he concluded that he was confident that the 'United States will, by appropriate means, extend to the free nations the support which the situation requires'. He also called for urgent action to restore the draft, which duly followed in August. The idea that Congress might endorse a defence commitment to Europe came in June 1948, when Vandenberg introduced a resolution in the Senate Foreign Relations Committee, calling on the United

States to associate with 'such regional and other collective arrangements as are based on continuous and effective self-help and mutual aid, and as such affect its national security'. Although this lacked legal force, it provided considerable encouragement to the administration as it conducted negotiations with Canada and the countries of western Europe throughout the winter of 1948–49.

As the negotiations proceeded, Truman at last came into his political inheritance. In one of the most spectacular upsets in electoral history, he defeated Thomas Dewey by 24,179,345 votes to 21,991,291. His inaugural address on 20 January 1949 looked forward to a 'collective defense arrangement' for the North Atlantic area. Four days later, he met his new Secretary of State, Dean Acheson, to review progress on the North Atlantic negotiations. On 4 April 1949, representatives of the United States, Canada, Britain, France, Belgium, the Netherlands, Italy, Norway, Denmark, Iceland and Portugal signed the North Atlantic Treaty, destined to be the cornerstone of American diplomacy for the next five decades. At its core was the commitment that should one of its members be attacked, the other signatories would come to her aid using 'such action as it deems necessary, including the use of armed force, to restore and maintain the security of the North Atlantic area'. Despite a last stand by a rump of isolationists, the treaty was ratified by the Senate on 21 July 1949. Four days later, Truman submitted a request to congress for $1,450 million in military aid to the countries of what was now known as the NATO alliance, $1,300 million being granted on 28 October. It was only four years since American and Soviet soldiers had embraced on the Elbe. On 21 September 1949, the diplomatic revolution was completed with the creation of the Federal Republic of Germany, uniting the three western zones, while on 7 October the Soviet zone became the German Democratic Republic. Once the Soviets brought their allies – 'satellites', as the West preferred to call them – into the Warsaw Pact in 1955, the division of Europe was complete.

Thermonuclear Weapons and NSC 68

In the autumn of 1949, two events combined to confirm the worst fears of American policy-makers. The first was the uncomfortable realisation of Mao's success in China. Only days before the proclamation of the People's Republic came the knowledge that the Soviet Union had successfully carried out tests on an atomic bomb, removing one of the two main props of American security, the other being her naval strength. Taken together, these events seemed to signal nothing less than a reversal in the balance of power (Nitze, 1989). A new, and more terrifying, weapon was in the course of development. Whereas the atomic bomb had been based on the principle of nuclear fission, since the 1930s scientists had also been working intermittently on weapons based upon nuclear fusion, which opened up the seductive possibility of blasts one thousand times the power of the atomic weapons detonated over Japan. The hydrogen bomb, as it came to be known, was regarded with deep suspicion by some, including Kennan and the scientist who had done as much as anyone to bring the atomic bomb to fruition, J. Robert Oppenheimer. Others thought differently. On 19 November 1949, Truman set up a Special Committee of the National Security Council to review the question. It came down in the end to the brutally simple proposition that if the Americans had the scientific knowledge to develop the weapon, then it had to be assumed that so, too, had the Soviets. On that basis, on 31 January 1950 Truman authorised the production of hydrogen weapons. It seems that Stalin had come to a similar decision three months before. At all events, the United States detonated her first thermonuclear device in November 1952, followed by the Soviet Union, possibly in 1953 and certainly in 1955. Confrontation between Washington and Moscow had acquired a potential for destruction which would assume an exponential growth over the decades to come, casting an understandable shadow over the minds of all who lived through them and gave more than a passing thought to world affairs (Nitze, 1989).

Truman's characteristically brisk decision to move ahead with the hydrogen bomb carried with it huge financial implications, not least in the light of the substantial assistance already being given to America's cash-strapped NATO allies, who were inevitably jittery over the Soviet atomic bomb. The direct result was a joint working party of the State and Defense Departments charged with directing a way forward. The result of their deliberations was 'NSC 68: United States Objectives and Programs for National Security', which reported to Truman on 14 April 1950. While students of American foreign policy have laboured over its assumptions, no one has seriously challenged its import for the future thrust of foreign and defence policies (May, 1993). NSC 68 was the product of a time when communist intentions had begun to assume an almost superhuman form. 'The Soviet Union', it argued, 'is animated by a new fanatic faith, antithetical to our own, and seeks to impose its absolute authority over the rest of the world.' Its design was nothing less than the 'complete subversion or forcible destruction of government and structure of society in the countries of the non-Soviet world and their replacement by an apparatus and structure subservient to and controlled from the Kremlin. To that end Soviet efforts are now directed toward the domination of the Eurasian land mass.' Current Soviet capacity would enable it to overrun western Europe, drive towards the oil-producing areas of the Middle East, launch air attacks against Britain, and 'attack selected targets with atomic weapons, now including the likelihood of such attacks against targets in Alaska, Canada and the United States'. All of these assertions were, of course, open to question.

Faced with such a terrifying vision, what was the United States, the only effective power in the western world, to do? Isolation was no longer an option. 'Containment' could only operate within a military framework: 'Without superior aggregate military strength, in being and readily mobilizable, a policy of "containment" – which is in effect a policy of calculated and gradual coercion – is no more than a

44

policy of bluff.' What was proposed was a heady formula. 'Our free society,' the paper contended,

> confronted by a threat to its basic values will take such action, including the use of military force, as may be required to protect these values. The integrity of our system will not be jeopardised by any measures, covert or overt, which serve the purposes of frustrating the Kremlin design, nor does the necessity for conducting ourselves so as to affirm our values in actions as well as words forbid such measures, provided only they are appropriately calculated to that end and are not so excessive or misdi-rected as to make us enemies of the people instead of the evil men who have enslaved them.

What might constitute the 'free world' was left eloquently undefined. Significantly lacking from NSC-68 was any price tag. Acheson estimated that what was envisaged was nothing less than an increase from the existing annual military budget of $13.5 billion to $50 billion. Critically, he recorded, 'it is doubtful whether anything like what happened in the next few years could have been done had not the Russians been stupid enough to have instigated the attack against South Korea and opened the "hate America" campaign' (Acheson, 1969). Two obvious points about NSC-68 need to be noted. 'Containment' was now firmly set in military terms, which had not been its author's original intention. Secondly, the repeated emphasis on 'Eurasia' as the focus of the Kremlin's ambitions set the widest possible boundaries to the implementation of containment. If not a blank cheque, it was pretty close.

Korea

The decision to locate the division between the American and Soviet zones in Korea at the 38th parallel meant the *de facto* partition of a country which decades of Japanese rule had left bereft of political leadership. In effect, Washington and Moscow became locked into the affairs of an unstable peninsula, the strategic value of which to either party was less than clear. Elections in the American zone in 1948 resulted in the formation of the Republic of Korea in July, with Dr Syngman Rhee as its president, proclaiming itself the national government. Castigating this as the work of American imperialism, Communists in the north, led by Kim Il Sung, announced the formation of the Democratic People's Republic of Korea, also claiming to be the legitimate voice of the whole country. The withdrawal of American and Soviet forces from their respective zones in 1948–49 seemed to confirm that Korea was not likely to become a source of confrontation, but the danger signals were there. Neither Rhee, a Christian convert who had lived most of his adult life in the United States, nor Kim, a doctrinaire Marxist, was much in tune with traditional Korean life, but each was a dedicated nationalist determined to pursue national unity. Tensions across the 38th parallel became so acute that the peninsula was in a state of barely concealed civil war. Particularly worrying to American and British intelligence was their belief that in the event of war between the two parts of the country, the North decisively held the balance of advantage. While the Soviets had assisted with the creation of a substantial military force, including an air arm, South Korea's military potential was judged poor by comparison (Lowe, 1997). Indicative of American thinking was a major policy speech by Dean Acheson before the National Press Club on 12 January 1950. Entitled 'Crisis in China – An Examination of United States Policy', Acheson used it to define America's defensive perimeter as running from the Aleutians, through Japan and the Ryukyu Islands to the Philippines – Korea, any other part of the Asian mainland, or Taiwan, being notably absent. The previous week, Truman had publicly confirmed that the United States would not provide aid to the KMT forces in Taiwan, in what was seen as China's unfinished civil war (Acheson, 1969).

All of this changed dramatically on 25 June 1950 when North Korean troops attacked along the 38th parallel. Precisely what prompted Kim's offensive remains conjectural, but it seems that in a visit to Moscow in April he secured Stalin's support (Lowe, 1997). There is no doubt that Truman and his principal advisers saw what was happening not in the context of Seoul, but of Munich. 'In my generation', he later recorded, 'this was not the first occasion when the strong had attacked the weak .... I remembered how each time that the democracies had failed to act, it had encouraged the aggressors to keep going ahead. Communism was acting in Korea just as Hitler, Mussolini and the Japanese had ten, fifteen years earlier' (Truman, 1956). Even if this may have the colour of Wordsworth's 'emotion recollected in tranquillity', there is no reason to doubt that it was the essence of his position. Key advisers were also telling him that the aggression in Korea was being seen as the test of the country's leadership across the world (Hamby, 1995). That an American military response would come was not in question, but it was important that it was done through the United Nations' sanction. On 25 June, in the absence of the Soviet Union, the Security Council voted to condemn the North Korean attack and demanded that their forces withdraw north of the 38th parallel. In discussion with his foreign policy and defence chiefs, Truman sent instructions that MacArthur should supply South Korea with arms, that the air force should defend the airport at Seoul, and that the Seventh Fleet should position itself in the Formosa Straits to prevent any attack on Taiwan or any KMT adventure against the mainland. There was to be no question of a wider Asian war. Two days later, a further Security Council resolution sanctioned the use of force by member states to aid the South Koreans. Such assistance was not thought likely to have much military value, but was considered politically important. In the event, 15 countries joined the American-led United

Nations force. Only the First Commonwealth Division, consisting of troops from Britain, Canada, Australia and New Zealand, was of major significance, confirming the British role as America's main ally (Lowe, 1997).

But the military and diplomatic response was essentially American. A further Security Council resolution on 7 July asked the United States to appoint a commander for the United Nations' forces. The choice inevitably fell on the 70-year-old MacArthur. While the North Korean and American forces were steadily pushed down the peninsula to a small perimeter at Pusan, MacArthur was planning a decisive counterstroke. On 15 September 1950, his troops landed at Inchon, west of Seoul, recapturing the city and reversing the course of the war, or so it seemed. Four days before the landing, Truman had prepared orders that MacArthur could conduct operations north of the 38th parallel with a view to occupying the whole peninsula. It was a fateful decision. Not only did it move beyond the mandate of the Security Council resolutions, it looked to the destruction of a communist state and presented the Chinese with the prospect of a victorious American army on their border. When the orders were conveyed to MacArthur on 27 September it was on the clear understanding that there was no Soviet or Chinese deployment in North Korea or threat that they should do so. As MacArthur's troops advanced towards the Yalu river, evidence began to accumulate that Chinese 'volunteers' were being deployed. On 24 November, MacArthur began an offensive, which, he claimed, would end the war. Instead, his forces were met with a massive attack by the Chinese army which threatened them with rout (Hamby, 1995; Lowe, 1997).

The Americans were now faced with a very different war, albeit undeclared, against one of the two principal communist powers. Two possible options were discounted. Although at a press conference on 30 November Truman had made reference to atomic weapons, he reassured Britain that he had not authorised their use. The second possibility, advocated by MacArthur, was to widen the war by bombing

Chinese supply lines across the Yalu and by supporting Chiang Kai-shek's intervention, for which the KMT leader was only too anxious. This, too, was ruled out. Truman and his general were increasingly at odds. On 24 March 1951, MacArthur sealed his fate by issuing a statement to the effect that China 'must by now be painfully aware that a decision of the United Nations to depart from its tolerant effort to contain the war to the area of Korea, through an expansion of our military operations to its coastal areas an interior bases, would doom Red China to the risk of imminent military collapse'. Stung by the challenge to presidential authority, Truman moved to dismiss MacArthur. On 5 April, MacArthur replied to a letter from Representative Joseph W. Martin advocating the use of KMT troops, by agreeing and concluding that there 'was no substitute for victory'. Five days later, MacArthur was relieved of his command. Returning to an America touched by anti-communist frenzy, he was given a hero's welcome, but his political ambitions came to nothing, the Republicans turning to a general with a less strident record (Truman, 1956; Hamby, 1995).

April 1951 saw the last intensive phase of the war, after which weariness seemed to set in all sides. But like most wars, it was not easy to end. Contacts with North Korea and China began in July 1951. In October, truce talks began in Panmunjom, but progress proved glacially slow and intermittent fighting broke out. Inability to end the war contributed materially to loss of public confidence in the Truman administration. In the course of these events, the United States had stabilised her position in other important respects, even if some of the results were questionable. With the war under way, in September 1950 Truman approved NSC-68, initiating the massive build-up of American forces which the document had advised. The war in Korea was further confirmation of the importance of Japan, accelerating moves towards a peace treaty. This was signed at San Francisco on 8 September 1951, confirming Japanese independence, though with Okinawa being retained by the

United States for 30 years. It was accompanied by a United States–Japan Security Treaty by which the Americans were allowed to retain their bases in the country (Smith, 1995). Events in Korea also had the effect of tying the United States in with Chiang's regime in Taipei, lending herself to the pretence that his government represented China when palpably it did not. America's relations with China were set into a pattern of sterility from which they were only ultimately rescued by Richard Nixon, though few would have guessed that from his stridently anti-communist attitudes at the time. They also contributed to Senator Pat McCarran's campaign against an array of distinguished Foreign Service officers, castigated as having helped 'lose' China to the communists, when, in truth, they had done nothing more than report the facts. The United States could ill afford to lose men of their stamp, especially since shadows were growing in other parts of Asia.

France's attempt to reimpose her control over Indo-China had, by 1950, embroiled her in a war which her tough Foreign Legionnaires and colonial troops were within no sight of winning. An attempt to pretend they were defending an independent Vietnam within the French Union under the Emperor Bao Dai convinced few. But Ho Chi Minh was increasingly seen in Washington as Moscow's agent in Southeast Asia. Ominously, by 1950 American analysts were prepared to speculate that a communist victory in Indo-China would have security repercussions throughout the region, including the Philippines and Indonesia. The resulting recognition of the Bao Dai government, coupled with the provision of increasing levels of aid to the French, marked the beginning of America's fateful involvement in the affairs of that country. Communism was to be contained in South-east Asia, even though Kennan warned Acheson on 21 August 1950 that 'we are getting ourselves into the position of guaranteeing the French in an undertaking which neither they nor we, nor both of us together, can win' (Kennan, 1972; Gaddis, 1987; Miscamble, 1992).

3

EISENHOWER: HOLDING THE FORT

> So we are persuaded by necessity and by belief that the strength of
> all free peoples lies in unity; their danger, in discord. To produce
> this unity, to meet the challenge of our time, destiny has laid upon
> our country the responsibility of the free world's leadership.
>
> Dwight D. Eisenhower, Inaugural, 20 January 1953

'I accept your summons. I will lead this crusade.' With
these words, Dwight D. Eisenhower, former Supreme
Commander of the Allied Expeditionary Force in Europe
during the Second World War, Army Chief of Staff,
Chairman of the Joint Chiefs of Staff and the first NATO
Supreme Allied Commander Europe (SACEUR), accepted
the GOP (Republican) nomination in July 1952. Eight
months later he was elected to the highest office in the
land, winning 442 electoral college votes to Adlai
Stevenson's 89, and carrying all but 9 states.

A newcomer to national politics, Eisenhower had been
courted since 1948 by both the Democrats and
Republicans. His decision to align himself with the latter
in late 1951 had much to do with the man he prevented
from becoming the Republican presidential candidate –
Senator Robert Taft (Lucas, 1991). Taft was hostile to
NATO and the Marshall Plan, supportive of unilateral
nuclear defence, and represented a section of the GOP
that embraced a neo-isolationist position mitigated only by
an inclination to regard Asia as a vital area of interest. A
Taft presidency threatened, in Eisenhower's view, to attack

the concept of collective security, destroy NATO and reduce America's involvement in Europe; in short, remove one of the key mechanisms for fighting the Cold War (Bowie & Immerman, 1998). Finally, it was the management of this war that compelled Eisenhower to stand as a Republican, for although he generally supported Truman's foreign policies, he was convinced that structurally, these needed to be revised and reorganised if the United States were to outlast the Soviet Union.

During his election campaign, Eisenhower highlighted a number of issues that would occupy him as president. Among the most significant was national security policy and Korea. The stalemated war, Eisenhower promised, would be brought to an end. On national security, he criticised Truman's massive spending, which he regarded as wasteful and unsustainable, and advocated instead long-term planning to protect and develop the economic and military might of the country. Careful not to alienate the more right-wing elements of the Republican Party, Eisenhower also endorsed a policy of peaceful liberation of captive countries or 'roll-back'. Also with this in mind, he selected for his Vice-President, Richard Nixon, a young, right-wing conservative who had made his name exposing Alger Hiss, a State Department official suspected of espionage and convicted of perjury.

Eisenhower brought a very clear agenda to his administration and probably more foreign affairs experience than any previous twentieth-century president. The identity, agenda and actions of the new administration were formed by Eisenhower's perception of the Cold War and his views on how this situation of global confrontation should be handled. The make-up of his foreign policy team reflected this mindset. For his Secretary of State he chose John Foster Dulles, grandson of one Secretary of State and nephew of another; author of the Japanese Treaty and, for the previous decade, Republican spokesman on foreign policy. Eisenhower and Dulles shared similar views about the Cold War and the Soviet Union although Dulles, a champion of the Republican Old Guard, advocated an Asia-first policy as opposed to Eisenhower, who firmly believed that Europe should be the United States' premier concern. Both men harboured deep suspicions about the Soviet Union and communism in general. They regarded the ideology and the political system they supported as aggressive, naturally expansionist and unstable. More ideological, doctrinaire and hardline than the president, Dulles increasingly became the focus of criticism of the administration's foreign policy. This was deliberate. Although often suspected of acting unilaterally, Dulles masterfully performed as Eisenhower's alter ego and as a lightning rod for some of the president's more controversial policies. Charles E. Wilson, whose credentials included heading one of the world's largest corporations, General Motors, was brought in to seize control of the unwieldy and fractious Department of Defense. Eisenhower appointed Robert Cutler as his special assistant for national security affairs to coordinate the revamped National Security Council, which he had expanded to include the Policy Planning Board tasked with preparing policy papers, and the Operations Coordinating Board with responsibilities for coordinating policy implementation. In a move that stressed the link between foreign policy and the intelligence establishment, Eisenhower chose Allen Dulles, brother of his Secretary of State (Gaddis, 1982; Bose, 1998). Finally, in his role of Staff Secretary to the President (a position initially held by Paul T. Carrol until his death in 1954), Andrew J. Goodpaster became Eisenhower's closest adviser and confidant.

Domestic Pressures

The new president was faced with two significant inherited challenges: the Bricker Amendment and the activities of Joseph McCarthy. Introduced in 1951 in response to

Truman's unilateral decisions regarding NATO and Korea, the Amendment sought to reduce presidential authority over foreign affairs and was vigorously opposed by Eisenhower in 1953 and 1954 before being finally dropped in 1956. Likewise, the activities of the junior Senator from Wisconsin were deeply distasteful to the president and caused him a great deal of personal angst. Nevertheless, Eisenhower consistently refused publicly to condemn McCarthy and avoided confrontation until the Senator's attacks on the army and his administration compelled the president to act. Even then, this intervention was indirect and largely hidden (Greenstein, 1994). Eisenhower's reluctance stemmed from his belief that McCarthy's appeal would soon diminish and that any presidential intervention would only serve to legitimise the Senator's actions and fuel his obsession (Schrecker, 1998). Moreover, Eisenhower was concerned that his involvement would split the Republican Party between the moderates in its eastern wing and the conservatives in its western wing, making it impossible for him to govern effectively. To a certain extent, Eisenhower was correct in his assessment. McCarthy's power did peak before censure and expulsion by the Senate in late 1954 precipitated his rapid fall from grace. But this was not before his crusade had purged almost all of the administration's Asian experts in the State Department. Although the individual had been condemned, the 'ism' had not been repudiated (Schrecker, 1998). Henceforth, policies not clearly anti-communist in content and tone would be judged with suspicion, if articulated at all. The implications for future drafting of foreign policy would be momentous and far-reaching.

The Cold War

In the months after the death of Stalin in March 1953, Eisenhower repeatedly eschewed the various peace feelers extended by the new leadership in Moscow. The president believed that the Cold War struggle could be won, but that this was most likely to happen as a result of the Soviet Union collapsing internally under the strain of major economic problems and over-extension in the sphere of foreign affairs. In his view fundamental fatal weaknesses would cause the superpower to implode. Eisenhower predicted that the Soviet threat would be long-term and constant. In contrast to the Truman administration, which perceived the Soviet threat as mainly military or nuclear, the Eisenhower–Dulles team perceived the danger in much broader terms. The solidification of the Cold War by the early 1950s brought challenges of not simply a military nature but threats that were economic, psychological and political. Furthermore, the new president viewed the Cold War as a bipolar struggle dominated by the two superpowers and their allies. With the world unofficially divided up between the East and the West, the remaining uncommitted or neutral states largely in the third world quickly took on greater importance in the eyes of the strategy-makers. This mindset transferred great importance to these non-aligned countries and compelled the administration to commit US prestige and personnel to preventing the Soviet Union from unsettling the balance of power in what was now an alarmingly fragile international system. So potentially significant was the loss of any US interests to communist encroachment that Eisenhower believed that this could lead to war. This prospect was all the more troubling given the advances made by the Soviet Union in developing nuclear technology. The successful testing of atomic and then hydrogen bombs created, by 1953, the permanent threat of nuclear war between the two rival camps. Remarkably, it was this horrific possibility, combined with Eisenhower's military background, that produced a willingness to deal with the Soviet Union pragmatically and realistically. The fact that he did not trust the Soviets did not prevent the president from attempting to maintain the peace.

National Security

Eisenhower's main priority was national security. This encompassed policies concerned with military defence, economic health, domestic stability and positive foreign relationships and was based on the premise that successful prosecution of the Cold War was only possible if the US maintained a robust and productive economy. The nation's wealth and industrial health were crucial in the struggle against communist attempts to dominate the free world. Although the country had experienced prosperity (reflected in the growth of GNP by 27 per cent between 1949 and 1953), the military increases undertaken by the Truman administration at the beginning of the Korean War had produced a number of worrying trends – a sharply rising national debt, surge in inflation, and tax increases. The massive increases in the military budget at the beginning of the 1950s bequeathed a vexing problem. The huge mobilisation was economically unsustainable and, if continued, would cripple the country. At the same time, Truman's adoption of the containment doctrine had committed the US to playing a permanent role in global affairs. For Eisenhower, the question was how to regain the initiative in the Cold War after the 'loss' of China and the stalemate in Korea, while at the same time reducing the amount spent on defence. These seemingly contradictory requirements compelled the new administration to undertake a review of national security policy.

Project Solarium and the New Look Policy

In order to conduct a thorough review of national security policy, Eisenhower established Project Solarium in May 1953. Task forces were invited to assess three possible policies. Led by the architect of containment, George Kennan, task force A was charged with reviewing this policy in the light of a new emphasis on defence economy. Task force B was assigned to look into nuclear deterrence and the Soviet threat. Finally, task force C had a mandate to examine the concept of liberation by 'roll-back' (Dockrill, 1996). The review produced little by way of consensus and was written up as NSC 162 – a draft policy paper that incorporated recommendations from all three task forces. The final draft (NSC 162/2), approved in October 1953, was less a blueprint (as NSC 68 had been) than a guide for future national security policy, and provided the basic framework for what became known as the New Look (Pickett, 1995; Bose, 1998).

The basic assumptions that underpinned the New Look differed in some ways quite considerably from the policy adopted by the Truman administration. To begin with, the New Look chose a middle ground between the aggressive liberation policy articulated by Eisenhower in the presidential election campaign and the containment policy pursued by the previous government. The new strategy asserted that the United States would do everything to maintain the current status quo balance of power, including meeting future communist expansionism and harassing Soviet satellites. Eisenhower wanted to regain the initiative in the Cold War, while at the same time reducing the crippling costs associated with massive mobilisation and defence spending (Dockrill, 1996; Bose, 1998). Of central importance was the decision to reduce conventional force spending in favour of building up a huge nuclear deterrent. This emphasis on nuclear weapons was considered both practical in economic terms (the 'more bang for buck' theory) and sensible in light of the defensive and offensive power of nuclear weapons. Moreover, it permitted the reduction and redeployment of conventional forces around the globe. Also inherent in the New Look doctrine was the importance of military alliances. With the United States shouldering the burden of providing non-conventional defence, it was thought that the allies should begin to take more responsibility for providing the conventional or forward force element – especially in the NATO area. Furthermore, the new thinking placed added emphasis on providing economic aid as well as developing and supporting mutual and collective security arrangements. Unlike the Truman administration, Eisenhower also stressed the desirability of expanding psychological and covert operations which necessitated augmenting the intelligence services. Finally, the New Look guidelines included the recommendation that the United States should seek opportunities to negotiate with the Soviet Union. Collectively, this revision of Truman's containment doctrine produced a guide for defence of not only the United States, but of the whole free world. America would choose when and where to meet Soviet aggression. Once the decision had been taken, US interests would be protected with any means, including nuclear weapons (Bowie & Immerman, 1998).

Europe

The administration's stated intention of initiating a massive nuclear strike in response to communist aggression, or 'Massive Retaliation', as it was soon dubbed, created a great deal of unease with the government and among America's European allies. Of more immediate concern to the Eisenhower administration was the fate of the European Defence Community (EDC), which had been signed by the prospective elements – France, West Germany, Italy, Belgium, the Netherlands and Luxembourg – in May 1952, but not yet ratified by all their governments. Eisenhower was committed to the EDC because it incorporated three of his goals for Europe: European unity, a rearmed West Germany tied to western Europe, and it would allow the United States to reduce troop numbers in Europe (one of the facets of the New Look rethinking). One of the president's first directives was to send Dulles to Europe in order to revive the stalled ratification process. There was, however, little that the

Secretary of State could achieve in talks with the French (the instigators of the treaty), who were now primarily responsible for its tenuous position. His degree of political leverage was severely hampered by the deepening crisis in South-east Asia where the French were still fighting their colonial war against the communist Vietminh. French threats of withdrawal threw up the unwelcome thought of possible US intervention in the region. Although Eisenhower and Dulles tried to link military assistance for Vietnam to French willingness to ratify the EDC treaty, in practice, they were not bargaining from a position of strength. Veiled French threats that they might be forced to abandon South-east Asia, claims that without military assistance they could not afford to contribute to NATO, evidence of growing anti-American sentiment in France and a change of government in early June changed the stakes, making it virtually impossible for the administration to pressure her truculent ally in any meaningful way.

Closely related to the EDC debate was the question of NATO force levels and rearmament. Even with the changes envisaged under the treaty, NATO still fell short of the troop numbers needed to defend Europe. The reluctance of the European Allies to spend more on conventional defence cast doubt in the minds of the Americans about the depth of their commitment. The related problems of introducing the New Look, with its emphasis on nuclear weapons, mutual security and troop reductions, and dealing with the reluctance of the Europeans to build up their own forces, compelled Eisenhower to consider extending America's new national security policy thinking to NATO. In August 1953, the administration began discussing a new approach to collective security that involved the use of tactical nuclear weapons by the Alliance. The basic concept of the New Look called into question in the minds of the Europeans the degree to which the Americans were committed to the defence of the continent. This, combined with the frequent warnings from Dulles that failure to ratify the EDC would spark an American reappraisal of its European policy, created an atmosphere of distrust and suspicion that put a great deal of pressure on the Alliance. Fearing that the Eisenhower administration was considering an isolationist or peripheral defence policy, the NATO allies doubted the president's assurances that his main foreign policy priority was Europe. Finally, at the end of August 1954, after months of delay and debate, the French vote for ratification was defeated, thus effectively ending any chance of life the defence community might have had. In response, Eisenhower asked for a resolution from Congress to help Germany rearm outside a European army context but within NATO. The New Look went into effect on 22 December 1954 and reduced US military divisions overseas to seven – two in Korea and five in Europe.

Korea

One reason for the eventual demise of the EDC was the deepening crisis in South-east Asia. But before Eisenhower was faced with this crisis, he had unfinished business to take care of in the Far East. Exchanging one set of stalled negotiations for another, Eisenhower turned his attention to the Korean War and the armistice talks that had been stalemated since 1951. Having made a promise in his election campaign to bring an end to the conflict, the new president signalled to the Chinese his resolve by threatening to 'move decisively without inhibition in our use of weapons' if the negotiations did not reconvene in a productive way. 'In India and in the Formosa Straits area,' he recorded in his memoirs, 'and at the truce negotiations at Panmunjon, we dropped the word, discreetly, of our intention. We felt quite sure it would reach Soviet and Chinese Communist ears' (Eisenhower, 1963). Eisenhower came under a great deal of pressure from various quarters, both inside and external to his administration, to adopt policies that ranged from an all-out military offensive against the Chinese to complete withdrawal from Korea. He was unwilling, however, to countenance either war (which would surely become nuclear) or surrender, and instead charted a course that accepted the concept of a military armistice and the country's partition. By early June 1953, the talks had moved sufficiently forward to allow agreement on perhaps the most intractable problem preventing the resolution of the crisis – the issue of prisoners of war. A ceasefire, it seemed, was close at hand. Eisenhower's negotiations with the Chinese, however, had angered Syngman Rhee who, fearing that events were moving rapidly beyond his control, voiced his frustration in dramatic fashion on 18 June by releasing some 25,000 North Korean troops in direct violation of the agreement that had been reached some ten days before. Eisenhower acted quickly to neutralise Rhee by threatening to withdraw US troops and military support from the Republic of Korea. He also warned that continued disruption of the peace negotiations would cost him a mutual defence pact and a substantial sum of reconstruction destined for South Korea in the event of a settlement. A placated Rhee acquiesced, and on 26 July a truce was signed in Panmunjon that represented, according to Eisenhower, 'an acceptable solution to a problem that almost defied, in view of world sentiment and the political situation, any solution at all' (Eisenhower, 1963). As with many of the difficulties faced by America in Asia, the final arrangement created more of a holding pattern than a long-term solution. Korea would continue to cause concern in Washington for years to come.

South-east Asia

The resolution of the Korean crisis did not allow Eisenhower to move far from Asia. By early 1954, even with the US supplying some 75 per cent of the French war effort in Vietnam, the burden was becoming intolerable. Although the president was willing to provide military assistance and personnel, he refused to contemplate the introduction of American combat troops into what had become another stalemated conflict. Eisenhower's adherence to the concept of mutual security permitted him to consider the possibility of bilateral intervention with a partner such as Britain, but failure to secure support for such a course of action forced him to reject any idea of unilateral intervention. As the situation continued to deteriorate, the president again came under extensive pressure to act decisively. Many, especially in the Republican Party, advocated stepping up assistance to the French. Others rejected the supposition that the loss of Vietnam would trigger a communist takeover of South-east Asia and stressed instead a policy of withdrawal. Eisenhower typically rejected both these courses of action, arguing a middle ground. He was convinced that Vietnam was a vital US security interest in the region and on 7 April outlined his thinking in a speech that used the fateful analogy of falling dominoes. Abandoning South-east Asia would, he told his audience, precipitate the loss of Indochina, followed by Burma, Thailand, Malaya and Indonesia (Ambrose, 1984). But while he was committed to preventing communist encroachment, Eisenhower was not prepared to fight a ground war in Vietnam. As the Geneva conference approached, the crisis ameliorated. At the isolated fortress of Dien Bien Phu, ten miles from the border with Laos, the French had massed some 10,000 troops in a fortified valley stronghold in anticipation of a battle with the Vietnminh (Billings-Yun, 1988). Resisting strong pressure to intervene, Eisenhower accepted what had become the almost inevitable defeat of his ally. By the time they finally surrendered on 7 May, after a lengthy and bloody siege, Eisenhower's thoughts had moved far beyond relief for the beleaguered French. Now emotionally reconciled to the idea of a divided country, his strategy involved a long-term effort to maintain a strong, pro-western government in the south of the country.

On 12 June the fall of the French government was quickly

followed by direct talks between the new premier Pierre Mendes-France and the Chinese Foreign Minister Chou En-lai. The Eisenhower administration distanced itself from these negotiations, the product of which was a ceasefire agreement followed by the temporary division of Vietnam along the 17th parallel and the promise of national elections within two years. The deal, which also included the prohibition of foreign aid to either North or South, any joining of alliances and the withdrawal of all foreign troops, was signed on 21 July at Geneva. Although the US opposed the agreement (which it refused to sign), Eisenhower recognised that it afforded him some time to construct what he had identified as the best way to halt the communist encroachment in the region – a defensive alliance based on the NATO model. After several weeks of intensive negotiations, Dulles had secured the participation of seven countries (in addition to the US) with security interests in the area – Britain, France, Australia, New Zealand, the Philippines and Pakistan – which signed the South-east Asian Treaty Organization (SEATO) on 8 September. The collective security treaty pledged to defend South-east Asia and extended protection to Laos, Cambodia and Free Vietnam, which were not permitted, under the terms of the Geneva agreements, to join the organisation. The following month, Eisenhower offered full US support to the Prime Minister of Free Vietnam – Ngo Dinh Diem – the anti-communist, pro-American, Catholic leader of the predominantly Buddhist country, also in contravention of the agreements (Ambrose, 1984). One direct consequence of his offer of assistance was the implicit recognition of the area south of the 17th parallel as a sovereign state. Also implied was the fact of US support for the new government's decision not to hold nationwide elections. By his actions, Eisenhower had committed the United States to Diem and South Vietnam. Another stage by which communism would be contained in Vietnam had been reached. By 1960, opposition to Diem had begun to take on a new dimension. The South

Vietnamese leader denigrated his opponents, calling them Vietcong, or Vietnamese Communists. But they, and their political arm, the National Liberation Front (NLF), had secured Hanoi's blessing to wage war against his increasingly corrupt and authoritarian regime. Before long, Diem was fighting what had become a civil war to maintain power in South Vietnam.

Crisis in the Taiwan Straits

A storm brewing in the Taiwan Straits began to give cause for concern when islands held by the Chinese Nationalist leader Chiang Kai-shek came under fire in early September 1954 from the People's Republic of China. Unlike Formosa and the Pescadores, which had been under Japanese rule for 50 years, the islands of Quemoy and Matsu had traditionally belonged to China. Chiang's fear was that the shelling of the islands was the precursor to a full-scale attack on Formosa. Although Eisenhower had inherited a commitment to defend the Chinese Nationalists on Formosa, no treaty existed to require this course of action. Eisenhower was torn. On the one hand, he was adamant that the United States had an obligation to protect the Chinese Nationalists. However, he also disagreed with Chiang and several of his own advisers who suggested that Quemoy and Matsu were vital to this end. Moreover, he was deeply reluctant to contemplate going to war over the islands. Insisting that congressional approval was needed in order to engage in military intervention in the Straits, he resisted calls from some quarters, including the Chairman of the Joint Chiefs of Staff, for an atomic strike against the communists. Instead, while Eisenhower stressed his commitment to defend Formosa against any direct attack, he remained deliberately obscure about his intended response to anything less. Throughout October and November the Chinese Communists continued to shell and build up what appeared to be an invasion force opposite the islands. In early December, Eisenhower signed a mutual defence treaty with Chiang that applied to Formosa and the Pescadores. Tensions continued to mount as the Communists attacked some remote islands held by the Nationalists. Mindful of the fact that American public opinion was deeply opposed to involvement in another Far Eastern conflict, Eisenhower sought from Congress a Resolution permitting him the unprecedented authority to take action in defence of Formosa, the Pescadores and closely related localities. The intentionally vague wording allowing the president the freedom to choose when and where US forces would go into action was passed in late January by 410 to 3 votes in the House and 83 to 3 in the Senate (Greenstein, 1994).

The Formosa Doctrine – the first blank cheque to be given to a president – was designed to deter the Chinese Communists from launching an invasion. Privately though, Eisenhower was committed to the defence of Formosa and Quemoy/Matsu only if the evidence suggested that the islands were stepping stones to the ultimate goal of seizing Formosa. His main concern was the morale of the Chinese Nationalists. If they decided to give up Eisenhower knew he would be faced with a stark choice – either go to war against the Communists or accept the repercussions arising from having abandoned an ally and allowed a vital region to fall into communist hands. In public, however, he kept his remarks deliberately obscure. Foremost in his mind was the knowledge that, according to Dulles, the US did not possess the conventional forces necessary to defend the islands and would have to resort to nuclear weapons in order to repel China. Although both he and Dulles publicly stated the government's intention to use any and all weapons at its disposal – including tactical nuclear weapons – the president was deeply reluctant to contemplate the evolution of the Straits crisis to such proportions. By the beginning of April, the administration calculated that the military assistance furnished to the Chinese Nationalists was sufficient to deter the Communists and was judged by Eisenhower to be a turning point in the crisis. On 23 April, before the Conference of Asian and African nations in Bandung, Indonesia, the Chinese Communists announced their desire not to go to war with the United States and suggested negotiations to resolve the crisis. Having committed themselves to securing the liberation of Formosa by peaceful means 'as far as this is possible', the Communists began reducing their shelling of the islands before stopping the offensive completely in mid-May. On 1 August talks began. Eisenhower's strategy of vague threats combined with military support had produced the desired result: Chiang retained the island network and the US commitment to the Chinese Nationalists had been strengthened without having to resort to war. The peace had been maintained, but at the price of the continuing division of China.

Intelligence

One of the criticisms of the New Look policy frequently articulated by both Democratic and Republican politicians was the perceived manner in which Eisenhower was waging the Cold War. Although periodically irritated and frustrated by the suggestion of weakness implicit in the attacks, the president rarely felt the need to dispel this illusion in order to set the record straight. Underpinning his confidence was the knowledge that the United States was pursuing an aggressive anti-Communist policy that drew its greatest strength from the fact that it was highly secret. Cognisant of the advantages afforded his country during the Second World War by the Office of Strategic Services, Eisenhower made it one of his top priorities, once elected, to expand and make more use of this resource. Thus, he ordered the development of the U-2 spy plane that debuted in 1956 and also pushed hard for the expansion of the intelligence agencies. The CIA, in particular, gained a new mandate designed to transform it into one of America's most powerful weapons in the Cold War struggle. The size and the scope of the agency increased dramatically under Eisenhower (Ambrose, 1984). Although propaganda, sabotage, subversion and intelligence gathering all featured strongly in the work of the Agency, it was in the realm of covert activity that perhaps the most significant developments occurred.

Covert Operations – Iran and Guatemala

The first major operation undertaken by the CIA under the new administration was in Iran. Its origins lay in a request by the British government for assistance in removing Dr Mohammad Mossadegh, who had nationalised the oilfields and refineries belonging to the Anglo-Persian Oil Company in May 1951. The ensuing diplomatic crisis did not directly involve the United States and indeed Eisenhower, when approached by Mossadegh for help, declined to intervene. The administration, however, believed the Iranian leader to be close to communists and feared that his sympathies made Iran vulnerable to Soviet encroachment. Ruling out overt force, in June 1953 Eisenhower approved in principle a plan to remove Mossadegh. As public order disturbances mounted and Eisenhower learned of the Soviet Union's financial assistance to the Iranian government, he ordered Operation Ajax to commence. The plan involved the use of millions of dollars to bribe Iranian army officers and to hire a crowd in Tehran; its objective was the replacement of Mossadegh with General Fazlullah Zahedi, who would be loyal to the pro-Western Shah, Mohammad Reza Pahlavi. On 22 August, after a shaky start that saw the Shah flee to Rome and Zahedi forced to hide out in a CIA safe house, Mossadegh was arrested by his own army and deposed. Emergency aid of $45 million sent by the United States cemented the coup (Roosevelt, 1979).

The success of the CIA's covert action in Iran convinced

Eisenhower that this was a Cold War asset that had tremendous value (Andrew, 1996). When faced with another unacceptable regime, this time in Latin America, the president again deployed the CIA. On this occasion the target was the president of Guatemala, Jacobo Arbenz Guzman, whose radical social reforms and a land distribution programme involving the appropriation of property owned by a number of large American multinationals, including the United Fruit Company, had sounded alarm bells in Washington. Critics of Arbenz pointed to his toleration of the Guatemalan Communist Party as further evidence of his sympathies. Private interests (some of the most prominent figures in the Eisenhower administration, such as the Dulles brothers, had close ties with United Fruit), and political concern about his left-wing tendencies, combined to create a strong desire to get rid of Arbenz (Ambrose, 1984). Using Ajax as a model, Operation PBSuccess was conceived with the aim of using deception to persuade Arbenz to leave the country by convincing him that the army had turned against him and was staging an American-backed coup. When the Guatemalan leader began to suspect a move against him and sought to arm a citizens' army in order to outmanoeuvre his opponents Eisenhower ordered 50 tons of weapons to be airlifted to the neighbouring pro-American dictatorships in Honduras and Nicaragua and declared a naval blockade of Guatemala. After calling for a meeting of the Organization of American States (OAS), he ordered Operation PBSuccess into action. Whilst propaganda from a CIA-controlled radio station in Honduras transmitted dispatches from the 'front' where fierce fighting was reported to be taking place between the Guatemalan army and forces controlled by Castilo Armas (the man chosen by the agency to replace Arbenz), intense diplomatic pressure and the naval blockade caused Arbenz to order martial law and turn to the Soviet Union for arms.

As the crisis intensified, Eisenhower tightened the blockade and ordered ships bound for Guatemala to be stopped and searched. On 19 June the *New York Times* ran a headline announcing that a massive revolt was under way in Guatemala. In reality, Armas and his 'invasion' force of 150 men had crossed the border from Honduras, advancing six miles into the country before striking camp to await news that Arbenz had fled the capital. Despite the massive propaganda campaign claiming that the country was in turmoil, Arbenz did not immediately capitulate, leaving the CIA somewhat at a loss as to how to proceed. When it became clear that the Guatemalan army had no intention of forcing Arbenz from power, the agency approached Eisenhower with a request to allow them to intervene. Anastasio Somoza, the dictator of Nicaragua, had offered to give two P-51 bombers to Armas if the United States agreed to replace them. Approving this arrangement, Eisenhower also allowed American bombers flown by CIA pilots to join in an air offensive. Meanwhile, supported by Britain and France, Arbenz tried unsuccessfully to have the UN Security Council put the crisis on its agenda. As the bombing raids continued, he fled.

At a press conference on 30 June, Eisenhower announced his 'great satisfaction' at the turn of events in Guatemala. The president clearly felt that a great deal was at stake in the country, as evidenced by his total commitment to installing a pro-American government. This courting of international crisis was highly unprecedented for Eisenhower. Not only did he cause outrage by his illegal blockade and stop-and-search tactics, unheard of in peacetime, he risked alienating his closest allies, Britain and France, who were strongly opposed to his actions at a time when the fate of SEATO and the EDC hung in the balance. Furthermore, he provoked accusations of gunboat diplomacy and jeopardised relations with the other Latin American countries which watched anxiously as their northern neighbour intervened, albeit surreptitiously, in the affairs of a democratic country. Finally, the propaganda victory associated with never having used the veto in the UN was sacrificed in order to prevent the crisis from being debated in the Security Council.

Eisenhower's fear that the domino theory was just as applicable to Central and South America as Asia had apparently compelled such a response. In July 1954, after a secret review of covert operations, Eisenhower justified the expanded use of this tool saying, 'It is now clear that we are facing an implacable enemy whose avowed objective is world domination . . . there are no rules in such a game' (Andrew, 1996).

1955

The year 1955 was one of some promise for relations between East and West. The long-anticipated formation of the Warsaw Pact on 14 May and the accession of West Germany into NATO five days earlier did little except formally acknowledge the accepted lines of division in the Cold War face-off in Europe. Moreover, the enunciation of 'peaceful coexistence' by Nikita Khrushchev (Party Secretary and dominant voice in the Politburo) signalled an end to the siege mentality of Zhdanov's 'two camps'. Arguing that war was not inevitable between East and West, he appeared ready to talk to Western leaders. Perhaps most surprisingly, the negotiations begun in 1946 to resolve the status of Austria came to an abrupt but positive end on 15 May, when the Soviets signed a treaty granting the country full independence and a neutral status. This unanticipated show of goodwill had some basis in the expectation of a summit meeting which was to be held in mid-July. The Geneva conference produced little by way of substance – the Soviets rejected Eisenhower's 'Open Skies' proposal and handed a clear propaganda victory to the United States. The result, apart for the much mooted 'Spirit of Geneva', was little more that an agreed commitment to 'work together to develop an acceptable system of disarmament'. It was something of a disappointment for Eisenhower who, having long been appalled by the implications of nuclear war, or 'race suicide', as he termed it, had been contemplating ways of making some concrete progress in putting an end to the arms race. His 'Atoms for Peace' initiative, launched in December 1953 in a speech to the United Nations General Assembly, had been rejected by the Soviets, who calculated that even such a small donation of uranium isotopes from their atomic stockpile would adversely affect their atomic programme. This unsurprisingly negative response ruled out any immediate redirection of the escalating arms race, but nevertheless afforded Eisenhower an opportunity to put a positive face on the production of atomic energy, while at the same time telling the US public and the rest of the world, including the Soviets, something about the size and strength of America's atomic capability. Failure in 1953 and 1955 to make progress in nuclear testing and disarmament meant that little movement would be likely until Eisenhower's second term in office.

Poland and Hungary

It was in Eastern Europe in 1956 that the Eisenhower administration first came face to face with the impotence of the new concept in national security. The publication via the CIA of an anti-Stalin speech by Khrushchev sparked riots and civil disturbances in Poland that had forced the disbandment of the old Stalinist Politburo. The new government, led by Wladyslaw Gomulka, an independent Communist whom the Soviets regarded as a Titoist, promised its own socialist politics and a democratic system of government, and warned that 'the Polish people would defend themselves with all means' (Ambrose, 1984). This defiance of the Soviet Union encouraged Hungarians (mindful of events in Yugoslavia and, more recently, Austria) to demand the restoration of Imre Nagy, who had been deposed by the Soviets in 1955. In a surprise move, Soviet Premier Nikolai Bulganin apologised for past Soviet behaviour towards her satellites, pledged non-interference in Hungarian affairs and promised the removal of Soviet troops. One day later Nagy, now reinstated, announced his country's intention to withdraw from the Warsaw Pact, declared Hungary's neutrality, and appealed to the United Nations for help. On 4 November a Red Army force of 200,000 troops and 4,000 tanks attacked Hungary where a new government under Janos Kadar was formed. Nagy, who had been promised safe passage, was seized, tried and later executed. The failed uprising resulted in the deaths of some 40,000 Hungarians and forced countless thousands to flee for the relative safety of neighbouring countries. Through the Voice of America, Radio Free Europe and resistance cells established by the CIA, the administration had encouraged the Soviets' client states to rise up against their captors. The tragedy of Hungary, however, demonstrated that America had neither the means nor the desire actively to support the liberation of captive peoples, especially when circumstances saw her opposing simultaneously the actions of her allies in the Middle East. For those who had heeded the calls for liberation the silence from Washington was devastating. Eisenhower was stung by the accusations of betrayal, but accepted that the United States's rhetoric of throwing off communist oppression had been largely without substance. In spite of this, however, the president refused to contemplate intervention of any kind, including covert CIA action. The whole affair was deeply frustrating, not to say embarrassing, for the administration. Eisenhower could only reiterate his desire to see the eastern bloc countries free from communist domination through peaceful rather than military means. American action was confined to assisting the fleeing Hungarian refugees (Eisenhower, 1965).

Suez

Eisenhower's embarrassment over Hungary was compounded by his fury over events in the Middle East. The

Arab–Israeli war of 1948–49 had resulted in a new radicalism in the Arab world, which, initially at least, the Americans hoped to harness. To that end, the CIA established contacts with the Free Officers' movement in Egypt, which seized power in July 1952. Gamal Abdul Nasser, who quickly emerged as the country's leader, was seen as a genuine nationalist who could be set against possible Soviet influence in the region (Copeland, 1969). At the same time that Nasser was being cultivated, the Eisenhower administration's relations with Israel got off to a shaky start. So concerned were the Israelis over the drift of events that in the summer of 1954 they mounted an ill-conceived operation designed to shake confidence in Nasser by setting off bombs at American offices in Cairo and Alexandria. When the Israeli agents responsible were arrested, the Americans refused to intervene on their behalf. Two were executed and the rest received long prison terms (Fraser, 1995).

Stung by this humiliation, in February 1955 Israel's David Ben-Gurion mounted a massive raid on Gaza, killing 38 Egyptian soldiers. With tension between Israel and Egypt now acute, Nasser looked to possible sources of arms. When the British and Americans were slow to respond, on 30 September he announced a major arms deal with Czechoslovakia, in effect the Soviet Union. While some Americans tried to hold to the line that Nasser was really only asserting a need for independence, Dulles and the State Department were increasingly angry over the Soviet Union's new influence at the heart of the Middle East. This was to impact upon Nasser's key project for the betterment of his people, the construction of a dam at Aswan on the upper Nile, which would provide regular irrigation and hydroelectric power. Much of the finance was to come from American and British grants. On 19 July 1956, Dulles announced that this would not be forthcoming, and the British immediately followed suit. Nasser's response was to announce the nationalisation of the Suez Canal Company, based in Paris, which operated the Suez Canal.

The crisis now spiralled out of control. The British prime minister, Anthony Eden, and his French counterpart, Guy Mollet, began assembling a massive task force in the eastern Mediterranean, the ostensible purpose of which was to restore the canal to 'international control'. But since the canal continued to operate normally, the mustering forces seemed increasingly purposeless, unless they were used to overthrow Nasser. Alarmed at the turn of events, on 31 July Eisenhower wrote to Eden warning him of the unwisdom of even contemplating military force. A resolution of sorts was concocted at highly secret meetings at Sèvres between 22 and 24 October, when it was agreed that the Israelis would attack in the Sinai desert, thus giving the British and French the pretext of intervening to protect the canal. The Israelis attacked on cue on 29 October. The Anglo-French military operation began on 5 November. Their sense of timing could not have been worse, since Eisenhower was facing re-election on the 6th, and the Red Army began their attack on Budapest on the 4th. Incensed by the crassness and obvious dishonesty of his allies' conduct, Eisenhower resolved to bring their adventure to an end. When, on the evening of 6 November, it was clear that the American Treasury was obstructing British attempts to sustain sterling in the International Monetary Fund, the British Cabinet found no alternative but to halt operations (Kyle, 1991).

It is hard to overstate the importance of the Suez–Sinai crisis. It left the French with a festering sense of grievance against the Americans. Britain remained stripped of any remaining pretensions to being a major power. Her new prime minister, Harold Macmillan, made it his major aim in foreign policy to rebuild the American relationship, but when he did so it was as the junior partner (Murray, 2000). In the Middle East, Eisenhower insisted that an extremely reluctant Israel surrender all her military gains in the Gaza Strip and the Sinai desert. Israel did so on the basis of a secret guarantee from Nasser to the Americans that he would not interfere with Israeli shipping in the Gulf of

Aqaba. The ostensible guarantee of this was the stationing of the United Nations Emergency Force (UNEF) in the Sinai and Gaza. It was the breach of these undertakings which was to trigger the next war in 1967. In January 1957, the president announced the 'Eisenhower Doctrine', which promised aid to any Middle Eastern country requesting help against communism.

The Third World

In the midst of the Hungarian and Suez crises, Eisenhower fought and won the 1956 presidential election, gaining 35,590,472 votes to challenger Adlai Stevenson's 26,022,752; an electoral college result of 457 to 73. At the beginning of his second term, the president highlighted what he believed to be one of the most pressing issues facing his administration and the country – the proliferation of newly independent states in the third world. Often unprepared both by their former colonial masters and their new leaders for democracy and independence, Eisenhower was concerned that these vulnerable countries would succumb to communism without help from the West. 'From the deserts of North Africa to the Islands of the South Pacific,' the president warned in his second inaugural address, 'one-third of all mankind has entered upon an historic struggle for a new freedom' (Eisenhower, 1965). Eisenhower understood that the power of nationalism, combined with the desire for better physical conditions, created a deep sense of need and put at risk not only fledgling democratic societies, but western access to the vital raw materials that they possessed. Moreover, he recognised the link between Third World prosperity and First World affluence and warned the US public that 'Not even America's prosperity could long survive if other nations did not also prosper.' With this in mind, the president made one of his major priorities in 1957 the passing of a Development Loan Fund and a Foreign Aid package worth $4 billion in total. It was a rejection of his 1953 policy of 'trade not aid' in favour of the concept of 'trade and aid'. Eisenhower found it extremely difficult to convince Congress, the American people and even some of his Cabinet secretaries of the necessity for giving large sums of money to promote development in distant and obscure regions of the world. Unwilling or simply unable to see the bigger picture, the legislative branch cut the proposed funding from $4 to $2.7 billion, handing Eisenhower one of the most bitter defeats of his presidency.

Defence Spending, Nuclear Testing and Disarmament

Dominating much of Eisenhower's time in both his first and second terms in office were the related issues of defence spending, nuclear testing and disarmament. The New Look, which demanded tightly controlled spending that favoured nuclear and high-tech weapons, a balanced budget, mutual security and reductions in conventional forces, created an environment of bitter dissension and discord, especially among the armed services and their political patrons in the legislative branch. Eisenhower's policy of redirecting money away from 'men' and into 'technology' came under constant attack from the services which were unwilling to accept these changes. The inter-service rivalry and political criticism that accompanied the implementation of this policy intensified as international developments such as the Hungarian and Suez crises highlighted the apparent weaknesses inherent in the strategy. Although increasingly concerned about the unanticipated costs associating with developing nuclear weapons, Eisenhower nevertheless approved multiple intercontinental ballistic missiles (ICBM) and intermediate-range ballistic missiles (IRBM) programmes in the hope that this would improve the chances of producing successful weapons and also mitigate the inter-service rivalry. At the same time, pointing out that the only way to reduce the budget, stop inflation and cut taxes was through disarmament, the president tried to focus public attention on the positive advantage held by the United States. Believing that 'in the long run, no country can advance intellectually and in terms of its culture and well-being if it has to devote everything to military buildup', Eisenhower badly wanted a test ban that would serve as a precursor to real disarmament. His deep distrust of the Soviets, however, compelled him to move cautiously, approving a top-level suggestion that disarmament commence in December 1957. Advised by his scientists that America could not afford to pass up on the opportunity to conduct nuclear tests, the president approved several series, the last of which, codenamed Operation Hardtrack II, began in April 1958. Eisenhower's reluctance to halt testing stemmed from his conviction that this would go some way to both reducing the effects of fallout and producing a 'clean' nuclear weapon. The possibility of progress seemed closer in June 1957 when the Soviets offered to drop their demand for a complete test ban in favour of a two- or three-year moratorium and suggested that they were prepared to accept a system of international control. In January 1958, the US put a new proposal before the United Nations that included, for the first time, a test-ban clause. Pressure from the Pentagon and the Atomic Energy Commission that any future agreement would be tied to a cut-off in weapons manufacture ensured that the American counter-proposal containing this and other conditions would be rejected.

Sputnik

In 1956, when he had been accused of allowing a bomber gap to develop that favoured the Soviet Union, Eisenhower had dismissed the criticism content in the knowledge gleaned from the U-2 spy missions that this was misinformation being peddled for political purposes. On 4 October 1957, the world was stunned to learn that the Soviet Union had successfully launched the first earth-orbiting satellite. In the United States the shock became panic, accompanied by hostile criticism of the government. Although Eisenhower had been anticipating such a development, the depth of the public outcry and dismay that followed Sputnik's launch – which created the impression that the country's fleet of B-52 strategic bombers was an inferior delivery system – took the administration by surprise. The psychological damage and the feelings of vulnerability that it created forced the president to act in order to allay the fears and concerns arising out of what his Secretary of Defense described as a 'a neat scientific trick'. Amidst the political fallout and 'Pearl Harbor' atmosphere, Eisenhower repeatedly refused to approve the massive increases in defence spending demanded by the Joint Chiefs of Staff, Atomic Energy Commission, Pentagon, Congress, Ford Foundation and the US public, warning that 'hasty and extraordinary effort under the impetus of sudden fear . . . cannot provide for an adequate answer to the threat'. Eisenhower's efforts to resist pressures to increase military spending were further hampered by the publication of extracts from the leaked Gaither Report on 'Deterrence and Survival in the Nuclear Age'. According to the authors, the Soviet Union was not only spending considerably more on defence but was experiencing a faster growth in GNP than the United States. The report painted a nightmarish picture of the devastating effects of a nuclear war and called for a massive increase in defence spending (of $44.2 billion) in order to shore up America's active and passive defences which were respectively labelled 'inadequate' and 'insignificant' (Snead, 1999). Nonetheless, Eisenhower's response was restrained. He allowed a limit of $1.26 billion in additional funds to go towards stimulating America's ballistic missile, ABM programmes, the production of more B-52 bombers and the protection of Strategic Air Command. As much as two-thirds of this, he admitted privately, was more to stabilise public opinion than to meet any real need. Pressure to 'retake' the lead in space also stimulated an intensive effort to launch a satellite (Explorer I) and the creation, in April 1958, of the National Aeronautics and Space Administration (NASA).

Eisenhower was more concerned with making progress on the issues of a test ban and disarmament. Dulles's suggestion in March 1958 that a declaration by the United States of a unilateral test ban would score an impressive propaganda victory was overtaken by the rise to prominence of Nikita Khrushchev, who took over as premier from Bulganin on 27 March and then promptly announced the commencement of a Soviet test ban. The president's scientific advisers now claimed that a test ban was in America's best interest as the country would lose its current superiority if the Soviet Union continued to test. On 28 April, Eisenhower sent a letter prepared by his Secretary of State to Khrushchev outlining a new proposal that did not tie any future weapons production to a test-ban agreement. This major position change was enough to persuade the Soviets to enter into negotiations beginning in July. In August, preliminary discussions between the technical teams agreed that it was feasible to create a 'workable and effective control system to detect violations of an agreement on the world-wide suspension of nuclear weapons tests', paving the way for test-ban negotiations to begin. By the end of August both sides had agreed to schedule talks to begin on 31 October. Little progress was made as disagreement set in about the nature of the agenda. With the talks stalemated and in recess, Eisenhower invited Khrushchev to visit the United States in the hope that some progress could be made at the highest levels.

The Middle East

Securing a test ban was not the only foreign policy issue to compete for the president's time in 1958. Three major crises rocked the administration, beginning in January 1958 with trouble in the Middle East. One of Eisenhower's deepest concerns – an arms race in the region – had become a reality with the US supporting Saudi Arabia, Iraq, Jordan and Lebanon; the Soviet Union supplying Syria and Egypt; and France giving arms to Israel. The formation of the United Arab Republic comprising Egypt and Syria, followed by the Arab Union alliance of Jordan and Iraq and the shift in power in Saudi Arabia in favour of pro-Nasser Crown Prince Faisal created a heightened sense of anxiety in the Eisenhower administration about the growth of Arab nationalism. In late April, a crisis in Lebanon sparked by President Chamoun's announcement that he intended to amend the country's constitution in order to allow him to seek another term in office prompted Eisenhower to consider intervention. He believed that the rioting and unrest accompanying the developments in Lebanon were orchestrated by pro-Nasser forces. His administration was divided, with Dulles suggesting that Chamoun's unlawful action offered no excuse for American intervention. By mid-July, a republican coup in Iraq and attempts to unseat King Hussein of Jordan persuaded Eisenhower to send forces to Lebanon. A great deal about the decision was surprising: the crisis in the country appeared to have passed when Chamoun gave up his aim of a second term, Nasser had contacted the US with a plan to defuse tensions in the region, and Eisenhower possessed little evidence that either Egyptian or Soviet elements were behind the unrest in the region. Finally, America had no vital interests in Lebanon. These, however, were not factors that influenced the president. Eisenhower, having secured the freedom to act from Congress, was determined to make a public demonstration of America's will, primarily to send a message to Nasser and his Soviet backers. The year 1957 had been a bad one for the president. Eisenhower had been criticised for letting the United States be overtaken by the Soviet Union in defence and technology. Intervention in Lebanon afforded him the opportunity to make a show of strength, proving to his domestic and foreign critics that his policies had made the country strong and able to respond to communist agitation around the globe. In many ways the conditions were ideal. Involvement limited in scope and duration posed little real threat of direct confrontation with the Soviet Union and was not thought likely to produce any local opposition to the arrival of the foreign forces who had been invited by the Lebanese president. By the end of August, having made his point, Eisenhower ordered the withdrawal of American troops which, together with a similar British effort on behalf of Jordan, had restored relative calm to the region.

A Second Taiwan Straits Crisis

The second crisis to assail the administration began towards the end of August when the Chinese Communists started shelling Quemoy and Matsu in response to the growing nationalist force build-up on the islands. Eisenhower was unchanged in his belief that Quemoy and Matsu were not integral to the defence of Formosa. So for the second time in four years, he was pressed with having to decide whether or not to employ nuclear weapons to prevent the fall of the islands and perhaps the seizure of the main nationalist stronghold. Once more threatening the use of force, Eisenhower sent Dulles to persuade Chiang to back down by removing some of his forces from the Islands. Although he failed in this, Chiang did agree to renounce the use of force to regain the mainland, a move that prompted the Chinese Communists to offer the bizarre concession of shelling Nationalist convoys only on odd days of the month. Before long, all attacks had ceased. According to his biographer, 'Eisenhower had used a combination of threats, firmness, and resolve, combined with a willingness to negotiate and be reasonable, to achieve an outcome satisfactory to him' (Ambrose, 1984).

Berlin

Europe was the setting of the third major crisis to confront the administration, which began with Khrushchev's announcement in early November that he intended within six months to sign a bilateral treaty with East Germany should the western powers fail to resolve the current question of Berlin. As the deadline approached, war-scare fever gripped the United States and Eisenhower came under intense pressure to increase military spending, stop planned troop reductions and order the mobilisation of US forces. Denying accusations that he was under-reacting to the crisis, the president dealt with the situation largely by refusing to accept that war was imminent. His approach was to stress both firmness (hinting that nuclear weapons would be used if the Soviets blockaded the city) and conciliation (willingness to negotiate and perhaps attend a summit). Moreover, Eisenhower conceded that the status of Berlin was, as Moscow had been claiming, abnormal, and signalled his desire to make progress in other areas such as the ongoing test-ban talks. The Soviets extended the May deadline before Khrushchev removed it altogether when he visited the United States in September 1959. Eisenhower had weathered the crisis without giving in to the myriad of pressures to act.

Cuba

The Berlin crisis was not the only problem facing the administration in 1959. That year saw the emergence of a problem in Latin America that would occupy much of the president's time until he left office in January 1961. Eisenhower's problems in Cuba began with the ousting of Fulgencio Batista by the charismatic leader Fidel Castro in January 1959. Castro, well-educated, politically astute and widely popular, was very much an unknown quantity in Washington, not least because it was extremely difficult to ascertain his communist sympathies. The new Cuban leader's proposed revolutionary changes – including free elections, economic development, and a programme of massive social reform – tweaked the antennae of officials like Allan Dulles who associated such policies with a communist world view. Although the Director of the CIA was quick to label Castro a communist, his own agency could not easily find the evidence to back up these accusations. Indeed, by the spring of 1960 it was still proving difficult to determine the extent to which the Cuban had embraced the politics and ideology of quite a number of his government. This was the case even though he had moved to make the Communist Party legal in Cuba, postponed elections, confiscated American property, and developed a habit of making anti-American speeches. Eisenhower did have genuine concerns that Castro was moving closer to the Soviet Union. But he was also moved by the growing demands of the other Latin American countries which refused publicly to condemn the Cuban leader but nevertheless used him as a pretext for requests for money and military aid in order to prevent his popular radicalism from spreading throughout the continent. In the end, the enigma that was Castro was judged by the president to be too risky to tolerate and he turned to the CIA to facilitate his removal from office. The official programme that they concocted had four main elements: the creation of a viable government in exile, a large-scale propaganda effort, development of covert intelligence and resistance cells in Cuba, and a paramilitary action force capable of launching an invasion of the island. Unofficially, plans for the assassination of the Cuban leader were also implemented (Andrew, 1996). This activity, together with economic and diplomatic initiatives, continued throughout 1960 with little success. In January 1961, the administration, having failed to remove Castro or even identify an alternative leader, broke off diplomatic relations with Cuba and left for Eisenhower's successor the unused invasion plans that he had tentatively approved. Henceforth, Castro would be Kennedy's problem.

Disarmament

As national politics began gearing up for the 1960 presidential election, Eisenhower's mind began focusing on the last chance he would have to make some meaningful progress on disarmament. Mindful of the approach of the May summit, in February he announced his willingness to accept a test ban comprising atmosphere, oceans, outer space and detectable underground tests. The Soviet Union responded positively, accepting for the first time the principle of a supervised ban, adding only one condition – that the United States agree to a voluntary ban on low-kiloton underground tests that could not be monitored. As the two sides inched towards a mutually acceptable framework, Eisenhower came under increasing pressure to increase military spending and resume testing (ironically, among his strongest support for not testing came from the Democratic hopefuls, John Kennedy and Hubert Humphrey). This pressure was magnified by the damning accusation that Eisenhower had neglected the nation's defence and allowed a missile gap to open up. Against the advice of the AEC, the Department of Defense, the Joint Chiefs of Staff, the intelligence community, scientists and Democrat and Republican politicians, Eisenhower agreed to the terms suggested by the Soviets. Only his science adviser, George Kistiakowsky, supported the president. Under acute pressure to allow the CIA U-2 programme to undertake one final set of missions before the summit, Eisenhower gave way and authorised a limited number of overflights with the proviso that none took place after the beginning of May. After several weeks of bad weather, the last flight took off on 1 May, two weeks before the summit was scheduled to begin. That evening the president learned that the plane was missing. Thus began one of the darkest episodes of his administration. Advised that the plane and its pilot would not have survived either an accident or a deliberate attack, Eisenhower waited for word. Five days later, Khrushchev announced that the Soviet Union had shot down an American spy plane, blamed the 'Pentagon militarists' for the flights and claimed that the president had been kept in the dark. On the assumption that Khrushchev had no evidence, Eisenhower ordered a cover-up, claiming that the plane was a civilian (NASA) weather research plane that had experienced technical difficulties. When the Soviets produced evidence of an aircraft that was clearly not a U-2, Eisenhower was convinced that the Soviet leader was trying to make mischief. Then, on 7 May, Khrushchev sprang his trap and announced that both the plane and its pilot, Gary Francis Powers, had been captured. Eisenhower was caught. Rapidly changing press statements only served to heighten the sense that the president had been lying to his colleagues, the press and the American public. Eisenhower handled the affair with uncharacteristic ineptitude. He passed up the opportunity to dispel the notion that he was not in control of his own government and the chance to occupy the moral high ground by pointing out that the spying missions were only necessary because of the closed and secretive nature of the Soviet Union. Finally, the president refused to silence once and for all those persistent voices that had criticised him for permitting a missile gap to develop. It was a bad call. Eisenhower was counting on his reputation for honesty to pay dividends at the May summit. His decision to launch a cover-up in order to protect the secret U-2 programme cost him this valuable commodity and created a deep sense of humiliation.

On 14 May, Eisenhower flew to Paris, still claiming that the prospect for positive talks remained bright. Khrushchev had decided otherwise. Perhaps because he realised that the Berlin issue was unlikely to be resolved satisfactorily or that a test ban would not only favour the United States but would reveal the true state of his country's defence capability, the Soviet premier chose to use the incident to ensure that the Summit was over before it had begun. When the president refused to apologise or pledge an end to the spying missions, the Soviet leader walked out of the talks. One month later the test-ban talks collapsed when the Soviet delegation returned to Moscow. Eisenhower's goal of reining in the escalating arms race was hopelessly out of sight. He spent a considerable amount of his last months in office travelling in fulfilment of commitments and invitations to visit numerous countries around the world. Dulles's death in May 1959, the failure of his arms control initiative (by the end of 1960, the United States was producing more bombs per year than the estimated total requirement had been in the mid-1950s) and the criticisms levelled at him during the 1960 presidential election combined to leave him deeply frustrated and disappointed (Ambrose, 1984).

4

KENNEDY: THE NEW FRONTIER?

> Let the word go forth from this time and place, to friend and foe alike, that the torch has been passed to a new generation of Americans – born in this century tempered by war, disciplined by a hard and bitter peace, proud of our ancient heritage – and unwilling to witness or permit the slow undoing of those human rights to which this Nation has always been committed today at home and around the world.
>
> John F. Kennedy, Inaugural, 20 January 1961

The 1960 presidential election was a close-run thing. Democratic Massachusetts Senator John F. Kennedy lacked opponent Richard Nixon's political experience and was burdened by the infamous wartime record of his billionaire father, Joseph P. Kennedy (if not the financial advantages that he provided). He was also Catholic. In his favour, Kennedy was strikingly charismatic. Much of his appeal rested on the idea, as much as the image, of a youthful, dynamic, and, above all, promising leader possessing the energy and vision to lift America out of the stalemated 1950s. Aided by the choice of Texan Lyndon B. Johnson as his running mate, Kennedy won 34,226,731 popular votes to Nixon's 34,108,157, making him the first, so far only Catholic, and youngest-ever elected president.

Kennedy's inaugural address was in stark contrast to the seemingly static and stalemated presidency of his predecessor. This was deliberate and carried on the vivid and vigorous anti-communist rhetoric of his election campaign in which he had criticised Eisenhower for not having done

enough to halt Soviet advances around the world. In particular, Kennedy accused him of having allowed a 'missile gap'
to develop and for permitting Fidel Castro to remain in
power in Cuba. Throughout his political career he had been
an outspoken critic of men and policies he perceived as
being 'soft' on this issue; as a presidential candidate, he had
been deeply concerned lest he be branded with such a fatal
tag. Once elected, Kennedy promised that under his leadership the United States would embark upon a new era of
activism and progress that would witness a reassertion of
American hegemony in the world. In part, this was a reaction
to the belligerent speech made a few weeks earlier by
Khrushchev, who had promised communist expansion and a
combative approach to international relations. Kennedy's
remarks also reflected the personal and political assumptions and beliefs of the new leader. He was keenly aware of
the need to achieve bipartisan support for his administration
and the backing of the almost fifty per cent of the electorate
who had not voted for him. Thus, while he was committed to
making and keeping America strong, especially in military
terms, Kennedy also spoke of cooperation and conciliation,
the search for peace and the avoidance of war by miscalculation. In short, his message offered peace, prosperity and
progress, while threatening confrontation and war. America,
he warned in his first State of the Union Address, was near-
ing 'the hour of maximum danger'. Under his administration, he promised, she would be prepared.

Kennedy's 'New Frontier' comprised liberals, moderates
and hardliners, reflecting both the complex nature of the
foreign policy challenges facing the new government and
the activism he had promised in his campaign. Under the
influence of former Secretary of State Dean Acheson,
Kennedy appointed Dean Rusk to head the State Department. Robert McNamara was brought in to rationalise the
Department of Defense; McGeorge Bundy became
Kennedy's National Security Advisor, while Allen Dulles
remained in charge of the CIA. Finally, in what became one

of Kennedy's most significant appointments, he named his brother, Robert, as Attorney-General. Unlike his predecessor, who had demanded a clear hierarchy of command, Kennedy preferred a very informal method of decision-making that accepted, even demanded, input from a wide range of sources including current and former officials, journalists, friends and acquaintances. One of the consequences of this youthful meritocracy was a highly energised style of policy formulation that exposed the president to a variety of opinions. The disadvantage was that by removing or downsizing formal decision-making mechanisms such as the National Security Council, Kennedy eliminated many of the safeguards that his predecessors had enjoyed. Like those who had come before him, his chosen style of government handed him both notable victories and embarrassing failures.

Latin America

Kennedy faced, according to Eisenhower, three immediate foreign policy problems: Laos, Berlin and Cuba. It was to Latin America (which had become a potentially divisive domestic political issue) that the new president turned first to arrest Moscow's influence (Rabe, 1999). Communism in the western hemisphere threatened not only America's national security but impeded her ability to act elsewhere. For many in the administration, including the president, Latin America was seen as a test: if US resolve failed successfully to challenge communism in America's traditional sphere of influence, other countries around the world – the uncommitted countries and those on the peripheries of the communist bloc – would be dissuaded from aligning themselves with the countries of the 'free world' or find it impossible to maintain neutrality. Such was his concern that Kennedy, even before taking office, had asked his aides to prepare a strategy for conducting the Cold War in Latin America. When produced, this plan

89

outlined a dual approach that presaged the Green Berets/Peace Corps approach that became the modus operandi of the administration.

The administration's answer was a policy with three parts: first, a financial aid plan, *Alianza para el Progreso* (Alliance for Progress), announced by Kennedy on 13 March 1961, was conceived as a ten-year commitment to the countries of Latin America. Heralded as a Marshall Plan for Latin America, it was designed to encourage economic development, while at the same time strengthening democratic principles and structures in the recipient countries (Brogan, 1996; Rabe, 1999). It was envisaged that the United States would underwrite the region's social and economic transformation during what Kennedy called 'the decade of development'. The new administration firmly believed that with America seriously and deeply committed to helping the Latin American countries to become strong, vibrant, self-reliant democracies, economic and social development would negate and eventually eradicate the influence of communism in the hemisphere. Moreover, the resultant economic, political and social stability would have rewarding benefits for the American economy and put to rest the national security threat generated by the existence of governments sympathetic to communism (or worse) in America's backyard.

While the Alliance for Progress aimed to eradicate the conditions in which communism was thought to flourish, the aims of the second and third policies were more direct and immediate. The second policy was constructed to help pro-democratic governments to combat communism by providing training for special police forces that included instruction in riot control, intelligence gathering and interrogation techniques. This project, code-named '1290-D', was designed to counter subversive communism at a local level. The third policy was US support for anti-communist forces plotting to overthrow actual, pro- or suspected communist governments in Central and South America. This largely centred on the removal of Castro and his revolutionary government, and, as such, the elimination of this communist influence in Latin America. For at the heart of Kennedy's policies in Latin America was the fear (that coexisted with the sanguinity that the US was omnipotent) that the region was susceptible to radical social revolution. This confidence that America had within her power the ability to help Latin America transform itself was 'mixed with alarm', largely because of the perceived impact of Castro's Cuba (Rabe, 1999). Without Cuba, it was thought, revolutionary communism had no real foothold in Latin America and would, therefore, cease to give the United States major cause for concern. Preparations for the removal of the Cuban threat had been in preparation for several years. The most recent plan had been born in the last year of the Eisenhower administration and involved the secret training by the CIA of Cuban exiles in Guatemala in order to overthrow the Castro regime. Kennedy's hawkish stance during 1960 (a departure from his earlier categorisation of Castro as a nationalist) left little political room for a reassessment of his campaign pledge to deal aggressively with the Cuban leader or, indeed, the rejection of the approval secretly given by his predecessor for such action.

The Bay of Pigs

Although the president-elect had been briefed about CIA plans for an invasion of Cuba, the operation that he eventually approved was fundamentally different from the one developed under Eisenhower. Concerned above all with the political fallout that might accompany an openly US-backed invasion, Kennedy rejected the small but full-scale invasion proposed by the CIA as 'too spectacular', and ordered that American involvement should be minimal (without the use of US troops) and, most importantly, covert. This was necessary in order to allow the administration plausibly to deny any involvement. Kennedy's order to 'reduce the noise level' of the plan prompted a revision of the scheme (Bissell, 1996). The new plan, codenamed Zapata, was scheduled to begin on 17 April 1961. Although the adjustments ordered by Kennedy increased the military risks associated with the invasion, no attempt was made to reconsider the venture (Higgins, 1987). The Bay of Pigs invasion was an almost immediate failure and a source of deep humiliation for the administration.

The plan itself was structurally flawed, perhaps most importantly, because without overt US air cover and troop support, the invasion was almost certainly predestined to fail. At Kennedy's request, the CIA had revised a plan that had taken months to develop inside four days because of pressures to execute the mission before Castro became too strong, America's allies in the Caribbean lost their nerve, the rainy season started and leaks exposed the plan. Zapata ruled out any overt US assistance even though it was believed that the exiles could not succeed unassisted. Victory rested on the fanciful expectation of a spontaneous uprising in Cuba. Unfortunately, however, the CIA's intelligence was poor and flawed. The loss of the US embassy in early 1961 and Castro's success in silencing potential and actual agents bore some responsibility for this. Moreover, the fact that the planned invasion was an open secret removed the element of surprise that the covert action demanded. Fatal mistakes, however, in the analysis of crucial photographic information, namely the labelling of dangerous coral reefs as seaweed, are less easily explained.

At the crux of the disaster lay the relationship between the CIA and the administration. There had been an almost total lack of serious criticism of the plan as top officials including the Joint Chiefs of Staff and senior members of the Department of Defense had all accepted it on the advice of the coordinating body responsible – the CIA. What dissent there was tended to be low-key and based on an incomplete grasp of the operation (Higgins, 1987). Kennedy, for his part, was anxious that the Castro threat be quickly and decisively removed from the Latin American arena. Having insisted upon secrecy and stealth as basic prerequisites for the operation's ultimate approval, he and his staff were confident that the Bay of Pigs would produce the desired results. For their part, Allen Dulles and senior CIA officials like Richard Bissell (Deputy Director for Operations), who had had drawn up the plan, believed that the president would ultimately sanction overt assistance once the invasion was in full swing (Freedman, 2000; Wyden, 1979). Both were wrong. Kennedy had been badly advised. Without full US support the plan was unworkable. Kennedy's controversial cancellation of the proposed second US air strike did not in itself doom the invasion and should not have surprised the authors of the plan. The president's primary concern was to minimise the political implications of the effort to unseat Castro. What the last-minute change did produce, however, was a dramatic excuse used by advocates of the plan and critics of the administration to explain what had gone wrong.

Although Kennedy publicly accepted blame for the disastrous affair (it was, ironically, a public relations coup that saw his approval rating actually rise ten points to 83 per cent), in private, he blamed all those whom he regarded as having failed him (Mahoney, 1999). His personal sense of betrayal and humiliation was sharpened by the immediate appreciation of the political damage the debacle would have on his presidency. Moreover, it heightened the desire to dislodge the Cuban thorn in his side. Kennedy ordered an immediate investigation conducted by General Maxwell Taylor to determine what had gone wrong. The affair deepened his distrust of the 'experts' in the military and, to a lesser extent, the CIA. As a result, he unofficially instructed his brother, Robert, and one of his advisers, Theodore Sorenson, to take on the roles of foreign affairs watchdogs in order to keep an eye on the formulation and execution of sensitive foreign policy matters. Kennedy also brought in his National Security Advisor, McGeorge Bundy, to take direct control of the intelligence information coming into the Oval Office so that the president often saw raw data even before the Director of the CIA. In effect, Kennedy created a small, private National Security Council apparatus, comprising his most trusted advisors and totally under his own personal control. Of immediate concern was his international credibility. In the eyes of the world (including America's allies), Kennedy knew that he looked weak and hesitant, even incompetent – a dangerous image for the new president – especially one soon to meet for the first time with his Cold War adversary, Nikita Khrushchev. Though shaken by the fiasco, Kennedy refused to contemplate abandoning his encounter with the Soviet premier.

Vienna

Kennedy was determined to meet with Khrushchev in order to disabuse the Soviet leader of any notion that he was not in control of his government. Khrushchev's recently renewed threat to sign a separate treaty with East Germany – a move that would force the United States out of Berlin – and an assessment from the American ambassador in Berlin that the risk of conflict was about 'fifty-fifty' because neither side believed the other would go to war over the city, convinced Kennedy that he needed personally to convince the Soviet leader of his commitment to defending Berlin and the Free World from communist expansionism. Judging miscalculation to be the most likely cause of a nuclear exchange, Kennedy reasoned that if Khrushchev clearly understood when, where and why the United States would act militarily, this would diminish the chances of the Soviet Union initiating a massive change in the status quo. Logically, he thought, this would diminish the chances of large-scale, destructive conflict.

The president also put great faith in his personal ability to reach agreement through his persuasive charm in face-to-face encounters. This allowed him to believe that a constructive meeting would allow progress to be made on improving Soviet–American relations, and other issues such as disarmament and Laos. He grossly underestimated, however, the degree to which the Bay of Pigs had convinced the Soviet premier that Kennedy was a weak leader, under constant pressure from a hawkish military in Washington. As a result, Kennedy was wrong-footed. He had studied for his encounter with Khrushchev the man, but had been insufficiently prepared for the intricate and compelling ideological arguments put forward by Khrushchev the communist. The Soviet leader dominated the discussions in Vienna, forcing the uncomfortable president on the defensive. Both in private and in public meetings, Kennedy found his opponent combative and unreachable. Khrushchev defended the right of the communist system to develop and made clear his support for other countries around the world which were fighting for change. Kennedy could have made the same argument himself but Moscow had already claimed the moral high ground. For Kennedy, communist-backed change was simply unacceptable. Thus, the president found himself having to argue against change. On the matter of Berlin, Khrushchev threw down the gauntlet. Under increasing pressure from his own hardliners and from the communist leader of East Germany, Walter Ulbricht, he announced that Moscow would sign a peace treaty blocking access to West Berlin. Concerned that his irrevocable commitment to Berlin had not been understood by the Soviet leader, Kennedy went back for one last 10-minute session. During this last exchange both men spoke of war. Kennedy left Vienna depressed and convinced that he had failed get through to Khrushchev (Reeves, 1994; Freedman, 2000).

The president was badly shaken by his encounter with the Soviet leader. He told journalist James Reston whom he met minutes after the talks had ended that he had been 'savaged' by Khrushchev; Reston thought the president was in shock. Senior American officials referred to the summit among themselves as a disaster. Kennedy was deeply concerned about his lack of ability to convince the Soviet leader of his serious intent to defend US interests, by going to war if necessary. He immediately prepared a speech in which he outlined to the American public the gravity of the threats made by Khrushchev and his commitment to meeting the challenge laid before him.

Laos

Kennedy's one success at Vienna was in reaching an agreement with Khrushchev on the issue of Laos (described by Eisenhower in a briefing to the president-elect as 'the cork in the bottle of the Far East'), where the United States was supporting anti-communist forces. By March 1961, the situation had deteriorated rapidly, forcing Kennedy to decide whether or not to commit US troops to prevent further communist encroachment. Reaffirming America's commitment to combat the communist 'push', he announced the deployment of American troops to the Thai–Lao border and ordered the Seventh Fleet to prepare to steam to Thailand with 1,400 combat-ready marines if the communist-backed Pathet Lao refused to agree to cease fire negotiations. Despite the tough talk, however, Kennedy's public substitution of a 'neutral' Laos for a 'free' Laos signalled a significant change in the nature of the US commitment.

By the end of April, this threat had apparently failed to achieve the desired ceasefire. Once again the president was presented with a policy heavily biased towards military intervention. The two choices placed before him – abandon Laos or commit troops – were two extremes. The latter, favoured by the military, was looked upon with suspicion by a chastened president who was, after the Cuban debacle, much more reluctant to go along with the military recommendations of his generals and less inclined to consider the huge commitment of ground forces. As he told one adviser, 'we would have troops in Laos right now if it weren't for the Bay of Pigs' (Reeves, 1994). Privately, Kennedy had decided that Laos was not a place where the US should or even could make a stand. If America had to fight in South-east Asia, he reasoned, then it would be in across the border, in neighbouring Vietnam. In early May, the president secretly formalised his decision not to try to 'save' Laos either at the conference table or by intervening militarily. Meanwhile, by posturing, using the threat of military intervention, copious troop movements and tough language, Washington hoped to force a negotiated settlement that guaranteed Laotian neutrality – at least for the time being. At the Vienna Summit Kennedy and Khrushchev agreed upon the principle of neutrality for Laos and the desirability of concluding a settlement reflecting this. In May 1962 a ceasefire supervised by the United Nations was brokered but remained intact for a matter of weeks. Again, Kennedy resorted to the threat of military intervention, ordering troops up to the Thai–Lao border. By this time, however, the conflict in Vietnam had supplanted Laos as the major theatre for Cold War confrontation in South-east Asia. Through secret correspondence, Kennedy and Khrushchev cemented the agreement reached at Vienna. Initial hesitation on the part of the US-backed forces was soon overcome when it was became clear that America intended to reach a settlement with or without the acquiescence of their 'hosts'. The 'Declaration and Protocol on Neutrality in Laos', signed on 23 July 1962, avoided war by postponing immediate confrontation in Indochina. When war finally arrived in Laos less than ten years later, it spilled over from neighbouring Vietnam, where Washington had chosen to draw the line.

Berlin

In early 1961, Berlin had been placed at the top of the new administration's list of dangerous places. According to Dean

Acheson, whom Kennedy had asked to prepare a memo on the subject, it was 'more than likely' that the USSR would make a move on the city within the year. His encounter in Vienna convinced him that a nuclear exchange was now frighteningly possible – a one-in-five chance – he told columnist friend, Joe Alsop. America and her allies had some 15,000 troops in West Berlin but a Soviet move to take over the city by force would be extremely difficult to resist, especially as the rail and road links went through Soviet-occupied East Germany. Kennedy knew that this physical vulnerability meant that he had at the most a few hours to decide whether or not to use nuclear weapons to defend Berlin. At the end of May, he delivered a second State of the Union Address asking Congress for an additional $2 billion, mainly for conventional military purposes, and to aid countries threatened by 'wars of national liberation' (Reeves, 1994). It was attempt to signal American resolve in the weeks before the Vienna meeting.

By the end of June, senior officials were warning of the probability of a grave test in Berlin, precipitated by the haemorrhaging of people leaving Soviet-controlled East Germany through Berlin for the affluence and freedom of West Germany. Conflict seemed probable because while it was in the Allies' interest to maintain the status quo, just the opposite was true for Soviet Union. The flight of the most talented, educated and economically productive members of society was a double-edged sword for the masters they left behind, exposing the fact that the reality of life in the regime bore little resemblance to the image portrayed by the communists. Moreover, the physical drain of vital resources was unsustainable. For Khrushchev, the loss of prestige in the eyes of the communist world was perhaps less damaging than the exodus itself which rapidly became a direct threat to the very existence of East Germany, especially in the weeks after the Vienna Summit, when numbers reached some 20,000. In Moscow, Khrushchev also faced steadily increasing domestic political pressures; following the emergent Sino-Soviet split and the recent agreement with the Americans over Laos, pressure from hardline opponents forced him cease demobilisation and resume the atmospheric testing of nuclear weapons.

On 25 July, Kennedy made public his response to the growing sense of crisis over Berlin. In a speech that called for a sharp increase in the military budget he also requested the authority to activate reserves, extend enlistment and mobilise the National Guard. An additional 40,000 troops were dispatched to Europe, and the civil defence fallout shelter programme was expanded. Like so many of the president's decisions, this was a compromise between calls for massive and immediate mobilisation preceded by a declaration of national emergency, advocated by the hawks, and the recommendation of the administration doves who favoured a firm stance that left room for negotiation (Freedman, 2000). Although Kennedy announced increases in military expenditure, he also limited America's commitment to West Berlin (Schild, in White, 1998). Notably, he neither called for German unification nor demanded guaranteed free travel from East to West Berlin. Indeed, the constant reference to *West* Berlin was also new and possibly an attempt to signal a potential solution to the problem. The military preparations had one aim: to convince Khrushchev that Washington was prepared to risk war over Berlin and that this risk was too great.

The immediate crisis came to a rather abrupt end on 13 August 1961 when the East German government began constructing a barbed-wire barrier that soon became a permanent wall. Without impinging upon the West's rights, the exodus leaving the Russian-controlled sector was halted. It was a crude yet effective move, the technicalities of which surprised many administration officials who had considered the possibility that Khrushchev might try to seal off the East but had judged this too difficult a task for it to be seriously considered as an option. The *fait accompli* left Kennedy with little choice; he told one of his aides: 'This is the end of the

Berlin crisis . . . . It's all over, they're not going to overrun Berlin' (O'Donnell & Powers, 1972). Washington protested the imprisoning of East Berlin but refused to contemplate war over what was undeniably a defensive move.

The citizens of West Berlin found it more difficult to accept the permanent physical division of a city long de facto divided. Kennedy was sensitive to their unique vulnerability and acknowledged a need to sustain morale in the isolated enclave. With this in mind he sent Vice-President Johnson with a convoy of 1,500 American troops as a highly visible sign of the United States' commitment to keep Berlin open to the West. In September, Kennedy received word that Khrushchev was not going to recognise the East German regime. This was made official at the 22nd Communist Party Congress in Moscow on 21 October, when Khrushchev removed the Berlin deadline. The potential for conflict, however, was not very far from the surface, as seen in late October, when Soviet and American tanks ended up eyeballing each other at the Friedrichstrasse checkpoint after the Head of the State Department mission in Berlin, Alan Lightner, had been harassed asserting US access rights across the city. Six days later, on 28 October, secret communications between Kennedy and Khrushchev, in which they both agreed to pull back their tanks, ended the stand-off and averted a crisis.

To some degree, the controversial and imperfect resolution of the Berlin problem transformed the Cold War in Europe and laid the foundations for détente (Freedman, 2000). Berlin, however, was never far from Kennedy's mind. Although by the end of the year he did not expect serious confrontation to develop over the city, it remained a potential hot spot. His famous 'Ich bin ein Berliner' speech, delivered during a visit in June 1963, was aggressively anti-communist and appeared to invite a challenge from the Soviet Union, which thankfully dismissed it as particularly colourful Cold War rhetoric. This was just as well. Kennedy himself admitted that he had been 'carried away' by the emotional reception he had received from the West Berliners. Neither wanting nor expecting war over Berlin, he had overcompensated with strong words.

Europe, NATO and the Grand Design

Kennedy had very mixed relations with his European allies. In Harold Macmillan, the British Prime Minister, he found a leader in whom he could confide. The two men had surprised observers with their warm friendship and frequent meetings. Macmillan, however, was the exception. Kennedy found Conrad Adenauer, the West German Chancellor, difficult to reach. But it was General Charles de Gaulle, the aloof French leader, who caused the president the most anxiety. Kennedy's Grand Design for Europe was unfortunately named. It implied a plan to be imposed by Washington on European countries unable adequately to see to their own needs. The Design comprised of a mixture of policies that were often self-contradictory. Kennedy strongly supported British entry into the European Common Market and acquiesced in Macmillan's determined pursuit of a special Anglo-American relationship, even though this damaged the United States' standing with the other European countries and especially with de Gaulle, who deeply resented the intimacy shared by the 'Anglo-Saxons'. In particular, Kennedy's decision to sell Macmillan Polaris submarines at the December 1962 Nassau Conference, after the United States had cancelled a missile system promised to Britain called Skybolt, provided the French leader with the excuse he had been looking for to deny Britain Common Market membership (Murray, 2000). Even the American offer of similar nuclear assistance could not frustrate de Gaulle's ambitions for France, both as a nuclear power and as leader of Europe.

Kennedy's problems did not simply relate to bilateral relations with allies such as France. The NATO alliance was also under pressure. One of the greatest threats to stability and cohesion within NATO was the divisive issue of nuclear weapons. The United States officially opposed nuclear proliferation and condemned small, independent nuclear forces like the British independent deterrent and the French *Force de Frappe*. However, they had helped and continued to help Britain with her deterrent while refusing to aid France. In addition, the new emphasis on the Doctrine of Flexible Response both confused and frightened the NATO allies, which believed that this strategy meant that the US would not defend Europe using nuclear weapons (Freedman, 2000). American suggestions that Europe concentrate on raising conventional force levels only strengthened this view and encouraged de Gaulle to pursue the costly French deterrent. The Multilateral Nuclear Force proposal that the administration peddled especially hard after the Nassau Conference was never warmly received in Europe. With the exception of West Germany, which came to favour the scheme (probably fearing that their refusal would result in reduced US military protection), none of the NATO allies expressed any enthusiasm (Winand, 1993). Even Britain, America's closest ally, agreed only to participate when, after months of prevarication, Macmillan and his Cabinet felt that refusal to discuss the matter might jeopardise the much-cherished 'Special Relationship'. The proposal had no real military value and did not increase the nuclear arsenal targeting the Soviet Union. For the administration, however, it would allow the European allies some measure of control of the nuclear weapons earmarked for their protection. It was a symbolic gesture that was never really intended as a power-sharing exercise (Murray, 2000). Kennedy wanted to retain complete control of America's nuclear weapons. He wanted France to give up the *Force de Frappe* and for Britain to assign her deterrent to NATO. The strategy failed largely because of the suspicion on the part of the European allies about America's resolve. The United States was willing to tell her NATO partners that they were wrong, but with words that were unconvincing and actions that were even less so.

Economic Foreign Policy

At the time of Kennedy's election, the United States was the strongest economic power in the world and at the apex of the dominant position she had assumed after the Second World War. All indications suggested, however, that while the Bretton Woods international economic system created in the 1940s (which established the gold–dollar exchange rate system that valued all currencies against the dollar and fixed the price of gold) was at last working effectively thanks to the recovery of Japan and Europe, America was now beginning to move into decline. By the end of the 1950s, it was clear that the continuing vast overseas military expenditure was creating a deepening balance of payments problem that was weakening the dollar and ultimately threatening the international stability rooted in Bretton Woods. The balance of payments problem (caused by a trade deficit that was running at around $5 billion by 1962) touched almost every aspect of Kennedy's domestic and especially his foreign policy decisions. He quickly grasped the link between economic power and his key policy goal of reasserting American hegemony in the world and resented the leverage other powers like France had because of their ability to deplete the American gold reserve. The debate within the administration centred on whether or not the United States would benefit from pursuing multilateral policies or neo-mercantilist policies. The president's advisers favoured the former because it would protect the interests of American exports and capital investment – the global interests of the multinational corporations, banks and investment houses.

A number of foreign economic issues faced the administration including the need to strengthen the dollar; the Trade Expansion Act (TEA) and the Kennedy round of trade negotiations; trade in agricultural products with Europe; the global military expansion of the United States and the effort to limit trade between Japan, Europe and the Soviet bloc (Paterson, 1989). Of these, the TEA was one of the most notable legislative successes of the Kennedy presidency. Passed in October 1962, it gave Kennedy the authority to negotiate up to fifty per cent reductions on tariffs on a wide range of goods and up to one hundred per cent reductions on goods traded mostly between Europe and the United States. The aim was to improve access to the European markets that were changing as a result of the Common External Tariff implemented by the emergent European Economic Community. Ultimately, however, the stance adopted by the administration was a largely defensive one that revolved around protecting the reserve currency status of the dollar and the Bretton Woods system. It was a strategy, according to some critics, that led to the long-term decline of American industry and the collapse of the system less than a decade later.

Middle East

During his election bid Kennedy had promised a presidential initiative to bring peace to the Middle East. He was committed to Israel's right to exist, while at the same time to preserving access to Arab oil (especially for America's European allies, which depended on the region for three-quarters of their petroleum). Once elected, the president announced an 'even-handed' policy that balanced support for Israeli security with greater tolerance of Arab nationalism in the hope that this policy would counteract Soviet influence in the Middle East. For the whole region the administration hoped to use economic aid to induce countries to follow the path of moderate reform rather than revolutionary change, believing that these so-called neutrals were more interested in economic development than revolutionary ideology. For Israel, in particular, Kennedy linked security assistance with the Palestinian refugee problem. Kennedy's attempts to court President Nasser of Egypt, a leading Third-World neutralist, alienated the traditional regimes of King

Hussein's Jordan and Saudi Arabia. When a palace revolt in Yemen led to a war which saw Nasser's United Arab Republic (UAR) fighting against Jordan and Saudi Arabia, Kennedy distanced himself from the Egyptian leader, moving closer to Saudi Arabia and Israel. By the end of his presidency Washington appeared to be heading for a showdown with radical Arab nationalism. A peace settlement in the Middle East had proved elusive.

Peace Corps and the Non-Aligned World

The Peace Corps was an archetypal Kennedy administration initiative. The idea of sending young Americans to live and work among some of the poorest people in the world appealed greatly to the president and to a generation who had come to age at the end of the staid and conservative Eisenhower era. The project (established by executive order on 1 March 1961) exemplified everything vigorous, dynamic and creative about the new administration and spoke to all that was good about the United States. Although in practical terms the appreciable benefits of the scheme were limited, the real success of the Peace Corps lay in the reflected glory that it projected on to the Kennedy administration and the confident, idealistic patriotism for which it provided an outlet. Aside from this, Kennedy was interested in policies that might make a difference in the struggle for the hearts and minds of the non-aligned countries that doggedly refused to commit themselves to one superpower or the other.

His attitude to countries such as India and the newly independent African states (19 of which gained their independence between 1960 and 1961) was certainly more sophisticated that of his predecessor, who had opposed the turbulent and often violent rush to independence, seeing Soviet intrigue and connivance behind the numerous nationalist movements (Schoenbaum, 1988). Kennedy also had a more high-profile interest in African affairs, having chaired the Senate Foreign Relations Committee's subcommittee on Africa and spoken out against colonialism in the Senate, attacking France's policy in Algeria.

Once elected, his administration was confronted with four sizeable problems in Africa, the first of which concerned non-neutral states. Unlike those countries whose neutrality was perceived as 'true', 'real' or 'objective' – the acceptable face of non-alignment – several non-neutral countries such as Ghana and Guinea displayed worrying pro-Soviet tendencies. The second issue involved constructing a policy towards the racist white minority government of South Africa. Thirdly, an anti-colonial revolt in Portuguese Angola appeared to create the ideal conditions for Soviet adventurism. Kennedy's efforts to entice Ghana and Guinea out of the communist camp produced mixed results (Noer, in Paterson, 1989). In South Africa, the United States criticised apartheid but refused to go as far as imposing economic sanctions on the mineral-rich state. Finally, the administration's pressure on the Portuguese was mitigated by the importance of the strategic Azores base and (as always) NATO and European solidarity.

It was in the newly independent country of Congo, however, that Kennedy faced his most intractable and pressing African crisis. Here, rapid decolonisation in 1960 had left a nation embroiled in chaotic civil war. After two years of negotiations, military threats and eventual intervention, the UN-sponsored mission succeeded in unifying the country under an anti-communist leader. Refusing to walk away from Congo or participate directly (arguments that divided his administration), Kennedy chose instead to support the efforts of the international community, while, at the same time, engaging in a considerable amount of public and private diplomacy. He was engaged with but did not engage the crisis. Direct American involvement would come elsewhere.

As with his approach to Latin America, Kennedy was able to empathise with the emerging nations and their desire for freedom, independence and prosperity. He knew that it was unlikely that their previous relationship with the West would predispose these countries to adopting a pro-western alignment and accepted that recent history combined with socio-economic considerations dictated the nature and direction of their interaction with the rest of the world. Yet despite this understanding, Kennedy was unable, ultimately, to free himself or his policy from Cold War constraints long enough to allow him to realise this commitment to Africa.

Cuba II: The Missile Crisis

Ironically, as it transpired, Kennedy was fascinated by and deeply torn about the use of assassinations as a political tool. This was the ultimate unconventional weapon – a surgical strike that could, with one fell swoop, remove a dangerous and unwelcome dictator and thus change the direction of politics in a country. Regardless, however, of the moral issues involved, great danger lurked in implementing such drastic action. While Fidel Castro was without doubt the most attractive candidate for this strategic strike, he was not the only leader in Latin America to be targeted. The CIA had been plotting for some time against Rafael Trujillo, the military dictator of the Dominican Republic. After the Bay of Pigs, Kennedy ordered that the US be protected from any complicity in these activities, while authorising continued support for the plotters. Although he expressed concern about who might replace an ousted Trujillo, and was not perhaps fully appreciative of the fact that there was little chance to remove such a figure without assassinating him, Kennedy continued to allow the CIA to operate. The plots succeeded on 30 May 1961 with the dictator's murder at the hands of dissidents armed with American-supplied weapons.

After the Bay of Pigs disaster the need to remove Castro became even more pressing. A White House team called the Special Group (Augmented), chaired by Robert Kennedy, had been entrusted with the government's 'top priority' – getting rid of Castro. In late 1961 an operational arm was added with the task of arranging a feasible plan. Operation Mongoose, as it was called, pursued a series of activities including espionage, sabotage, propaganda and assassination with the overall aim of toppling the Cuban leader (White, 1999; Andrew, 1996). By early 1962, Mongoose was Kennedy's chief and most expensive foreign policy initiative. Combined with the numerous other projects, such as the CIA's ZR/Rifle which was designed to have standby capabilities for assassinations, it represented the 'massive activity' directed against the regime that was demanded by the president (Bissell, 1996; Andrew, 1996).

By the summer of 1962, it was clear that something was happening in Cuba. Despite growing evidence (including the arrival of large number of Soviet technicians and military personnel) that the Soviets were constructing missile sites on the island, it remained unclear from the U-2 spy flights whether these sites were defensive installations or in fact the early stages of offensive Medium-Range Ballistic Missile (MRBM) sites. Assurances from Moscow, the lack of historical precedent and the sheer audacity of the gamble gave succour to the majority of those within the administration who believed that the activity in Cuba was a purely defensive reaction to increased activities directed against the Castro regime. Although criticised by Congress and the media, Kennedy prevaricated, publicly promising action if the sites turned out to be offensive weapons installations. In private, Operation Mongoose was stepped up. Preparations for an invasion of Cuba scheduled for the end of October were also set in motion.

On 16 October, Kennedy learned that the Soviets had placed offensive missiles in Cuba. Shocked and outraged, his immediate reaction was to consider a massive strike against Cuba in fulfilment of the action he had earlier promised (Allison & Zelikow, 1999). Within hours, however, he had established a special secret group of advisers, the Executive

Committee of the National Security Council ('ExComm'), to manage the crisis, dubbed 'Cuba II' by those involved. Comprising key officials including the Secretaries of State and Defense, McGeorge Bundy, Under-Secretary of State George Ball, Special Adviser Arthur Schlesinger, Jr, CIA Director John McCone, and Robert Kennedy, Excomm would meet almost continuously for the duration of the crisis.

On the morning of 16 October, the group discussed four possible courses of action: surgical/strategic air strike, general air strike, invasion, and blockade. By the afternoon, the preferred option had moved from a surgical to a general strike. Two days later, the group began to lean towards an invasion. By 19 October, when it became clear that none of the offensive options under discussion could guarantee the elimination of the missiles, the blockade proposal began to gain momentum (Fursenko & Naftali, 1997). Gradually, Kennedy became convinced that a blockade, coupled with a demand for withdrawal of the missiles, was the best way to manage the crisis. Threatened with the prospect of a confrontation that might become nuclear, Kennedy calculated that the Soviet leader would back down (May & Zelikow, 1997). The president chose to relay his message in a televised broadcast to the American people on 22 October, rather than in a communication to the Soviet leader. This was deliberate and signalled his determination to prevent Khrushchev from engaging in a public debate about Washington's Cuba policy and Cold War geopolitics. The public phase of the Cuban Missile Crisis had begun (White, 1996). Two days later, as the Soviet ships continued to make their way towards Cuba, the United States military went on DEFCON 2 – the highest degree of mobilisation before nuclear war. As the world watched the progress of Soviet ships, secret talks between American journalists and administration officials (including Robert Kennedy), and Soviet intelligence agents and embassy staff, discussed ways to end the crisis (Fursenko & Naftali, 1997). Although several of the

Russian ships began to turn back, new evidence confirmed that the missiles already in place were ready to launch against the United States.

On 26 October, Kennedy received a letter from Khrushchev offering to remove the missiles in exchange for a promise not to invade Cuba. The following day, a U-2 plane was shot down over Cuba. The sense of crisis deepened further when a second communication from Khrushchev arrived demanding the removal of the American Jupiter missiles stationed in Turkey as a precondition for an end to the standoff. Unsure as to who was actually in control in Moscow, the Kennedy team elected to reply to the first letter in the hope that this would provide the necessary conditions for constructive dialogue (Kennedy, 1969). The strategy worked. On 28 October, Khrushchev announced his acceptance. The deal struck allowed for Soviet withdrawal of the missiles in exchange for a pledge from the United States not to invade Cuba. In secret, Kennedy also agreed to remove the Jupiter Missiles from Turkey. On 20 November, after arrangements were made to remove the Russian weaponry from Cuba, Kennedy announced that the crisis was over (Freedman, 2000). Both Washington and Moscow claimed victory.

The Cuban Missile Crisis was, in crisis management terms, a triumph. It was also a near-miss. True, Kennedy avoided rushing into confrontation with the Soviet Union. Moreover, his tactics allowed him to adopt a strategy that was both imaginative and flexible enough to facilitate a resolution to the crisis. The crisis, however, could have escalated any number of times as a result of developments unknown to or even outside his administration's control. These 'X' factors were numerous and included uncontactable Mongoose teams active in Cuba during the crisis and inaccurate information about both the type and readiness of the missiles on the island and the numbers of Soviet personnel stationed there. Moreover, Washington was unaware of either the authorisation order that permitted Cuban soldiers to fire on

American aircraft or the fact the Soviet command chain had broken down in Cuba. These unknowns, and the fact that the two sides were not in direct contact, augmented the risks involved as the crisis played out. It was the most dangerous type of crisis management and embraced a strategy that could have resulted in the most horrific of confrontations – nuclear war.

Kennedy's handling of the confrontation is also diminished somewhat by the fact that his Cuban policy was largely to blame for creating the possibility of some kind of crisis in the Caribbean. The covert activities of Mongoose and the anti-Castro rhetoric emanating from Washington had substantially increased tensions in the region. Indeed, Castro's fear of invasion (or worse) had provided greater impetus for deepening ties to the Soviet Union. Of course, responsibility for providing the catalyst belonged to Khrushchev. By early 1962, the Soviet leader was coming under pressure from a number of sectors. For one thing, the Sino-Soviet split was becoming more visible with Beijing openly criticising Moscow for its handling of the Berlin crisis. Another concern was Stalinist Albania's refusal to toe the Soviet line. Domestically, a fifth year of bad harvests was the cause of socio-economic and political instability (Garthoff, 1989). This coincided with a double blow from the US: first, the revelations from Washington that the oft-cited missile gap was actually in America's favour, coupled with Kennedy's public commitment to increasing his country's nuclear arsenal, had deeply damaged Khrushchev. Finally, the knowledge that the Jupiter missiles in Turkey had become operational in the spring of 1962, and the fact that the Soviet Union could not afford to build additional long-range missiles, combined to persuade the Soviet leader to take bold action (Fursenko & Naftali, 1997).

Kennedy admitted after the crisis that he would never again have such an opportunity to invade Cuba. Such a move could have been easily justified but, given the nature of the crisis, would certainly have been much more difficult to implement successfully. The end of the immediate crisis did nothing to resolve Kennedy's problem of Castro. Shut down after the standoff, Operation Mongoose was reconstituted soon after as the National Security Council Standing Group. Its goal – the removal of the Cuban dictator – was pursued throughout 1963. Towards the end of the year, frustrated by the group's lack of progress and aware that Vietnam was becoming his most pressing problem, the president began exploring secretly a new approach that included the possibility of rapprochement with the Cuban leader. At the time of Kennedy's death, however, neither policy had borne fruit (Freedman, 2000; White, 1999).

Nuclear War, Testing and the Partial Test-Ban Treaty

The Massive Retaliation Doctrine adopted by the previous administration had, by the end of Eisenhower's term, been replaced, at least in theory, with the concept of Flexible Response. This became the centrepiece of Kennedy's Cold War strategy and the rationale behind increases in Defense Department expenditure which rose from $41.2 in fiscal year 1960 to $49.8 billion in fiscal year 1964, when total outlays for national security reached a post-war high of $54.2 billion. The president also ordered ten additional submarines carrying Polaris SLBMs and 400 Minuteman missiles. All in all, by 1964, the United States possessed 1,100 ICBMs, 800 ICBMs and 250 Polaris missiles. Although this expenditure was significantly higher than that approved by the Eisenhower administration, the actual percentage of GNP spent on defence declined under Kennedy – falling from 9.1 per cent in 1961 to 8.5 in fiscal year 1964, largely due to the rapid rise in GNP over the period. The number of military personnel grew gradually, from 2.5 million in 1960 to 2.7 million in 1963.

The Cuban Missile Crisis had a sobering effect on Kennedy. His comprehension of nuclear war before the crisis had been understandably abstract. Having castigated Eisenhower in 1960 for allowing the Soviets to open up a missile gap, at Vienna, the president had discussed the chances of war by miscalculation with Khrushchev. Afterwards, Kennedy had been appalled to discover that America's nuclear war plan for fiscal year 1962 (SIOP-62) made no distinction between the various communist states and turned the conduct of war, once authorised by the president, over to the military. Furthermore, he had been troubled by the bellicosity of his Soviet counterpart and worried that, if the US did not maintain her nuclear superiority over the Soviet Union, this would be an invitation to Khrushchev to risk such a cataclysm. In the aftermath of Cuba II, the spectre of nuclear holocaust was not easily shed.

A short time later, acting in concert with Britain, Washington entered into dialogue with the Soviet Union on nuclear testing. Although he had developed a deep interest in nuclear testing and had explored the possibility of reaching some kind of test-ban treaty since the creation of the Arms Control and Disarmament Agency in September 1961, Kennedy had not been prepared, however, to relinquish the lead gained by the US in nuclear technology (even though this was a good one to two years off) and felt compelled to refute any charge of weakness by starting to test again after the Soviet Union ended the three-year moratorium in August 1961. Critics denounced the president's refusal to make use of the moral victory the Soviet move had handed him. Kennedy was prepared to negotiate but not from a position of weakness. The nuclear testing and military build-up was necessary in his mind before he could safely and productively begin negotiations with the Soviet Union.

On 5 August 1963, a Partial Test-Ban Agreement negotiated by a joint Anglo-American team was signed in Moscow ending nuclear tests in space, the atmosphere and under water (Freedman, 2000; Oliver, 1998). France and China refused to sign. This was made possible because of a number of new developments. First, the United States had fulfilled its testing requirements and no longer had any real use for the kinds of tests banned under the new agreement. The introduction of new, smaller warheads was also a consideration. Furthermore, the discord between communist China and the Soviet Union had deepened to a point where it is possible that Khrushchev saw more advantage in dealing with the United States than in trying to please his Chinese counterparts whom he increasingly feared as a nuclear player. Towards the end of his presidency, Kennedy attempted to build on this. In perhaps his most famous 'peace speech', given to the American University at Washington, DC in early June 1963, he called on the American people to re-examine their attitudes towards the Soviet Union. For some, it signalled a new direction in the president's conduct of the Cold War; for others, it was simply a lull in the familiar cycle of crises that had typified US–Soviet relations since the late 1940s.

Vietnam

'There are limits to the number of defeats I can defend in one twelve-month period', Kennedy told his aides. 'I've had the Bay of Pigs, and pulling out of Laos, and I can't accept a third' (Reeves, 1994). He committed the US to the struggle against communist subversion in South Vietnam that far surpassed the degree of support received under Eisenhower. But the tenor of the debates surrounding the Vietnam issue was typified by heated disagreement and widely divergent perceptions of the needs, aims and projected outcomes of involvement in the country. Kennedy recognised early on in his presidency that Vietnam was potentially the worst crisis that faced his administration. In the aftermath of the Bay of Pigs debacle, Kennedy's growing concern with South-east Asia prompted him to establish a secret Vietnam task force headed by the Deputy Secretary for Defense, Roswell Gilpatric, with the aim of preventing the communist domination of South Vietnam. This was formally embodied in

NSAM 52, approved in May 1961. Within months Kennedy had approved more than fifty recommendations made by the Vietnam Task Force. Collectively, their basic premise was deceptively simple: to prevent communist domination of South Vietnam through military, political, economic and psychological action, and included the training of South Vietnamese guerrilla units and 'Special Forces' and the establishment of a penetrative intelligence network in the country (Reeves, 1994). In addition, an effort was made to increase support for the South Vietnamese President Diem. Finally, Kennedy approved plans to ascertain the necessary size and composition of US forces required should America decide to become more directly involved in the war.

Aside from authorising covert, non-conventional strategies (like the Green Berets, whom he sent to Vietnam ostensibly as military advisers in October 1961), Kennedy was undecided about his Vietnam policy. He came to rely less on his diplomatic staff in Saigon and in particular, Ambassador Frederick Nolting, appointed to evaluate President Diem but who had, in Washington's eyes, become too close to the quarrelsome leader. Constantly craving more information about events in Vietnam, Kennedy increasingly came to depend upon reports and assessments solicited from friends, colleagues and others who had been sent by him or who had business in or near the country. The president regularly dispatched teams of officials, often comprising men known by Kennedy to hold opposing views on the problem, so that the widest range of opinions possible would be on offer. Consistently, however, the president was reluctant to commit ground combat troops. Both in public and in private, Kennedy pointed out that the advice given to him by several influential and respected military and political figures not to commit US forces to Vietnam was compelling. That said, he was totally committed to preventing South Vietnam from being overrun by communists. His preferred course of action was to support the Diem regime in this struggle without getting drawn into a full-scale military conflict. Although he did not rule out negotiations, Hanoi's flouting of the Geneva Accords caused Kennedy to doubt if they would adhere to an arrangement worked out for Vietnam (Freedman, 2000).

What is perhaps most significant about Kennedy's Vietnam policy is the fact that it was to a large extent a reactive or responsive policy. The situation was almost always fluid and constantly changing; crisis was never far from the surface and threatened on a regular basis to change the context of the conflict. As time passed, the debate within the administration centred on whether or not the United States should stay committed to Diem, who was becoming deeply unpopular at home and uncooperative abroad. By the end of December 1961 there were 2,067 American military advisers in Vietnam; they had been given the first official authorisation to use their weapons in self-defence and the first US soldier had been killed in the jungle. Kennedy had put in place a system that allowed him to make day-to-day decisions on the use of US forces without leaving a paper trail. Within a year of taking office, the president was directing a high-stake and increasingly less covert operation in Vietnam. In January 1962 he authorised subversive counter-insurgency activities, putting this strategy on the same footing as conventional warfare. In May, this was supplemented with the 'Strategic Hamlet' policy designed to separate rural villagers from the Vietcong. At the end of 1962 there were 11,500 American military personnel in Vietnam – almost 9,000 more than at the beginning of the year.

Although in the latter part of 1962 and early 1963 Washington had been receiving favourable reports (Kennedy had ordered contingency plans for withdrawal of troops, and in April told his team in a top-secret meeting that they should be prepared for an opportunity to reduce American involvement even though this might be some time off), by the spring of 1963, the crisis in Vietnam appeared to be spiralling (Bird, 1998). The brutal repression of the Buddhist monks in South Vietnam and the widespread corruption within the Diem regime had created a situation of deep unrest. This widespread disaffection with the Diem government was manifested in the death of a Buddhist monk, Thich Quang Duc, who burned himself to death in the streets of Saigon in June 1963 to protest against Diem's treatment of his people.

After the McNamara–Taylor mission in October 1963, Kennedy felt he had achieved consensus within his administration and found a strategy for the prosecution of the war. After months of deliberation he decided that America would not actively encourage the removal of the Diem government but would position itself to closely appraise coup prospects and the likely replacement regime. The McNamara–Taylor report had also recommended a plan for US troops to be replaced with Vietnamese forces and a deadline of 1965 for total withdrawal. The thought of announcing actual dates, however, caused too much disagreement and Kennedy approved a change that saw the predictions announced as part of the McNamara–Taylor report (which was introduced to the public as US policy) rather than as part of a specific presidential statement. Kennedy officially sanctioned the report (including the proposed deadlines) in NSAM 263. The much-anticipated coup against Diem that finally came on 1 November, and his subsequent assassination, gave birth to a period of turmoil fuelled by the resultant power vacuum in South Vietnam. The degree of American responsibility for Diem's overthrow created an obligation to deal with the consequences (Freedman, 2000). Kennedy's assassination three weeks later ensured that this burden would not be his to carry.

5

JOHNSON: THE FRUSTRATION OF POWER

> I will repeat today what I said on that sorrowful day in November
> 1963: 'I will lead and I will do the best I can.' ... For myself, I ask
> only, in the words of an ancient leader: 'Give me now wisdom and
> knowledge, that I may go out and come in before this people: for
> who can judge this thy people, that is so great?'
>
> Lyndon B. Johnson, Inaugural, 20 January, 1964

John F. Kennedy's assassination on 22 November 1963
passed to Lyndon B. Johnson the only government position
he yet aspired to, but in circumstances that would encumber
him professionally and personally. The slaying of the popular and charismatic president; the manner, timing and place
of his death precipitated, with the aid of close Kennedy
friends and family, the creation of a cult of personality that
elevated the late president to a position that dwarfed the
corporal entity of his successor. In the early days of Johnson's
administration, the resentment, frustration and nagging
feelings of inferiority that this inflicted were largely
subsumed by his determination to secure the legacy of
America's lost leader. As crises mounted, however, so did his
inability to escape fully from the presence of JFK.

In the last six months of the Kennedy administration,
Cold War tensions had become noticeably reduced and relations between the two superpowers looked more normal
than they had done for years. Johnson's first priority was to
make sure that the transition from Kennedy's administration

to his own would be seamless. Conscious of the immense popularity of his predecessor and his family, the new president felt it incumbent upon himself to reassure the country and the rest of the watching world that the essence of the Kennedy presidency would be carried on in his own. The success of this attempt to preserve continuity would depend largely on the willingness of the staff Kennedy had brought to his administration to stay on and work under Johnson. To this end, he embarked upon a hugely successful effort to secure the allegiance of the men who had served his predecessor. In some ways, however, this judgement, while highly understandable given the circumstances, tied Johnson to a group of people that he had not chosen and with whom relations were often strained. Driven by a desire for unity and consensus and hindered by deep feelings of insecurity, distrust of his advisers and in particular the military men, like most presidents Johnson was also motivated by a determination to secure his own place in history. Despite his 32 years in politics which saw him rise from Congressional secretary in 1931, to Congressman, Senator (Speaker of the House) and finally Vice-President in 1961, he was not well known to the American public, only 5 per cent of whom claimed, at the time of Kennedy's death, to know 'very much' about the new president (Dallek, 1998).

The Great Society

Foremost in his mind were the bills such as foreign aid, civil rights, tax reduction, higher minimum wage and Medicare that his frustrated predecessor had not managed to push through a hostile Congress. The highlights of these were the 1964 Tax Reduction Act and the Civil Rights Act of the same year that were arguably the most significant bills that came to fruition under the new Johnson administration. In particular, the broad Civil Rights Act attacked segregation, banned discrimination in public accommodation, and eliminated restrictions in job opportunities. His success in securing the passage of the logjammed Kennedy bills was largely due to a combination of factors: congressional sympathy stemming from the brutal assassination, public pressure to honour the late President and Johnson's own skills as a negotiator and builder of consensus among congressional friends and foes. Once this legislation had been safely shepherded through his attention turned to expanding the liberal policies he cared most deeply about – the continuation of Franklin D. Roosevelt's New Deal – an ambition that became known as Johnson's Great Society (Dallek, 1998).

The Great Society was conceived as a powerful collection of legislation designed to address the problems and in particular the poverty experienced by growing numbers of Americans. However, Johnson's initial success in achieving what had ultimately eluded his predecessor belied the deep social, economic and political changes that were already under way in the United States at the beginning of the 1960s. The confident, hopeful and proactive mood that had inspired the nation during much of the Kennedy presidency seemed to melt away after the shocking murder of the 35th president.

Despite Johnson's natural inclination towards domestic politics, he was deeply conscious of the need to preserve the firm Cold War Realpolitik practised by Kennedy. Infused with and driven by the Cold War mindset of his recent predecessors and contemporaries, he felt compelled to maintain America's stance against expansionist and aggressive communism around the world. In his first congressional address Johnson assured his audience that he would uphold American commitments 'from South Vietnam to West Berlin'. In particular, he was determined to stand firm in Vietnam. He told his biographer: 'everything I knew about history told me that if I got out of Vietnam ... then I'd be doing exactly what Chamberlain did in World War II. I'd be giving a big fat reward to aggression' (Goodwin, 1991). Any change in policy or sign of weakness would leave him open to the accusation of betraying Kennedy, and, perhaps more troubling, that he was an 'unmanly man' – a coward. On the other hand, Johnson had a duty to his own administration to establish his credibility in foreign affairs.

Tragically, although his passion for social reform dominated much of his thinking, foreign policy issues that were altogether less familiar consumed his mind and energy. If he hoped that his retention of the powerful and skilful Kennedy foreign policy team of Rusk, McNamara, Ball and Bundy would allow him room to realise his Great Society dreams, he was gravely mistaken. Johnson's aspirations were slowly eroded as he found himself increasingly confronted by foreign policy crises, all of which were eventually eclipsed by the war in Vietnam. The irony, not lost on Johnson, was that a war for which he had initially little interest ultimately came to dominate, define and defeat his administration. His plans for the Great Society to a large extent influenced his Vietnam decisions in that the president was cognisant of the need to keep congress on board and public opinion on side. But as Johnson committed the United States to an ever-widening war the conflict ultimately absorbed the money, energy and goodwill needed to achieve his ambitious legislative proposals, leaving bitter disappointment and dissent instead.

Vietnam: Early Decisions

Two days after Kennedy's death, Johnson had his first meeting on Vietnam which reaffirmed the United States' commitment to South Vietnam and reassured the generals who had overthrown Diem that they had the full support of his government. The Vietnam imbroglio was deeply troubling to the new president, not least because of his reluctance to alter significantly Kennedy's policies before he had secured a personal mandate in the 1964 presidential election to lead the country. The recent assassination of Diem had created a power vacuum in which a new government led by General Duong Van Minh (a leading figure behind the coup that had removed Diem) had unsuccessfully attempted to restore some semblance of order and stability. The ousting of Minh and his co-conspirators less than two months later attested to the fragility of politics in South Vietnam and compelled a now familiar reassessment of America's commitment to supporting Saigon's war effort. The president was warned of a rapidly disintegrating situation that was at best likely to result in a neutral South Vietnam and, at worst, a communist-controlled state. Johnson was torn; he wanted to appear strong and in control but he did not want to risk losing the 1964 election because his actions as a caretaker president had alienated the public still in mourning for their slain leader. Ironically, Kennedy had successfully resisted a substantial and public escalation of the war. Johnson was convinced, however, that this predictably unpopular decision was becoming increasingly unavoidable and would most likely fall to him.

At the beginning of 1964, Johnson's attention was momentarily diverted by the outbreak of violence in Panama fuelled by long-running tensions in the Caribbean country. The following month Cuba took centre stage as Castro attempted to force the United States to give up Guantanamo Naval Base by cutting off the water supply, prompting Johnson to build a desalinisation plant to circumvent the Cuban leader's plan. Meanwhile, deepening crisis in South Vietnam forced the president to re-examine his policy options. He could either seek a negotiated peace and accept the neutralisation (or worse) of South Vietnam, continue the present strategy of anti-guerrilla warfare and increase military and economic aid to South Vietnam, or expand the war (Woods, 1998). The first option was dismissed out of hand. The third was also rejected because Johnson refused to escalate overt attacks against North Vietnam, wanting the status quo to be preserved without obliging the US either to escalate the conflict or withdraw from it. Although the 30 per cent of

South Vietnam controlled by the Vietcong at the time of the Diem coup had increased to almost 45 per cent by March, Johnson still ruled out massive intervention because of the costs to America's international image, impact on domestic politics and cost (McMaster, 1998). He chose instead the middle ground and allowed the provision of military, economic and technical aid to carry on in the hope that this degree of assistance would be sufficient to maintain Saigon. As a compromise measure, in early January, he secretly approved a recommendation to augment clandestine operations – specifically Operation Plan 34A, which extended covert action to include the support of South Vietnamese raids against the coastline of the North and DeSoto missions, whose aim was to provoke the North Vietnamese into revealing their coastal radar capabilities to waiting US intelligence-gathering ships.

While Johnson's stated goal was to prevent South Vietnam from losing the war, his military advisers (notably the Joint Chiefs of Staff) were committed to securing a military victory. These mutually incompatible war aims were not reconciled or even clearly acknowledged until much later in the war. In the meantime, Johnson increasingly relied on his Tuesday luncheon meetings with permanent members Rusk, McNamara and Bundy to coordinate Vietnam policy (these had begun as informal, wide-ranging meetings in 1964 and later evolved into the primary instrument for management of the Vietnam War) (Herring, 1995). According to Walt Rostow, who took over from Bundy in 1966, the assembly contained only 'those whose advice the president most wanted to hear' (Rostow, 1972). No military adviser was a regular participant until 1966, when congressional opinion forced Johnson to include the Chairman of the Joint Chiefs of Staff, Earle Wheeler (McMaster, 1998).

By the summer, Johnson remained undecided about a full military commitment, admonishing his top advisers that he wanted more diplomatic ingenuity and the option of being able to disengage from South Vietnam. In an attempt to halt the slide towards deepening crisis, he changed the team in South Vietnam, replacing General Paul Harkins, the Chief of the US military mission, with General William Westmoreland and Ambassador Henry Cabot Lodge with General Maxwell Taylor. Although the new team quickly established a strong presence in South Vietnam, the situation continued to deteriorate, prompting calls from a number of Johnson's advisers for consideration of attacks against the North.

The Gulf of Tonkin

Meanwhile, on 30 July the *USS Maddox* was en route to the Gulf of Tonkin with orders to engage in a DeSoto patrol. Intelligence reports indicated that the North Vietnamese were likely to attack the ship, believing that its purpose was linked to the 34A operations that had been stepped up in the area. The anticipated attack came on 2 August when an exchange of fire between North Vietnamese torpedo boats and the *Maddox* resulted in the enemy PT boats being driven off, with help from planes assigned as cover from a neighbouring aircraft carrier. The American forces suffered no casualties in the skirmish. The incident was reported to Washington where Johnson and his advisers debated the rationale behind the attack and the consequences it would have for his presidential bid. They concluded that Hanoi might have misjudged the situation, given the hostile activities being carried out in the area, and decided against retaliatory action (Johnson, 1971). Nevertheless, Johnson ordered the Navy patrols and the secret 34A activity to continue, warning the North Vietnamese that any further unprovoked attacks would have dire consequences. Two days later amidst a violent thunderstorm, the *Maddox* received flash traffic from the National Security Agency that another attack was imminent. The ship's radar confirmed the presence of three patrol boats some thirty miles away and within an hour both radar and sonar were picking up multiple craft and torpedoes. Believing an attack was under way, even though the atrocious weather and darkness prevented any visual sightings to confirm this, the *Maddox* and another ship, the *C. Turner Joy*, returned fire and informed Washington. Within hours of the news reaching the White House, intercepted radio traffic from Hanoi appeared to confirm the attack. Content that it was 'probable but not certain' that the second attack had occurred, McNamara and Rusk both recommended retaliation (McNamara, 1995). On this basis, Johnson ordered limited air strikes against targets in North Vietnam based on McNamara's strategy of graduated pressure (McNamara, 1995; 1999).

The following day, the president submitted to Congress his request for a 'free hand' in expanding the conflict in Vietnam. Johnson had long been concerned about the need at some point to obtain congressional approval for military and other action in Vietnam and had ordered a document prepared for such an eventuality (Johnson, 1971). He had been reluctant to put the resolution to Congress before the November election for fear that it would damage his domestic legislation bills and create 'war fever' on Capitol Hill. The alleged second attack, however, resurrected the document and ensured its rapid and almost universal approval by both Houses. The South-East Asian or Gulf of Tonkin Resolution, as it was later called, gave congressional support for the president to 'take all necessary measures to repel any armed attack against the forces of the United States and to prevent further aggression' (Johnson, 1971). Although it was not intended as a blank cheque for escalation of the war effort, this was how it came to be perceived.

One deeply troubling and highly contentious aspect of the Tonkin affair and the Resolution to which it gave birth is the fact that the administration had substantial evidence within hours of the second attack that a mistake had been made. No one had actually seen enemy ships and no torpedoes had been sighted or felt. Indeed, the captain of the

Maddox advised Washington that an electrical storm, poor visibility and an over-excitable crew might have combined to create the impression of an attack where none had existed. Moreover, the radio traffic intercepted from North Vietnam that had appeared to confirm this also turned out to be misleading. Mistakes in translating and transcribing the reports had incorrectly identified the cables relating to the first and corroborated attack on 2 August as evidence of a second incident two days later. All told, considerable doubt surrounded the legitimacy of the second incident. Nevertheless, McNamara and other senior officials went before Congress and briefed the legislative branch without revealing their doubts about the verity of the second attack or indeed the connection between the 34A Operations and the North Vietnamese retaliation on 2 August. What had begun as an honest mistake quickly became a deliberate fudging of the situation for political purposes (McMaster, 1998). The truth was that the Gulf of Tonkin incidents offered an attractive opportunity for Johnson to gain congressional backing for his handling of the war in Vietnam, at a time when a lack of uniformity and consensus among the branches of government could have seriously damaged his chances of winning the 1964 election. Indeed, the fact that the administration pushed ahead with the retaliatory air strikes and the Tonkin Resolution is testament to the need felt by Johnson to capitalise on events in order to secure a mandate for the prosecution of the war. Moreover, the Tonkin incident provided him with the opportunity to stress both his 'peace candidate' image and his ability to act decisively, even presidentially, effectively outmanoeuvring his right-wing Republican presidential rival Barry Goldwater and those critics who accused him of being 'soft' on communism (Gardner, 1995). Having used the incident to apply the concept of graduated pressure, Johnson resumed his election campaign, confident that it would serve as a holding strategy until he was securely elected. He had chosen the 'path of least resistance' in order to prevent a wider escalation of the war and to avoid a humiliating US defeat (McMaster, 1998). It was a decision taken with political, not military considerations in mind. Ultimately, policy was dictated not by how much it would cost but by how much Johnson was willing to give. The military consequences of this decision were never fully costed or debated within the mainstream decision-making process. Ironically, the reprisal which was aimed at convincing Hanoi that a wider escalation of the war would not be permitted was based on the mistaken assumption that this underpinned Hanoi's approval of the 2 August strike. Years later, McNamara would learn not only that a second attack had not in fact occurred, but that the first incident had been carried out without orders from Hanoi, in response to the DeSoto and 34A Operations in the area (McNamara, 1999).

On 3 November 1964, Johnson won a landslide victory, gaining an outstanding 42,995,259 popular votes to Goldwater's 27,204,571 and an Electoral College result of 486 to 52. This huge popular mandate gave him the confidence and determination to put into operation plans for a myriad of social reforms that went far beyond the measures he had shepherded through Congress on behalf of Kennedy. In the immediate aftermath of the election Johnson, now elected in his own right, spoke passionately about the war that he was going to prosecute – not Vietnam but a war much closer to home – a war against poverty, social deprivation and despair. Vietnam intruded very little in the weeks of frenetic activity that kicked off Johnson's drive to realise his Great Society. Quietly, however the first regular North Vietnamese troops began crossing into the South, signalling a new dimension to the war (Bird, 1998).

Escalation

By early 1965, Johnson was still desperately searching for a consensus on how to meet the deteriorating political and military situation in South Vietnam. A working group under William Bundy began a review of the conflict on election day and met continuously for two weeks, producing the most wide-ranging and comprehensive review of Vietnam policy yet undertaken. Its recommendation supporting graduated escalation with a view to securing meaningful negotiations failed to gain universal approval among Johnson's top advisers, who remained divided over the direction of the war.

Although he instinctively distrusted the military assessments that frequently called for a massive effort to be directed against the North, Johnson was also aware that America's lengthy and public commitment to the fight against communism in Vietnam had tied his country's national honour to the struggle. The situation he faced was grave – attacks on US personnel and installations had been rising at a steady rate since the Gulf of Tonkin incident. Clearly, the resources devoted to pursuing the war effort had not been enough. Disengagement was an option but not one that was very seriously considered. The loss of American prestige was thought to risk such a rise in communist aggression around the world that only a very small number of officials, like George Ball, advocated such a dangerous reversal in policy (Bill, 1997). The majority of opinion recommended air strikes as a prelude to a sustained bombing campaign against targets in the North (Woods, 1998). Greater intervention was acknowledged as a difficult and risky strategy, but ultimately embraced because Johnson believed it would signal to Hanoi his determination to remain committed to South Vietnam. Slowly, a consensus emerged supporting the intensification of the Graduated Pressure strategy.

The trigger was a surprise attack on Pleiku, a heavily protected US base in Vietnam's central highlands, that killed nine soldiers and wounded more than one hundred and twenty others. The carefully coordinated strike on 7 February also destroyed sixteen helicopters and six planes. Telling the American public that no wider war was sought, Johnson approved the commencement of a pre-existing bombing programme codenamed Flaming Dart. Three days later another attack prompted Johnson to order a second round of retaliatory strikes. Less than a week later, on 13 February, the President authorised the first widespread bombing of targets in North Vietnam in Operation Rolling Thunder, which began on 2 March. Finally, on 8 March the first combat troops – two Marine battalions – arrived at Da Nang with the mission to protect the US air bases that had been targeted by the Vietcong attacks. Within weeks it became clear that bombing alone would not force the pace of the war, compelling Johnson to authorise sending more troops to Vietnam. He also approved a new mission for the Marines already deployed in-country, allowing them to engage in offensive ground combat and not just in defensive actions. An American land war in Asia now seemed a certainty.

The long post-election months of agonising about the war had seen Johnson move slowly to favouring a stronger military commitment. But he was deeply desirous of proceeding with a consensus of opinion. This dictated that all options be considered and debated and resulted in a delay in formulating a clear policy for the conduct of the war. Pleiku and the raids that followed, however, in many ways forced consensus and limited the appeal of the voices advocating diplomatic initiatives. The February decision to initiate 'continuing action' against the enemy was an incremental move in the gradual escalation of the war, but it was deeply significant. Within a few weeks, the nature of the US commitment had radically changed as the administration settled on an agreed strategy of greater military involvement.

It is striking that the bombing campaign and the introduction of combat troops were not underpinned by a clearly defined set of aims. This confusion about the purpose of the escalation prevented any effective review and development of this new policy. Whether or not the Joint Chiefs of Staff actively pointed out the obvious link between the commencement of a prolonged bombing campaign and the need for ground troops remains controversial. What is not contested, however, is the fact that this policy change over which Johnson and his team had agonised for months was not announced in a major public address, as many of his advisers had expected, but at the end of a routine speech on 17 February (Bird, 1998). The president had chosen to escalate the war without formally announcing his intention to either the American public or indeed their elected representatives. He was not untroubled by this decision as a brief remark in his diary indicates: 'I can't get out. I can't finish it with what I have got. So what the hell can I do?' (Gardner, 1995).

In April, Johnson attempted to exorcise some of these doubts by responding to calls from NATO and the non-aligned countries to talk to Hanoi. In a speech carefully weighted with carrots and sticks, the president stressed the continuity between his Vietnam policy and that of his predecessors. Offering to 'go anywhere', and 'talk to anyone' about peace, Johnson held out the incentive of a billion-dollar economic rehabilitation programme for South-east Asia once the conflict had ended. Should this 'Marshall Plan' for the region be rejected, however, he warned that the United States would not be defeated, nor would he order a withdrawal, 'either openly or under the cloak of a meaningless agreement'. This message was reinforced less than twenty-four hours later when 15,000 more troops left for South Vietnam. Whether seriously intended or not, as US bombers began striking the North once more, Hanoi let it be known that Johnson's Great Society would not be transplanted to Vietnam (Dallek, 1998). Though less than convincing, the president's olive branch succeeded, to an extent, in settling Johnson, making him more confident about pursuing the steady escalation that he had already approved.

Crisis in the Caribbean

In the Dominican Republic a counter-coup on 24 April 1965 removed from power Donald Reid y Cabral who himself had ousted former President Juan Bosch (the first democratically elected president since the overthrow of dictator Raphael Trujillo). The crisis in the country escalated rapidly, prompting Johnson to order the speedy evacuation of the American citizens caught up in the conflict. A new military group claiming to support free elections had emerged to take power and requested the assistance of US marines to restore order. However, within hours the US embassy was under fire and claiming that military intervention was needed to protect the evacuees. Johnson was concerned about the reaction of the other Latin American countries to his military action. American intelligence was ambiguous about the depth of communist involvement in the Dominican Republic and the existence of pro-communist elements within the continent as a whole. Ordering 400 marines (followed by an additional 1,500) to the island, he informed the Organization of American States (OAS) and Congress of his limited humanitarian objectives – to protect the lives of American and other foreign nationals and to administer badly needed food and medicines.

The deteriorating situation in the Dominican Republic led Johnson to forego the traditional channels of information and communication that were proving too slow and ineffective. In order to obtain more data he ordered the CIA to deploy 50 agents to report on developments on the ground. As Johnson and his team debated the crisis reports began to reach the president of the involvement of as many as 1,500 armed Communists in the capital city of Santo Domingo and some 4,000 in the country as a whole. This information prompted Johnson to order the 82nd Airborne Division to proceed to Santo Domingo to support the US forces already there. He also ordered some 25,000 troops to be sent to the country to contain the crisis. These were to occupy an 'international security zone' which would separate the warring factions and sustain the ceasefire demanded by the OAS. Johnson also authorised diplomatic efforts, centred on the reappointment of Kennedy's former ambassador to the

Dominican Republic. The strategy was to saturate the country, overwhelming the factions in order to bring a rapid conclusion to the crisis. Once peace and stability allowed for free elections, the US would withdraw. By mid-May US forces had managed to limit the conflict to the capital; Bosch had been kept on board but at a distance; an OAS-sponsored Inter-American Peace Force had arrived to supplement the US troops; and with all sides having agreed to accept a provisional government, amnesty and free elections, the country appeared to be stabilising. The following year, a popular moderate, Joaquín Balaguer, was elected president. By October 1966 all foreign troops had been withdrawn.

Although the crisis was rated by Johnson as one of the highlights of his presidency, he was strongly criticised both during and after it for his heavy-handed approach. His relative lack of foreign policy experience saw Johnson exaggerate the nature and depth of the crisis in order to justify his actions. While the president was aware that the communist nature of the crisis was deeply questionable, he nevertheless used it as a pretext. Johnson's overcompensation only succeeded in confirming the perception that he was weak in foreign affairs and left him more resolved than ever to prove his mettle in Vietnam.

Aside from its psychological implications, the Dominican crisis allowed Johnson to avoid a congressional review of his Vietnam policy while at the same time exacting what was tantamount to a reaffirmation of the Gulf of Tonkin resolution (Gardner, 1995). In asking for a small appropriation of funds to deal with the crises in the Dominican Republic and Vietnam, he challenged Congress to refuse to support American soldiers already in combat. Congress's almost unanimous approval of the funding request granted de facto approval of the policies that led to the conflicts in both countries (Vandiver, 1997). This political manoeuvring was highly suspect but it got Johnson past an awkward political spot. But only just. Before long, congressional dissent, led by Senator William Fulbright, would coalesce into a formidable force.

Into the Quagmire

As June arrived in South Vietnam, a new government emerged headed by General Nguyen Van Thieu. In Washington, after the failure of the May bombing halt which brought criticism from both the political Left and Right, Johnson was faced with another major decision. Reports from Vietnam pointed to large increases in the operational strength of the North Vietnamese forces, compelling General Westmoreland to request massive intervention beginning with a boost of some 41,000 with a view to increasing numbers to 200,000. His message to Washington was stark: the US had to decide whether or not it wanted 'in' or 'out' of Vietnam. For the next month Johnson ordered his staff to review his Vietnam policy. He began to realise that the low-cost, graduated-pressure strategy that deferred the crucial decision of whether to stay in or get out had become infinitely more complex. With US air and ground forces engaged in Vietnam this decision had de facto already been made. Johnson felt constrained by the deteriorating situation and limited options available to him. The pessimistic scenario painted by Ball and the small group of advisers who argued against escalation and for diplomatic initiatives to allow the US to escape a quagmire in Vietnam touched Johnson. He continued to doubt the confident predictions of the military men but trusted his Secretary of Defense, who was in agreement with much of the statistical evidence they had supplied him with. After much deliberation and encouraged by the warm support for deeper commitment that came from his 'wise men', a group of 16 prominent Americans periodically called together to advise him, Johnson decided to approve Westmoreland's request for more troops and America's involvement grew deeper.

On 28 July 1965, Johnson announced his intention to increase troop levels from 75,000 to 125,000 and to send more as and when needed. By the end of October these numbers had risen to over 200,000. This decision (revealed in a press conference rather than to a joint session of congress) amounted to an 'all-out limited war' (Herring, 1995). It marked a turning point in the commitment to South Vietnam, signalling that the terms of engagement were loosely defined and open-ended. Johnson's pledge to 'stand in Vietnam' provoked no sense of urgency or crisis (Bird, 1998).

Indonesia

In September, the administration was buoyed by events in Indonesia where a coup against the non-aligned leader President Ahmed Sukarno, whom the United States suspected of moving into the communist camp, brought to power the pro-western, anti-communist General Suharto. In the bloody rout that followed, the new government (with the help of American embassy intelligence) targeted and killed over 100,000 suspected communists. In total, perhaps as many as one million people died as Suharto consolidated his power. Johnson made no protest at what the CIA termed 'one of the worst mass murders of the twentieth century' (Bird, 1998). America had a new, key, strategic ally in South-east Asia – right in the heart of the struggle against communism.

Doubts and Dissent

In November 1965, 30,000 marchers descended on Washington and newspapers and columnists not known for professing anti-war sentiments began to publish pieces questioning government policy in Vietnam. Dissent was also evident within the administration. Late in the year the architect of graduated pressure, Robert McNamara, had begun to suspect that the statistics behind the decision to escalate were increasingly contradictory. This was partly because the formula used by the military to calculate enemy strength and numbers produced artificially low figures (understated by as much as

50 per cent according to conflicting CIA reports), so as not to turn the American people against the war effort (Bird, 1998; McNamara, 1995). A trip to Saigon confirmed his fears that the numbers they had been discussing only weeks before could not now guarantee victory. He and his advisers had consistently minimised difficulties and underestimated North Vietnamese capability and resolve, refusing to contemplate a situation in which the enemy could and would match the forces committed by the United States (Herring, 1995). It was a harrowing moment of realisation for the Secretary of Defense, who found himself advising Johnson that he could expect more than one thousand American soldiers to be killed every month without any end in sight to the conflict. Now increasingly unconvinced that the military approach adopted by the administration could result in the successful completion of the war, his influence began to wane. In mid-December, however, Johnson acquiesced with his Secretary of Defense who was advocating a Christmas bombing halt. The president ordered a diplomatic initiative – a 'peace offensive' – in the hope that this pressure might force Hanoi to the negotiating table. The initiative failed; Ho Chi Minh denounced Johnson's efforts as 'deceitful' and demanded that the US withdraw from Vietnam. Johnson responded by approving a troop request for 30,000 more men.

In his State of the Union address in January 1966, Johnson described Vietnam as 'the center of our concerns'. While public opinion polls suggested that the majority of Americans agreed with this assessment (with 60 per cent rating Vietnam as the country's most urgent problem), they were unconvinced that the administration was making any progress in ending the war (Dallek, 1998). Growing public disquiet was mirrored in the Senate Foreign Relations Committee (SFRC) Hearings, led by Fulbright, which openly questioned Johnson's Vietnam policy. Although the majority of Congress still supported the government, the hearings opened up a crack in the middle-class support for Johnson's war and facilitated the gradual erosion of the political centre. The administration's official line confidently articulated by officials like Walt Rostow, McGeorge Bundy's replacement, attempted to convince people that the war of attrition was being won. Yet, by the summer of 1966, McNamara had come to just the opposite conclusion – a position supported by CIA estimates that continued to insist that the air campaign had failed to dent the resolve and capability of the North Vietnamese (Herring, 1993).

The ever-widening credibility gap was highlighted by the media which took an increasingly hostile line that frequently contradicted the official government version of the war (Woods, 1998). Heavily criticised, for example, was the government's claim that it would 'negotiate at any time without reservations', which was dismissed in the media as a political ploy because of the administration's repeated refusal to talk to the Vietcong. Johnson's decision to conceal the cost and scale of American involvement in Vietnam for the sake of the Great Society widened and deepened the chasm between rhetoric and reality.

By early 1967, support for the war among working- and middle-class Americans dropped sharply as draft calls started to exceed 30,000 per month and the news media saturated homes with images of burning villages, wounded and dead soldiers and children burned by napalm. Although the massive troop increases since 1965 had managed to prevent the military collapse of South Vietnam, they had clearly not been sufficient to secure the victory such a war of attrition was thought would achieve. Hanoi had been able to match the piecemeal increases in American forces by drawing upon the estimated 200,000 North Vietnamese who reached draft age each year (Woods, 1998). The evidence which suggested that the two sides were stalemated was confirmed by General Westmoreland's admission at the Guam Conference in March, where Johnson met with Thieu to discuss the war, that the US faced the possibility of an indefinite engagement.

Exhausted and convinced that his policies had failed, McNamara left the administration and was replaced by veteran presidential adviser and establishment man Clark Clifford, thought to be a Vietnam hawk. Significantly, when faced with the prospect of an expanded, indefinite war, Johnson's refusal to contemplate extrication was influenced by a number of factors. First, he had made the Vietnam War his war and to admit that the US could not win would be admitting that he had been wrong – his pride, prestige and political credibility were at stake. Second, the strong opposition of his rival, Senator Bobby Kennedy, made it difficult for him to consider adopting a policy that forced him to share a platform with Kennedy, whom he had long disliked and resented. Finally, the administration's publicity campaign that stressed positive developments in Vietnam seemingly convinced Johnson to stay the course.

The Six-Day War

However compelling that might be, events elsewhere in the world were not standing still. Since Eisenhower's intervention in Lebanon in 1958, the Arab–Israeli conflict had presented a deceptive calm, but when in 1965 Palestinians began mounting raids into Israel tensions in the region rose. The immediate origins of the Middle East war of 1967 lie in a muddle caused by the Soviet intelligence services, who mistakenly passed to President Nasser their belief that Israel was about to attack Syria in retaliation for Palestinian attacks and artillery bombardments on her territory from the Golan Heights. Nasser's response was to deploy his troops in the Sinai desert and demand a limited withdrawal of UNEF. His move did not include the critical areas of the Gaza Strip, nor, more importantly, Sharm el-Sheikh, the key to Israeli shipping through the Straits of Tiran. Relying on Nasser's secret guarantees to the United States in 1957, the Israelis had always insisted that interference with this shipping traffic would be regarded as a *casus belli*. When United Nations Secretary-General U Thant acquiesced in Nasser's demand, and the straits were blockaded on 23 May, the Americans were suddenly presented with a situation which threatened to spiral out of their control. As both Egypt and Israel mobilised their forces, the Americans searched for a diplomatic solution in tandem with the Soviet Union. With Soviet assurances that Nasser was not intending a war, the administration believed it had the space to avert a conflict. In an attempt to reassure the Israelis, Johnson told them, 'You will not be alone unless you go alone.' When Israeli foreign minister Abba Eban came to Washington on 25–26 May, Johnson and Rusk strongly urged the Israelis to undertake no unilateral action. They were not heeded. As Egypt, Syria and Jordan formed a united military command, the pressures on Israel proved too great. On 4 June, without informing the Americans, the Israeli Cabinet decided to mount a massive pre-emptive strike the following morning. The result was one of the most spectacular military victories in modern history, Israel gaining control of the Sinai desert and the Gaza Strip from Egypt, the Golan Heights from Syria, and the West Bank, including east Jerusalem, from Jordan.

The war did not leave Israeli–American relations unclouded, since on 8 June Israeli jets and patrol boats attacked the surveillance ship *USS Liberty*, leaving 34 sailors dead and 171 injured. Although the administration chose not to follow up this incident, it cut a scar on relations between the two countries, which were never totally healed for the rest of the Johnson administration. Even so, Johnson saw the need to move forward. In a public address on 19 June, he outlined his 'five principles' for a settlement: an end to threats against the existence of any nation, justice for the 'refugees', an end to interference with maritime rights, restrictions of the arms race, and peace based on recognised boundaries. On 22 November 1967, these formed the basis of United Nations Security Council Resolution 242, which was designed to provide a framework for an Arab–Israeli peace based upon mutual recognition, an Israeli withdrawal from 'territories' she had recently occupied, and a just settlement for the refugees. But the task of negotiating such a settlement rested with the United Nations. When by 1969 it had become clear that the international organisation lacked the muscle to bring such bitter adversaries together, it was clear that this would fall to the United States, a matter which would increasingly preoccupy Johnson's successors. From the American perspective, the crisis had confirmed two sobering facts. The first was that their absorption with Vietnam did not mean that the administration could afford to ignore other potential trouble spots. The other was that the best efforts of Johnson and Rusk had failed to prevent a war in this strategically vital region. That the Middle East became a priority for all subsequent administrations is hardly surprising. (Fraser, 1989; Quandt, 1993)

The Six-Day War briefly forced US–Soviet relations to the front of Johnson's agenda and helped bring about the first and only high-level meeting between the two superpowers. In June 1967, the President met with Soviet Premier Alexsei Kosygin at Glassboro, New Jersey, where they discussed tensions in the Middle East and Vietnam. The talks produced no substantial agreements but hinted, in Johnson's mind, of an improvement in relations between East and West. The détente that he glimpsed would not, however, materialise during his time in office.

1968: Tet, the Presidential Election and New Moves for Peace

By the beginning of 1968, government officials were cautiously upbeat. Johnson, convinced that he might soon be in a position to force the North Vietnamese to come to the negotiating table, began to press his aides for a withdrawal strategy. Within a few weeks a new threat emerged when the *Pueblo* – a US intelligence ship – was seized by

North Korea on 23 January. Seven days later, this crisis was eclipsed by the massive Tet (New Year) offensive launched by the North Vietnamese, which struck at more than one hundred cities and towns in South Vietnam, including Saigon.

Tet was a tactical defeat for the North Vietnamese. The attack, which was quickly repelled by South Vietnamese and US forces, cost the North the cream of its fighting force, believed to be as high as 40,000 men. Furthermore, the government of South Vietnam did not collapse nor did the people rise up in support of the North. Strategically, however, the offensive was a massive victory that proved that America was not winning the war. Tet was a disaster on many levels because it shattered two long-held beliefs. The first myth shattered was that 500,000 men (a number whispered in 1964 as the highest the US would have to go in order to defeat the enemy) was not enough to preserve the status quo, let alone win the war. Secondly, the idea that a sustained bombing campaign would disrupt the flow of men and supplies into the South was shown to be an overly optimistic assessment. Moreover, the official line that the US was engaged in a limited conflict assisting the army of South Vietnam was exposed as a lie. Although Tet initially provoked a surge of public support for the government, this quickly dissipated. Perhaps most damning was the perception of futility and defeat that was broadcast into the homes of Americans. This lingered long after the pictures had ceased to be broadcast – images of the US embassy in Saigon under the control of Vietcong troops, running battles in the streets of South Vietnamese cities, pictures of the holy city of Hue being battered by all the power mustered by American forces. The hostile media coverage confirmed years of deepening distrust of and animosity towards the government. CBS Vietnam correspondent Walter Cronkite's assertion that the war was clearly stalemated and could only be ended through negotiation symbolised the rupturing of relations between the government and the media. His 'defection' prompted Johnson to remark, 'If I've lost Cronkite' (described by surveys as 'the nation's most trusted person'), 'I've lost Middle America' (Dallek, 1998). Lastly, the SFRC hearings taking place at the same time accused Johnson and his staff of misleading Congress and the American public, adding to the hurt inflicted by the Tet offensive. By March Johnson's approval rating had reached an all-time low of 26 per cent (Dallek, 1998).

The conflicting reactions of Johnson's civilian and military advisers highlighted the sense of unreality that clung to the administration in the months following the offensive. While the civilians fought demoralisation and despair, the military urged Johnson to allow them to take the initiative and step up the war effort in a bid for total victory (Divine, 1994). Westmoreland's request for 200,000 more troops (which necessitated expanding the draft and calling up the reserves) prompted the first major debate about the course of the war since the watershed 1965 decisions.

The year 1968 was that of the election. Johnson's poor showing in the New Hampshire primary against Senator Eugene McCarthy, followed by the announcement that Senator Robert Kennedy had decided to join in the presidential race, caused the president to begin to reconsider his political career. On 25 March, Johnson's Wise Men reversed their earlier assessments of the war and advised the president to get out of Vietnam. Five days later, he announced a bombing halt and, unbeknownst to all but a very small number of his closest confidants, chose to end his address with the version of the speech that announced his decision not to seek the presidential nomination. Johnson had at last accepted that his policies (and those of Kennedy before him) had failed. The desire to win the war politically had excluded the possibility of pursuing a feasible military strategy; the possibility of failure had been thought too ridiculous to merit serious consideration. Johnson's definition of US aims and objectives in Vietnam had created a no-win situation as surely as if he had announced the very fact himself.

To abrogate responsibility for South Vietnam would fatally damage America's ability to challenge the Soviet Union and the global threat of communist encroachment. To negotiate a peaceful settlement would send out the same signal. Confidence in the far superior technology and warmaking capability of the US had convinced Johnson that a limited, controlled and managed war would ultimately result in victory. This thinking was fatally flawed. A limited war (fought out of consideration for the sensibilities of the US public, the needs of the Great Society, charges of imperialism and racism, and the deep belief in the superiority of the US military capability) was incapable of realising victory not least because it gave the enemy a chance to prepare for each new American step and enabled them to match the incremental increases. On the other hand, Johnson himself argued that his options were limited. It is highly unlikely that he would have successfully obtained congressional or indeed public support for a full-scale war in Vietnam. Moreover, the president's devotion to another war made him reluctant to contemplate this difficult course of action, knowing that this would fatally wound his domestic policy dreams.

The initial burst of activity that followed Johnson's shock announcement quickly gave way to a protracted period of stalemate as the major players argued about the location, timing and substance of the proposed talks. It was not until June that these basic differences had been resolved, enabling discussions to get under way in Paris. Within weeks the talks had deadlocked. In August, the Soviet military intervention in Czechoslovakia, followed by the announcement of the Brezhnev Doctrine which committed the USSR to protecting all socialist states from western subversion, ruled out any possibility of the East–West summit meeting, hoped by Johnson to facilitate some progress on Vietnam.

Finally, in late autumn a breakthrough occurred when Hanoi indicated that it would not object to the presence of representatives of the Saigon government at the talks. Any hope, however, of getting serious negotiations under way before the US presidential elections were dashed when Thieu refused to participate in the talks – it later emerged that he had been approached by the Nixon team and promised a better deal if he held off until after the election. The feeling that the Saigon government had been influenced 'beyond the bounds of justifiable political conduct' by the Republicans left a rancorous aftermath, and has led to the suspicion that Thieu felt that Nixon was obligated to him (Clifford, 1991; Bundy, 1998).

Marked as it was by Johnson's decision not to seek re-election, the emergence of the populist Right led by former Democrat George Wallace, and the riots in the streets of Chicago during the Democratic National Convention, the presidential campaign of 1968 turned out to be one of the most dramatic, indeed traumatic, in the country's history. The sense of national crisis was heightened by the assassination of two of the country's leading political personalities, the Civil Rights leader Martin Luther King, and Robert Kennedy, who was fast emerging as the Democrats' main hope. Left with little real choice between Hubert Humphrey, who had committed himself to the continuation of Johnson's policy with hints of a dove-like attitude and a last-minute commitment to bring the war to a speedy end, and Richard Nixon, who promised his own secret plan, the US electorate narrowly voted for the former vice-president. His victory was hugely unconvincing but it secured for him the ultimate political prize – the presidency. The war that Nixon inherited had cost the US upwards of 29,000 men and some $70 billion.

6

NIXON: THE PEACEMAKER?

The greatest honor history can bestow is the title of peacemaker.
This honor now beckons America – the chance to help lead the
world at last out of the valley of turmoil, and onto that high ground
of peace that man has dreamed of since the dawn of civilisation.
Richard M. Nixon, Inaugural, 20 January 1969

The 1968 election saw Richard Nixon narrowly succeed
against Hubert Humphrey, an innately decent Minnesota
liberal, but indelibly linked to Johnson and the war. Nixon
gained 31,785,480 votes to Humphrey's 31,275,166. But a
comment on the times was that the American Independent
team of segregationist George Wallace and Curtis Le May,
with his idiosyncratic views on nuclear weapons, attracted
9,906,472 votes. Nixon had fought his way back to the centre
of political power after his defeat by Kennedy in 1960,
followed by a humiliating rebuff at the hands of the
California electorate two years later. While it would not be
convincing to claim that Nixon was one of the great
American presidents, he was certainly amongst the most
remarkable. No president had to face such disgrace as he was
to suffer over the Watergate cover-up and consequent resignation, but in 1969 this unprecedented train of events lay
well in the future. A proud, solitary and suspicious man,
capable of colouring his fierce ambition with acts of spontaneous generosity, of all twentieth-century presidents Nixon
is the most difficult to place with certainty. Enigmatic is the
adjective which best describes him.

Nixon's Vietnam Inheritance

Nixon's most pressing foreign policy problem had to be Vietnam. When he took office, American troop strength in the country was approaching the 543,000 figure set by his predecessor, but the war was far from won. It was estimated that 65 per cent of the population, 80 per cent in rural areas, was under Vietcong influence (Kissinger, 1979). The Paris negotiations with North Vietnam were failing to develop any momentum, in part because of the South Vietnamese government's refusal to attend. Nixon knew that his narrow victory had partly turned on the belief of sufficient Americans that he had the capacity to end the war. In the course of the election he had been careful to offer no specific plan, beyond the repeated pledge that he would end the war and win the peace in the Pacific (Bundy, 1998).

But he also believed, quite correctly, that Johnson's almost total preoccupation with Vietnam had led to a serious neglect of other key areas of American foreign policy. As he saw it, the war had to be ended and there were three ways in which this might be done. The first was through outright military victory, which might be achievable through intensified bombing of North Vietnam, by the use of tactical nuclear weapons, or a renewed conventional campaign. Any of these options carried the risk of endangering his hopes for improving relations with the Soviet Union and China, while domestic support for the level of casualties likely to be sustained was highly unlikely. A plausible, and probably popular, alternative would be to declare that this was a war created by Kennedy and Johnson, and announce a phased withdrawal. Nixon rejected such a possibility on the basis that if the United States simply sacrificed an ally when support became unpopular or difficult, then the country would no longer be trusted by its friends. With escalation or withdrawal ruled out, that only left the pursuit of a negotiated settlement which would preserve South Vietnam's independence under President Thieu. How North Vietnam's

agreement to this condition was to be secured was dangerously opaque. Equally intangible was South Vietnam's viabil-
ity as an independent state without American military
support, always the great unanswered question of the war.
One problem facing Nixon was that opinion in the army and
the CIA was divided over Saigon's military potential, with the
latter noticeably pessimistic (Bundy, 1998). Nixon claimed
that he had been prepared to devote most of his first year in
office to bringing about a settlement on the above basis;
events were to show that he was gravely underestimating a
tenacious enemy which scented victory and was quite unin-
terested in retaining South Vietnam (Nixon, 1978).

Nixon and the Communist Powers

If events were to prove just how frustrating the achievement
of this Vietnam strategy was to be, Nixon cannot be denied
the perception that the war had become a miserable and
bloody affair which was being pursued to the detriment of
other American interests. However serious the human cost to
all concerned, Vietnam was not ultimately an area of vital
American concern, but in engaging in the war there to the
exclusion of virtually everything else Johnson had neglected
areas which were. Amongst these Nixon numbered the
decline in the NATO alliance, the linchpin of American security. Europe had not featured prominently amongst
Johnson's concerns, despite the brutal Soviet and Warsaw
Pact suppression of the 'Prague Spring' of 1968 in Czechoslovakia. At the same time, the Soviet Union had been
dramatically increasing its strategic nuclear arsenal. Whereas
at the time of the Cuban Missile Crisis the United States
could deploy 229 ICBMs and 144 SLBMs against 50 Soviet
ICBMs and 97 SLBMs, by 1970 the Soviets had 1,427 ICBMs
and 289 SLBMs to the Americans' 1,054 ICBMs and 656
SLBMs (Nitze, 1989). While these figures disguised the
American strategic bomber force, as well as the British and

French nuclear deterrents, they clearly confirmed Moscow's intention to match the Americans in the realm of intercontinental missiles, which it did in 1971. There were also significant potential developments in missile systems. Since 1964, the Soviet Union had been developing an antiballistic missile (ABM) system. The American response was to set in hand multiple independently targeted re-entry vehicles (MIRVs), missiles with multiple warheads which could be used to deluge any ABM system, though they also initiated an ABM programme of their own. These developments, not least their cost, led Robert McNamara to the conclusion that arms limitation was needed, though negotiations had not gone far by the end of the Johnson administration (Bundy, 1998). These circumstances demanded a policy of positive engagement with the Soviet Union, no matter how much Nixon distrusted its purposes. One area where the Soviet Union appeared to hold a stronger hand than the Americans was in the strategically and economically important countries of the Arab Middle East. If the Arab–Israeli conflict were not addressed then Soviet military support for Egypt and Syria might lead to confrontation. By 1969, the Jarring mission, which sought to build an Arab–Israeli peace agreement on the basis of Security Council Resolution 242, was clearly going nowhere. One potential opportunity for movement seemed to be the widening split between the Soviet Union and China, but here Nixon would have to fight to overcome two decades of almost total freeze between Washington and Beijing (Nixon, 1978).

Nixon, Rogers and Kissinger

Nixon regarded foreign affairs as his principal area of expertise. To his credit, Eisenhower had gone to considerable pains to ensure that his vice-president would be as fully involved in affairs as possible (Ambrose, 1987). Both in office and during his political exile he had travelled widely, maintaining a formidable range of contacts with world leaders. He was determined that the direction of foreign policy would be firmly in his hands, something which helped determine the choice of William Rogers as his Secretary of State. A former Attorney-General under Eisenhower, Rogers was seen as a keen negotiator and able bureaucrat who would carry forward Nixon's plans. Distrustful of the East Coast 'Establishment', Nixon believed that the Department of State needed a strong hand. Given the extent of troop deployment in Vietnam, the new Defense Secretary Melvin Laird, an experienced congress-man with strong political links, was next in the hierarchy (Nixon, 1978). Both men were to oppose some of Nixon's key initiatives, ineffectively, as it turned out. The making of policy was to rest firmly in the White House, and to assist him in that task Nixon revived the almost moribund position of National Security Advisor, or, more accurately, Assistant to the President for National Security Affairs. His choice for what proved to be the most pivotal appointment of his administration was Dr Henry Kissinger, a professor of government at Harvard, whose publications on foreign policy had caught Nixon's attention and who had acted as adviser to his Republican rival, Nelson Rockefeller. A Bavarian Jew who had fled with his parents to the United States in 1938, Kissinger brought to his adopted country that sense of commitment which had been such a distinguishing mark of the Jews of Germany until Hitler threw it back at them. Given the nature of his brief, tensions and rivalries with Rogers were bound to arise; Nixon described their ultimate relationship as 'combative' (Nixon, 1978). Kissinger steadily gained the upper hand. Nixon, with his expe-rience and range of contacts, and Kissinger, a trained acade-mic, were to become one of the most remarkable partnerships in the history of American diplomacy.

Détente

When assessing Nixon's conduct of foreign policy, it is useful to acknowledge both the narrowness of his domestic political base and the fact that Vietnam had raised fundamental questions about the nature of America's place in the world. Not only had he been elected by the slimmest of margins, but the Democrats retained their long-standing majorities in both Senate and House, though it is true that he could usually rely on the support of a number of conservative southern Democrats. He did not enjoy a particularly warm relationship with his own party, to the extent of toying with the idea of forming a new one. Worst of all, in the course of his political rise he had aroused a particular level of dislike in his political opponents, reflecting a mutual antipathy with the liberal elite, which made it harder for him to build the alliances every president needs (Nixon, 1978; Kissinger, 1999). He also had to contend with a growing feeling, reflected in Arthur Schlesinger's influential book *The Imperial Presidency*, that the power of the executive had become too great and that consequently the legislative branch needed to assert itself more effectively (Schlesinger, 1974). Several of Nixon's policies, foreign and domestic, were to fuel such sentiments. In fact, many of Nixon's key ideas for the future of American foreign policy were not initially so far apart from those advocated by some who were counted amongst his critics. In 1966, Senator J. William Fulbright, Democratic Chairman of the Senate Foreign Relations Committee, published *The Arrogance of Power*, a powerfully argued liberal critique of recent events. Although eloquently criticising involvement in Vietnam, Fulbright did not advocate what he called a disorderly withdrawal, but instead offered an eight-point plan for ending the war on the basis of the neutralisation of both North and South Vietnam. He also argued for a new approach to China, and a policy of reconciliation, or détente, with the Soviet Union (Fulbright, 1967).

Détente, the word which was to assume such sigificance in the conduct of foreign policy under Nixon and Kissinger, was a term which had been washing around for some time, not least in Europe. It was, after all, a French word, as

President Reagan somewhat dismissively observed (Reagan, 1990). Eisenhower had used it after the death of Stalin, but it then resurfaced in the mid-1960s. In 1965, Soviet Foreign Minister Andrei Gromyko referred in Paris to the 'breeze of détente' between France and the Soviet Union. By the later stages of the Johnson presidency, the term was gaining favour as a means of describing the desirability of easing relations between East and West, a prospect which the Soviets temporarily stifled with their invasion of Czechoslovakia. Seeing him, quite correctly, as a dedicated anti-communist, European leaders assumed Nixon to be an opponent of détente (LaFeber, 1993; Kissinger, 1979; Gromyko, 1989).

The pursuit of détente formed an important part of Nixon's discussions with fellow Alliance leaders during a visit to Belgium, Britain, Federal Germany, Italy and France, which began on 23 February 1969. This early overseas visit was intended to send out a number of important signals about the new administration's future directions, not least that America was breaking free from the obsession with Vietnam and was determined to rebuild the sagging NATO alliance. While his meetings in Britain and Germany were useful in reassuring key allies about his intentions, the real thrust of Nixon's mission was to court President Charles de Gaulle. Two factors lay behind this. The first was that de Gaulle had made France NATO's prickliest member, withdrawing his country from the alliance's integrated military command in 1966. He also stood in the way of America's cherished ambition of seeing British membership of the Common Market. Despite this, Nixon saw the French as able to take on a key role in possible overtures to China and North Vietnam, since they had diplomatic relations with both countries. In his discussions with Nixon, de Gaulle pressed for a policy of détente with the Soviet Union, advised opening links to China, and a phased end to the Vietnam War. Nixon responded positively to his advice to open direct conversation with Hanoi, in the belief that this would be channelled to the North Vietnamese embassy in Paris. But if

Nixon had pinned any hopes of de Gaulle acting as some kind of conduit to Beijing and Hanoi, this was confounded by the French leader's resignation two months later (Nixon, 1978; Kissinger, 1979).

The Bombing of Cambodia

Nixon's European visit was accompanied by a North Vietnamese escalation of the war, which he interpreted as a test of the new administration. Judging that subsequent negotiations would be coloured by the nature of his response, he decided that retaliation was necessary. Since a return to the bombing offensive against North Vietnam would not be supported by domestic public opinion, Nixon and his advisers turned instead to an option which would in time arouse even greater controversy, the bombing of Cambodia. Cambodia's neutrality was not in doubt; neither was the fact that parts of her territory had been turned into a base area for North Vietnamese operations in the South. American commanders had for some time been advocating air strikes against these positions. On 16 March 1969, Nixon authorised attacks by B-52 strategic bombers on North Vietnamese bases inside the Cambodian border. These were launched the following day and continued with increasing regularity over the next 14 months. They were undertaken in secrecy. This was later justified in terms of protecting the position of the Cambodian leader, Prince Sihanouk, though Nixon was candid enough in his memoirs to concede that possible domestic reaction had also played its part. How Nixon imagined that such secrecy could survive the obvious fact that it was no secret to the Cambodians and North Vietnamese, or journalists, is unclear (Shawcross, 1979; Ambrose, 1989). When the inevitable leaks appeared in the press, the Federal Bureau of Investigation was authorised to tap the phones of a number of suspected officials and news-papermen. Kissinger later admitted that the administration had been unwise not to have been more frank with congressional leaders. But the secret bombing of Cambodia, and the domestic actions which it spawned, ultimately worked against the administration's credibility. Neither, of course, did it help the country which until then had just about managed an uneasy neutrality in the South-east Asian conflict. Before long, Cambodia was to spiral into tragedy (Nixon, 1978; Kissinger, 1979).

Vietnamisation and the Nixon Doctrine

If Nixon hoped that by sending the right signals, backed up by his bombing campaign, he could either force or induce Hanoi to bring a speedy end to the conflict then he was soon disabused, since the North Vietnamese held stubbornly to their insistence that President Thieu be removed and American forces unilaterally withdrawn. In an attempt to break the deadlock, Nixon made public his negotiating position in a televised address on 14 May 1969. This committed the United States to the participation of the Vietcong in South Vietnamese politics, free elections, and simultaneous withdrawal by American and North Vietnamese forces under a precise timetable. The absence of any response brought Nixon up against the hard reality that the North Vietnamese saw no need to compromise, and it led directly to the beginning of American disengagement. The option favoured by Laird was 'Vietnamisation', in short, the replacement of American combat troops by South Vietnamese. The outline of Vietnamisation was agreed by Nixon on 15 March 1969, based upon an optimistic assessment of the extent of the population under Saigon's control (Bundy, 1998). Nixon presented this unwelcome development to Thieu at a meeting on Midway Island on 8 June, announcing the withdrawal of 25,000 troops. It was the defining moment in America's retreat from Vietnam. Both Thieu and the American commanders in the country were deeply unhappy, knowing that this was the start of a process which must inexorably lead to total disengagement. Henceforth, the army was conducting a holding operation rather than fighting for victory, with all the implications for morale and motivation (Nixon, 1978; Kissinger, 1979). It is safe to assume that the North Vietnamese knew this, too.

Nixon now moved on two diplomatic fronts, one public, the other secret. The first emerged, not entirely by design, on 25 July in a press conference on the island of Guam. Aware that their actions over Vietnam were having a profound impact on a whole network of agreements and relationships in Asia, Nixon and Kissinger had been reviewing the future direction of policy in the region. The thrust of the latter's advice was that these countries would have to supply the policies and resources, that this could not be done by Washington, but that what was needed was to relate each country to overall American security needs. In his press conference Nixon indicated that while America would abide by her treaty commitments, she would expect problems of internal security and military defence to be handled by the Asian nations themselves. With the exception of a nuclear threat, American assistance would be confined to military supplies and economic aid. This quickly became codified as the 'Nixon Doctrine', as articulated by the president in his Foreign Policy Report of 18 February 1970: 'we shall furnish military and economic assistance when requested and as appropriate. But we shall look to the nation directly threatened to assume the primary responsibility of providing the manpower for its defense' (Nixon, 1978; Kissinger, 1979). While it provided a rationale for Vietnamisation, the doctrine also signalled a significant readjustment in America's perception of the nature and extent of her overseas commitments. There were clear implications for parts of the world other than Asia. Although its importance can be overstated, the Nixon Doctrine meant that American commitments were being reined back from the rhetorical promises of the Kennedy Inaugural or Johnson's open-ended commitment to South Vietnam.

Another initiative was taking place well away from the public gaze, at the Paris apartment of the former French Delegate-General in Hanoi, Jean Sainteny, who had already acted as a conduit for messages between Nixon and Ho Chi Minh. On 4 August, Kissinger met Xuan Thuy and Mai Van Bo, seeking to convince them of Nixon's hope that by 1 November they could make serious progress towards ending the war. Central to the North Vietnamese response were the linked demands of the complete withdrawal of American forces and the replacement of Thieu's government by a coalition which would include the Communists. The latter position was to act as the principal obstacle to substantive negotiations over the next three years (Kissinger, 1979). A month later, Ho Chi Minh died and was replaced by Pham Van Dong, but this was not accompanied by any change in North Vietnamese policy. As domestic protests against the war continued, in Congress, in the press and on campus, Nixon announced in mid-September that a further 40,500 troops would be withdrawn by 15 December. This failed to win him any plaudits with the war's opponents, who announced a national protest, the Moratorium, beginning with a mass rally in Washington on 15 October. With his 1 November goal now clearly beyond reach, Nixon sought to defend his policies in a speech on 3 November, which he used to appeal to what he called the 'silent majority' of Americans to support him. While he was heartened by the response, he was well aware that all he had done was buy himself some time, and that a Vietnam settlement was no closer than before (Nixon, 1979).

The Rogers Plan and 'Black September'

While these events were unfolding, Rogers and the State Department were working on a peace plan for that other area of abiding tension, the Arab–Israeli conflict. The Americans had been privately assured by Jordan's King

Hussein that he and President Nasser were prepared to work towards a settlement with Israel, much as Resolution 242 had envisaged. The Rogers Plan, unveiled on 9 December 1969, attempted a major definition of what had been implied by key phrases in Resolution 242. At its core was the question of borders. Here, Rogers insisted that 'any change in the pre-existing lines should not reflect the weight of conquest. We do not support expansionism.' What he envisaged were 'insubstantial alterations required for mutual security'. His speech also moved on from the language of Resolution 242, which had simply referred to 'refugees', by acknowledging 'a new consciousness amongst the young Palestinians'.

These were not messages which the Israeli government would find enticing. They reacted with moves to build up the Jewish population of east Jerusalem, expropriating Arab land and moving ahead with 25,000 flats for Jews. In Washington, their case was taken up in Congress, with pro-Israeli resolutions supported by both Democrats and Republicans. Privately, Nixon assured the Israelis that they had no need to worry. The Rogers Plan did not survive the determined opposition of the Israelis, reinforced by their political muscle on Capitol Hill, and helped by Nasser's inability to think strategically. But the problems of the region did not go away. In September 1970, Nixon was forced to deal with a new, and potentially highly volatile, crisis. On 6 and 9 September, the left-wing Popular Front for the Liberation of Palestine hijacked American, Swiss and British airliners to Dawson Field in Jordan. All the hostages were released, but King Hussein, determined to assert his authority, turned his army on the Palestinian guerrilla bases in his country. Syrian armoured forces, though not supported by their air force, crossed the Jordanian border, threatening to provoke an Israeli counter-move. Nixon's response was to deploy airborne forces and the carriers of the Sixth Fleet in the Mediterranean. On 23 September, the Syrians withdrew. Given Syria's close relationship with the Soviet Union,

Nixon was to compare his action with that of Kennedy over Cuba. Though this was stretching the point, it had been, at the very least, a dangerous affair which demonstrated that the tensions of the Arab–Israeli conflict were ignored at their peril. Even so, the process of disengagement from Vietnam was to leave the Middle East in something of a limbo once again. This was a pity. In the course of what became known as 'Black September', Nasser died while trying to mediate between King Hussein and PLO Chairman Yasser Arafat. His successor, Anwar el-Sadat, saw the United States as the key to unlocking the diplomatic impasse, despite the fact that Washington and Cairo still had no diplomatic relations (Fraser, 1989).

Allende and Chile

September 1970 saw another unwelcome development, this time in Chile, whose position close to the junction of the Atlantic and Pacific oceans gave it a pivotal strategic importance. Presidential elections were won by the Marxist Dr Salvador Allende, with 36 per cent of the popular vote against a divided opposition. Allende had been in America's sights for years as a possible threat. Appalled at the prospect of a second Marxist regime in the Americas, Nixon authorised a covert CIA operation to thwart Allende's ratification in Congress, unsuccessfully as it turned out. The CIA's attention then turned to assisting Allende's opponents, channelling covert financial assistance to political parties, newspapers and trade unions. As the country's economic position deteriorated, in September 1973 the army led by Augusto Pinochet seized power. Allende perished in the course of the coup and hundreds of his supporters were executed. Internationally denounced for violations of human rights, Pinochet's regime secured America's interests in the 'southern cone' of Latin America (Kissinger, 1999).

Intervention in Cambodia and Laos

By September 1970, Nixon was in need of a diplomatic success, since the year had so far seen a further serious escalation of the war, with bitter and tragic domestic consequences. Once again, Cambodia provided the trigger when, on 18 March 1970, Prince Sihanouk was deposed in a right-wing coup led by General Lon Nol. Events did not go the general's way, and within a month North Vietnamese and communist forces had his government on the run. The prospect now opened up a communist Cambodia, which, some felt, would confound any American hopes for an independent South Vietnam remaining after a peace settlement, particularly since a salient of Cambodian territory, the so-called 'Parrot's Beak', reached to just over thirty miles of Saigon. In fact, the main Cambodian communist movement, the Khmer Rouge, was aligned with China rather than with North Vietnam. Counsel in Washington was divided, with Rogers and Laird, as well as some of Kissinger's staff, strongly against intervention in the country, arguing that an invasion would result in substantial American casualties with no permanent strategic gain. Nixon knew perfectly well that any extension of the war into Cambodia would provoke a widespread hostile reaction at home, but he was increasingly convinced of the need to intervene. The decision to intervene was, it seems, very much his own (Haldeman, 1994; Bundy, 1998). On 20 April, he announced a further troop reduction of 150,000 at the same as holding urgent discussions over the deteriorating Cambodian situation. Six days later, the critical decision to invade was reached, even though Nixon would not concede the term 'invasion' (Ambrose, 1989). On 30 April, Nixon announced a combined American–South Vietnamese operation against communist positions in Cambodia, essential, he claimed, for the policy of Vietnamisation to succeed (Nixon, 1978; Kissinger, 1979).

As a major offensive got under way, the anticipated domestic reaction set in with a vengeance. Press opinion overwhelmingly saw the invasion as committing the country to an ever-deeper involvement in war in South-east Asia, a sentiment increasingly echoed in Congress. As protests erupted on a number of college campuses, an irritated Nixon dismissed the demonstrators as 'bums'. This maladroit remark came to haunt him on, and after, 4 May, when National Guardsmen opened fire on unarmed student protesters at Kent State University in Ohio, killing four, two of whom were not even on the demonstration. The effect on other colleges and universities of this tragedy was electric, while Nixon's stance over Cambodia was made no easier by the revelation that his two most senior Cabinet officers had opposed the invasion (Nixon, 1978; Haldeman, 1994). By any yardstick his presidency was passing though an acute crisis. Ominously for Nixon, congressional opposition to his policies grew to dangerous levels. Senators Frank Church (Democrat) and John Sherman Cooper (Republican) introduced amendments to the Foreign Military Sales Bill to deny funds for ground and air activity in Cambodia after 30 June. Faced with information that their amendment was likely to succeed, Nixon was left with a stark choice (Bundy, 1998). On 30 June, American troops evacuated Cambodia, allowing Nixon to claim that this had been a limited operation, which had impaired the military potential of 74 North Vietnamese battalions and taken the pressure off Lon Nol's government. The facts were otherwise. Kissinger later conceded that the 30 June evacuation date had been a panic decision taken under domestic pressure (Kissinger, 1979). It is difficult to see the invasion of Cambodia as doing other than confirming the extent of opposition to the war and that America was, in effect, conducting a retreat. The North Vietnamese forces had been damaged, but not mortally, and increasingly saw events moving their way. Domestically, Nixon had undermined, probably terminally, the image he had created of a carefully crafted disengagement from South-east Asia. A further consequence of the Cambodian affair was to speed up the repeal in the senate of the Gulf of Tonkin Resolution. Though this had ceased to be a matter of any immediate relevance, it inevitably brought into question once again the legal basis for the war (Bundy, 1998).

The beginning of 1971 saw Nixon at the midway stage of what he hoped would be his first term, and, by his own admission, at a low point, not least because his foreign policy initiatives, far from ending the war, had stirred the domestic pot. Things did not immediately improve. Hanoi's negotiating position continued to be nothing less than an American and South Vietnamese surrender, something the administration refused to contemplate. Moreover, like some hydra-headed monster, the war seemed capable of growing new dimensions. By the end of 1970, the main source of communist supplies had switched from Cambodia to the well-established Ho Chi Minh trail through the jungles of Laos, almost certainly in preparation for a spring offensive which would test the reality of Vietnamisation. The American command in Saigon proposed to disrupt this by an offensive into Laos by the South Vietnamese army with American air and logistical support. Like many such plans it read well, but failed to take into account the ability of the South Vietnamese forces to undertake a sophisticated operation outside their home territory (Kissinger, 1979). Nevertheless, Nixon determined to press ahead. On 8 February 1971, the South Vietnamese attack began, but it soon became embarrassingly clear that their troops were out of their depth. On 18 March, they began to withdraw. There is always a fine line between an orderly retreat and a rout, and some units undoubtedly crossed it. American audiences were treated to the spectacle of South Vietnamese soldiers fighting to hold on to helicopters as they evacuated. While Nixon inevitably argued that the operation had been a military success by disrupting enemy supply lines, which was true enough, the operation had been a dismal advertisement for Vietnamisation. It was also the last major offensive operation of the war, as it happened (Nixon, 1978; Ambrose, 1989).

Nixon and China

At the same time as the Laotian operation was maturing, another, more positive, foreign policy initiative was taking shape. For some time, Nixon had been signalling his interest in improving relations with China, which were still solidly set in the frozen mould they had been in since the Korean War. He had come to this comparatively late in life, having as a young Congressman been a strident critic of the Truman administration over the 'fall' of China. As late as October 1967, he was still pointing to the clear threat from 'Red China', though this may have been to reassure conservative supporters. What appears to have changed his perception was the serious military clash between Chinese and Soviet forces along the Ussuri river in March 1969. Though this would have to be delicately handled, it indicated that a new pressure point against Moscow might be exploited (Bundy, 1998). At the beginning of 1971, premier Chou En-lai sent a message to the effect that he would welcome an American move, even a visit from Nixon. It brought into focus tentative contacts which had been passing between the Chinese and Americans over the previous year, surviving even the Cambodian crisis. There was a clear mutual interest, potentially at least. For the Chinese a warmer relationship with Washington could be set against their quarrel with Moscow, while for Nixon and Kissinger a move towards China opened up a range of new diplomatic possibilities. The trick was how to do this without giving the Soviets the impression that a rapprochement between Washington and Beijing would result in a strategic threat, something their diplomats were quick to point out once they learned what might be afoot (Kissinger, 1979).

Nixon responded to Beijing's signals with an important one of his own when his Foreign Policy Report of 25 February 1971 for the first time officially used the term 'Government of the People's Republic of China', adding that 'it will find us receptive to agreements' (Stebbins & Adam, 1976a). The significance of the terminology was not lost on the Chinese, who responded in a manner as unconventional as it was imaginative. The occasion was an international table-tennis tournament in Japan, in the course of which the Chinese team invited their American counterparts to visit China. On 14 April 1971, the young Americans were treated to a full reception by Chou En-lai in Beijing's Great Hall of the People. This 'ping-pong diplomacy', as it was inevitably termed, was intended to confirm China's readiness to explore a new relationship with the United States (Kissinger, 1979). This was reinforced more formally on 27 April when a message from Chou, routed via Pakistan, informed the Americans of China's willingness to have direct discussions with them, including the president. Nixon's positive response produced, on 2 June, a formal invitation for a presidential visit to be preceded by a secret advance meeting with Kissinger (Nixon, 1978).

Kissinger's preparatory visit to Beijing from 9 to 11 July set the scene for Nixon's historic announcement on the fifteenth that he would be travelling to China. The major stumbling block in the way of opening a fruitful dialogue was, of course, America's long-standing relationship with Taiwan and, in particular, support for her position in the United Nations. By the time Nixon made his announcement, he had already come to the conclusion that Beijing would win the next United Nations' vote. What really mattered was that a quarter of the world's population could no longer remain in a state of isolation. When the United Nations voted on 25 October to admit the People's Republic to membership and expel Taiwan, one of Nixon's problems was solved, though he had to head off moves from his own right wing to suspend funding to the international organisation.

Such was the fate of the once-feared China Lobby (Kissinger, 1979; Haldeman, 1994).

The way was now open for Nixon's visit to China, now chiefly remembered through John Adams's opera, but in its day seen, quite rightly, as a move of historic significance. Like most such visits it was stronger on style than substance. Nixon set the tone on his arrival in Beijing on 21 February 1972 by pointedly shaking hands with Chou, thus setting to rights the slight when Dulles had refused to do so in 1954. In fact, as Kissinger later conceded, the message was what the visit was really all about. The sight of their president in easy conversation with Mao, so long castigated as the embodiment of revolution, or visiting the monuments of Chinese civilisation, was intended to convey to the American public that the People's Republic was no longer the pariah of the international system. It was also designed to send a clear, if coded, signal to Moscow that the bipolar world which had persisted throughout the Cold War was at an end. The final communiqué, while acknowledging that the two countries differed over Vietnam, Korea and Japan, stated that 'progress toward the normalization of relations between China and the United States is in the interests of all countries', and that 'neither should seek hegemony in the Asia-Pacific region'. More significant was the warning that they were 'opposed to to efforts by any other country or group of countries to establish such hegemony', a barely veiled reference to a common stance against the Soviet Union, which had, of course, been an objective of both parties from the beginning (Bundy, 1998).

On Taiwan, the Chinese government reaffirmed that this was the crucial barrier to the normalisation of relations. It confirmed that China was one country with the People's Republic as its sole government, and demanded the withdrawal of all American forces from the island. For its part, the American government acknowledged that China was indivisible, that its interest was 'in a peaceful settlement of the Taiwan question by the Chinese themselves', and that its ultimate objective was the withdrawal of all its forces (Stebbins & Adam, 1976b). Despite the differences, and the more strident tone of the Chinese position, it was clear that Mao and Chou regarded Taiwan as an issue to be resolved later rather than sooner. In retrospect, Nixon's visit may be seen as a belated American recognition of the reality of the People's Republic. So, of course, it was, but this should not be allowed to detract from the fact that, with the war in South-east Asia still unresolved, Nixon had pushed ahead with the initiative in the knowledge that it would unsettle many of his core supporters on the right (Ambrose, 1989). Once the Vietnam accords were reached the following year, the two countries established Liaison Offices in Washington and Beijing, before moving to full diplomatic relations in 1979. It was a significant advance from the sterilities of the 1950s and 1960s, but it was only a first step and it would require the authority of a strong president to move the relationship forward (Nixon, 1978; Kissinger, 1979).

Détente with the the Soviet Union

China was only one leg of Nixon's policy of détente. The other, and more important, was the Soviet Union. If events in Asia and the Middle East had so far grabbed the headlines in the administration's conduct of foreign policy, this did not mean that this key issue had been neglected. From the start, Nixon and Kissinger had agreed on three core principles in their dealings with Moscow: a willingness to negotiate over clear, concrete issues; to work for a policy of mutual restraint; and, finally, the concept of 'linkage', whereby good relations had to be based upon progress over a broad range (Kissinger, 1979). Ever the pragmatists, the Soviet leaders were willing to explore a relationship with Nixon, his anti-communist record notwithstanding. The starting point for any new relationship was the control of nuclear weapons, which lay at the heart of the administration's approach to Moscow. Strategic Arms

Limitation Talks (SALT) began in Finland in November 1969, but they soon ran into difficulty on the vexed question of definition. The Soviet negotiators pressed for a definition of 'strategic' which would take in weapons capable of hitting the national territory of the other. It was not a matter of semantics. This would take out of the equation their missiles and bombers aimed at NATO targets in Europe, a gambit transparently aimed at the Alliance's solidarity, but also one which took into account the changing nature of the strategic relationship (Kissinger, 1979).

The growth in the Soviet strategic arsenal under Brezhnev meant that the focus of any possible nuclear exchange had changed from western Europe to the continental United States. The Soviet Union had, in short, become a world power with global reach, a development which forced a re-evaluation of American defence and foreign policy priorities. The extension of Soviet power posed an obvious question mark over the stability of the NATO alliance. Simply put, would the United states be prepared to sacrifice her cities in the defence of western Europe? Viewed in that light, Nixon's dogged determination not to be seen to be abandoning South Vietnam assumes a rather different perspective (Kissinger, 1979).

Nixon started exploring the idea of a summit meeting with the Soviet leaders as early as 1970, not least because he saw this as a way of countering his domestic critics, but the hope that this could be linked with agreement in the SALT negotiations was frustrated through lack of progress. Nor was it made any easier by the level of domestic political controversy over the nature of the nuclear arsenal, the acrid nature of which seemed to reflect the country's deeper malaise. At issue in the SALT negotiations were issues as complex as they were vital to world peace. The Soviet position had come to rest on the principle that any agreement should be confined to ABM systems, while American negotiators insisted that strategic offensive weapons should also be included. Negotiations were being conducted at two levels, the official SALT talks as well as a secret dialogue between Kissinger and Soviet ambassador Anatoly Dobrynin, to which not even Rogers was privy. It was out of the latter channel that the principles for an agreement came; namely, that in return for limiting ABMs there would be a freeze on the development of offensive nuclear weapons. This was what Nixon announced on 20 May 1971, though, while confirming agreement on ABM deployment, he confined himself to saying that the two sides would 'agree on certain measures with respect to the limitation of offensive strategic measures' (Nixon, 1978; Kissinger, 1979). Even so, his announcement was widely recognised as a significant milestone on the path to arms limitation.

An early sign that détente might amount to something more than mere rhetoric came on 3 September 1971 in the shape of a new four-power accommodation over Berlin, which allowed for easier access from West to East, even if not in reverse. On the ground, this eased the beleaguered position of West Berliners, while indicating that East–West progress was possible on other issues. That this was the case was confirmed on 12 October when Nixon announced that he would visit Moscow the following May. Nor was the war between India and Pakistan in December 1971, in which the Indians were supported by the Soviets and the Pakistanis by the Americans, allowed to deflect the developing relationship. This conflict, which saw the emergence of Bangladesh, had to do with the unfinished legacies of Britain's partition of the subcontinent in 1947 and should not have exercised the two superpowers. Nixon saw the war as aggression by a Soviet-supported state, India, rather than what it really was, the irretrievable breakdown of Pakistan (Nixon, 1978; Ambrose, 1989). With the war's end, the Indian subcontinent, home to a quarter of the world's population, was allowed to slip back into diplomatic obscurity, leaving relations with Moscow untouched. The affair had confirmed how Nixon, in common with many Americans, had a curious inability to engage with the world's largest democracy.

The Moscow Summit and the SALT Treaty

The preparations for the summit meeting were completed in a secret visit Kissinger made to Moscow in April 1972. His discussions with Brezhnev turned on American plans for ending the Vietnam War and fine-tuning the details of the SALT agreement. Although the broad outline of an agreement was in place, two substantive issues remained: the number of ABM sites to be permitted, and restrictions on Submarine-Launched Ballistic Missiles (SLBMs). Kissinger's mission resolved both. Brezhnev agreed that each side would be allowed two ABM sites, one to protect its capital and the other an ICBM site, and that there would be a limit of 950 SLBMs (Kissinger, 1979). Nixon's arrival in Moscow on 20 May marked a new development in the Cold War. He had been there 13 years before, and Roosevelt had gone to Yalta, but since this was the first presidential visit to the Soviet capital Nixon was conscious of its historic import. Nor was it entirely a formality, since details of almost Byzantine complexity about the nature of missiles to be included remained to be solved, and there was hardly likely to be a meeting of minds over Vietnam. On the latter, the two sides simply agreed to disagree, though the disagreements were feisty enough (Kissinger, 1979).

The climax of the summit was the signing of two agreements on arms limitation, SALT I as they became known. The first, on ABMs, pledged the two signatories to limit such systems to two, separated by 1,300 kilometres, one for the capital and the other for an ICBM site, which in the American case was at Grand Forks, North Dakota. By agreeing 'not to deploy ABM systems for a defense of the territory of its country', the two powers had codified the principle of 'mutual assured destruction' (MAD). The second was the Interim Agreement on the limitation of strategic offensive arms, to last for five years. This committed the signatories not to construct additional ICBM launchers after 1 July 1972, and froze the number of such missiles at 1,054 for the

United States and 1,618 for the Soviet Union. They also undertook not to convert land-based launchers for light or older ICBMs into launchers for heavy ICBMs. Finally, the number of SLBMs was restricted to the number operational or under construction at the time of signature: in effect, 656 for the United States and 740 for the Soviet Union. Notably absent from the Interim Agreement was any restriction on MIRVs, which, it can be argued, left a yawning gap at its core, though one which was to America's advantage, given her lead in MIRV development. Absent, too, was any limitation on strategic bombers, an area where the United States dominated, and the British and French nuclear weapons were not included (Stebbins & Adam, 1976b; Nixon, 1978; Ambrose, 1989). The Interim Agreement was seen as only the first stage in nuclear arms control, and the United States had not come out of it too badly, though conservative critics of détente did not agree. The summit also produced a document setting out the 'Basic Principles of Mutual Relations' between the two countries, which signalled the limits of détente. While confirming that they would 'do their utmost to avoid military confrontations and to prevent the outbreak of nuclear war', the relationship was to be 'on the basis of peaceful coexistence'. The latter phrase, insisted upon by Soviet negotiators, was understood to mean that the Soviet Union would continue its policy of confrontation with the United States by all means short of force (Stebbins & Adam, 1976b; Bundy, 1998). The year 1972 had seen Nixon record diplomatic triumphs in Beijing and Moscow, which would have ensured his re-election without recourse to trick or subterfuge. Few presidents have been as fortunate as Nixon seemed to be that year.

7

NIXON, FORD AND THE AMERICAN CRISIS

Let us pledge together to make these next four years the best four
years in America's history, so that on its two hundredth birthday it
will be as young and vital as when it began, and as bright a beacon
of hope for all the world.

Richard M. Nixon, Inaugural, 20 January 1973

Endgame in Vietnam

Buoyed by his reputation in foreign policy, Nixon could look
forward with confidence to the realisation of his overseas
goals. He declaimed in his Second Inaugural in January
1973: '1972 will be remembered as the year of the greatest
progress since the end of World War II toward a lasting
peace in the world.' It was a record he believed he could
build upon. But before anything could be attempted on the
wider canvas of relations with Moscow and Beijing, the war
in South-east Asia had to be ended, or at least America's
direct involvement in it. Not that it was much of an American
war any more, since Nixon's rolling policy of troop withdrawal had progressively brought military strength to some
69,000 by the spring of 1972. On 29 August, he announced
a further reduction to 27,000. Even so, American air power
was still formidably deployed in support of the South
Vietnamese forces. In March 1972, the North Vietnamese
army began a sustained offensive in the South. Nixon's
response was to assemble a major force of B-52 bombers and

aircraft carriers to attack targets in North Vietnam. Then, on 8 May, he announced the mining of all North Vietnamese ports and attacks on their communications network. At the same time, he outlined America's conditions for a settlement; namely, the return of American prisoners and an internationally supervised ceasefire throughout Indochina. This would be followed by a complete American withdrawal within four months (Stebbins & Adam, 1976b). While these military measures did not stop the North Vietnamese campaign, they undoubtedly blunted its effectiveness, and enabled the South Vietnamese forces to stabilise the situation. Significantly, in August 1972 the Hanoi government at last sanctioned moves for a negotiated settlement (Isaacson, 1992).

This decision opened the way to what proved to be the final phase of negotiations. On 11 September, the Vietcong announced their acceptance of the principle that a solution for South Vietnam must acknowledge the reality of two administrations and two armies in the country. The various elements in the equation began to come together in Paris on 8 October at a meeting between Kissinger and the chief North Vietnamese negotiator, Le Duc Tho, in which the latter set out Hanoi's response to Nixon's proposals of 8 May. It was immediately clear that there had been a significant shift in their position. What Le Duc Tho offered amounted to the essential elements of a settlement: a ceasefire without the precondition of the removal of the South Vietnamese government, and the return of prisoners, followed by an American withdrawal. There would be an Administration of National Concord, formed from the South Vietnamese government and the Vietcong, while the two bodies would continue to administer the areas their forces controlled. From the American perspective, the critical concession was that a ceasefire was no longer contingent on the removal of Thieu's government. An American withdrawal would not be seen as the betrayal of an ally (Stebbins & Adam, 1976b; Kissinger, 1979; Isaacson, 1992).

This was not how President Thieu and his government saw it, however. For them, the National Council would amount to the coalition government they had long resisted. More importantly, while American troops would withdraw from the country, 145,000 North Vietnamese would not. A visit by Kissinger to Saigon on 16 October signally failed to win Thieu over, and further movement had to await the result of the presidential election on 7 November. In domestic political terms, Nixon's visits to Beijing and Moscow undoubtedly boosted his political standing in a presidential election year, confounding his critics and clouding over the fact that the war was still continuing. His re-election was virtually ensured when changes to the Democrats' nominating process resulted in the selection of Senator George McGovern from the left wing of the party. Nixon had little trouble in convincing the electorate that he spoke for mainstream America, coasting to a margin of 47,169,911 to McGovern's 29,170,383. He now had a clear electoral mandate to bring the war to an end on his terms. With the election safely behind him, Nixon sought to reassure Thieu that the United States was not proposing to abandon him. Writing on 14 November, Nixon conceded that North Vietnamese forces would remain in the country, but continued:

> Far more important than what we say in the agreement on this issue is what we do in the event the enemy renews its aggression. You have my absolute assurance that if Hanoi fails to abide by the terms of this agreement it is my intention to take swift and severe retaliatory action . . . . I repeat my personal assurances to you that the United States will react very strongly and rapidly to any violation of the agreement.

Thieu was far from convinced (Stebbins & Adam, 1976b; Nixon, 1978).

While trying to convince a sceptical South Vietnamese government of American good faith, Nixon and Kissinger were finding it frustratingly difficult to conclude the final details of an agreement. By mid-December, talks between Kissinger and Le Duc Tho were once again badly stalled. The only path to an agreement, it was argued, was to make the North Vietnamese, and by extension the South Vietnamese, aware of the full weight of American air power. In what Nixon described as the most difficult decision he had to make in the course of the war, on 14 December he ordered full scale B-52 raids on military targets in Hanoi and Haiphong. In addition to the obvious fact that such high-level bombing could not avoid hitting civilians, heavy anti-aircraft defences around the two cities carried serious risks for the American aircrew. In the event, 15 B-52s and 11 other aircraft were lost, with 93 of their crew. In Hanoi, some 1,318 people were killed. Nixon's action was widely denounced at home and abroad, though key Republicans like Ronald Reagan supported his action. On 26 December, as the heaviest raids of the war took place, the North Vietnamese indicated their willingness to take part in a meeting in Paris on 8 January. Three days later, the bombing stopped (Nixon, 1978; Kissinger, 1979; Ambrose, 1991).

The Paris Agreement

The final negotiations resumed, as agreed, on 8 January. Three days before, Nixon warned the South Vietnamese of the grave consequences should they break with the United States (Stebbins & Adam, 1976c). The historic 'Agreement on ending the war and restoring peace in Viet-Nam' was signed in Paris on 23 January 1973, just three days after Nixon's second inauguration, to come into effect four days later, bringing to an end over four years of tortuous negotiations. Under its provisions, all hostilities were to end at midnight on the 27th. Within 60 days all American troops and military advisers were to be withdrawn from the country and military bases dismantled. All captured military and civilian personnel were to be returned. On the future of South Vietnam, the country's right to self-determination was declared to be 'sacred, inalienable, and . . . respected by all countries', her political future to be decided 'through genuinely free and democratic general elections under international supervision'. Immediately after the ceasefire, the two South Vietnamese parties would form the National Council of National Reconciliation and Concord, which would organise 'free and democratic elections'. The agreement also contemplated the reunification of Vietnam through 'peaceful means on the basis of discussions and agreements between North and South Viet-Nam, without coercion or annexation by either party, and without foreign interference'. Finally, the United States agreed to assist with the 'post-war reconstruction of the Democratic Republic of Viet-Nam and throughout Indo-China'. By a bizarre irony, the day before the agreement was concluded, one of the war's more eminent victims, Lyndon Johnson, died. In announcing the agreement to the American people, Nixon used the phrase 'peace with honor'. He undoubtedly did so with conviction. Had he thought of the last statesman who had used these words, Neville Chamberlain, he might have hesitated, but for Americans, if not the people of South-east Asia, what mattered was that the long agony of Vietnam was over (Stebbins & Adam, 1976c).

Watergate and Détente

On 18 June 1972, five men were arrested while breaking into the Democratic National Committee at the Watergate complex in Washington. They were, it emerged, attempting to bug the office, and one of them was an employee of the Committee to Reelect the President, CRP to the Republicans, but, predictably, CREEP to the Democrats. So began the Watergate scandal, which, curiously, did nothing to prevent Nixon's re-election, but consumed, and ultimately destroyed, his presidency. Although the twists and turns of Nixon's attempts to escape the snares of Watergate lie beyond the scope of this volume, they set the scene for his direction of foreign policy. The combination of Watergate and the humiliating end to the Vietnam War saw the United States pass through a crisis unprecedented in modern times. As the Watergate affair relentlessly unravelled in the course of 1973, Nixon's prestige and credibility eroded so swiftly that as early as May the Chinese and Soviets were speculating about his position. As the authority of the White House waned, Kissinger's rose, since even Nixon's enemies knew that the country's foreign policy needed purpose and direction. While Nixon's wounds over Watergate were largely self-inflicted, he tried not to let his prolonged humiliation affect his conduct of foreign policy. Détente with the Soviet Union continued to be the lodestone of his strategy, with Kissinger convinced that détente had the potential to deliver both containment and coexistence (Kissinger, 1982). But when Brezhnev came to the United States in June 1973, what should have been a productive sequel to Nixon's Moscow visit took place under the cloud of imminent critical Watergate hearings, postponed for a week on account of the summit. Little of substance emerged from the visit, in the course of which the two leaders had marked differences of views over the terms for settling the Arab–Israeli conflict. Brezhnev later admitted to his worries over the drift of events in the Middle East, while disclaiming any foreknowledge of the military plans maturing in Cairo and Damascus (Burr, 1999). He could not have missed the gathering sense of peril surrounding the Nixon presidency. Watergate was already making its mark on international affairs. One other symptom of the administration's changing priorities was Rogers's replacement by Kissinger on 22 August. No Secretary of State of the modern era has ever enjoyed such authority, especially since he retained his role in the National Security Council (Nixon, 1978; Isaacson, 1992).

War in the Middle East

Confirmed by the Senate on 21 September 1973, Kissinger was immediately tested, as few of his 53 predecessors had been, by full-scale war in the Middle East. Arab pride had been stretched beyond its limits by the failure of any diplomatic attempt to secure the return of the territories occupied by Israel in 1967. Anwar el-Sadat knew that the United States was the key to unlocking the situation, but was unclear as how this might be done, especially since diplomatic relations had been severed in 1967. In July 1972, he ordered the Soviet Union to withdraw her military advisers from Egypt, but this failed to generate a response from Washington. This set the scene for intense military preparations for an attack on Israeli positions on the Suez Canal and Golan Heights in conjunction with Syria's Hafiz al-Assad, planned to begin on 6 October. American and Israeli intelligence failed to anticipate what was maturing until the 5th, when the families of Soviet advisers in Syria were flown out. An Israeli request that Washington warn Egypt and Syria not to attack was accompanied by an intelligence appraisal that war was not imminent. On the morning of the 6th the Israelis revised their opinion, but their Cabinet decided against a pre-emptive strike to help preserve American support. When the combined Syrian and Egyptian assault began later that day, it succeeded beyond the Israelis' worst imagining. On the Golan front, the Syrians captured the key position of Mount Hermon and a full breakthrough was only prevented by the sacrifice of 40 Israeli aircraft. The Egyptian crossing of the Suez Canal captured Israel's Bar-Lev Line. Within hours, their Second and Third Armies were deployed along the east bank (Fraser, 1995).

These dramatic events could hardly have caught the administration at a worse time. Not only was Kissinger finding his feet as Secretary of State, but the Watergate investigations were at a critical phase. On 20 October, the Watergate Special Prosecutor was dismissed, followed by the resignation of the Attorney-General and resolutions in Congress for Nixon's impeachment. To add to the administration's woes, on 10 October Vice-President Spiro Agnew resigned as he was about to be indicted on tax charges, to be replaced by Gerald Ford, the Republican leader in the House of Representatives. On the constitutional front, long pent-up frustrations in Congress over the actions Johnson and Nixon had taken over Vietnam and Cambodia also reached their climax. On 4 October, a War Powers Resolution was introduced in both houses. This required the president to report to congress within 48 hours situations where 'imminent involvement in hostilities' demanded the use of armed force. This then triggered a 60-day limit on their use, unless Congress declared war, extended the 60-day period, or had been unable to meet because of an armed attack. The Resolution was passed by the Senate on 10 October, and by the House two days later. Condemning it as 'unconstitutional and dangerous to the best interests of our Nation', on 24 October Nixon vetoed the Resolution. But the measure of his decline came on 7 November when the Senate, by 75 votes to 18, and the House, by 284 votes to 135, voted to override his veto. It was exactly one year since his triumphant re-election. The Resolution never remotely fulfilled its sponsors' hopes, most presidents honouring it in the breach. The definition of what constituted 'hostilities' proved elastic. Some have argued that the Resolution actually increased the scope for presidential action, while others feel that it did significantly alter the balance between president and Congress in favour of the latter (Stebbins & Adam, 1976c; Johnson, 1995; Bundy, 1998).

As these events were unfolding on Capitol Hill, the largest tank battles since 1943 were being fought in the Middle East. For the first time in her military history, things were not going Israel's way. By 9 October, she had lost 49 aircraft and 500 tanks. Although they were slow to appreciate, or be told about, the extent of Israel's losses, Nixon and Kissinger were able to react to the crisis on the basis of back-channel assurances from Sadat that he was waging a limited war for the return of territories lost in 1967, to be followed by a peace conference (Fraser, 1989). It was not until the 9th that the Israeli government made an urgent request to Washington for a re-supply operation, vital if she were to deploy her reserves of aircraft, tanks and ammunition. Various pressures were operating on Nixon and Kissinger, not least the nature of Israel's possible response if her military setbacks continued. While they could not abandon a close friend in the Middle East, they were anxious not to trigger an Arab oil embargo. Nor did they want to see the war end with an Egyptian and Syrian defeat on the lines of 1967, which would once again stifle hopes of diplomatic progress. Nixon agreed that Israel's losses should be made good, but the initial scale of the response left the Israelis resentful. American supplies were flown to the Azores, leaving El Al's seven jets to complete the final leg. Phantom jets were replaced at the rate of one and a half a day. It was not until the 13th that Nixon ordered American Galaxy transports to fly direct to Israel. Once the airbridge began to operate, it did so on a massive scale. The following day, the Israelis inflicted a major defeat on the Egyptians in the Sinai desert, while on the 16th a force under General Ariel Sharon crossed the Suez Canal, opening up a dangerous gap between Egypt's Second and Third Armies (Fraser, 1995).

Kissinger and the Ceasefire

The fighting had to be ended in such a way that a diplomatic path would open up. Urgent action was necessary, since the Soviet Union was threatening to respond with her own re-supply operation to Egypt and Syria, while on 17 October the Organization of Arab Petroleum-Exporting Countries (OAPEC), condemning America's actions, instituted a cut in oil production. This was followed by a total oil embargo on the United States and the Netherlands, the key to the supply of western Europe. The potential consequences of the Arab 'oil weapon' was another powerful inducement for the Americans to pursue a negotiated settlement. With the fighting turning Israel's way, Soviet premier Alexsei Kosygin convinced Sadat of the need for a ceasefire. On the basis that any ceasefire included the Palestinian issue, Kissinger was invited to Moscow. On 21 October, Kissinger and Brezhnev agreed the terms of Security Council Resolution 338, and, as such, a key text in signalling the way forward. It provided for a ceasefire in the positions then occupied, hence allowing the Egyptians and Israelis to retain their respective bridgeheads. The parties were then charged with implementing Resolution 242 'in all its parts', and with starting negotiations for 'a just and durable peace in the Middle East'. Knowing that the Israelis would resent a formula which prevented them exploiting their recent gains, Kissinger had to fly to Israel to reassure them (Fraser, 1989).

Shocked by the scale of their initial defeats, the Israelis were only too anxious to press home the advantage of Sharon's bridgehead. Kissinger hinted that they might consolidate their positions by allowing the time of the ceasefire to overrun. He clearly did not anticipate what actually happened, a major offensive on the west bank of the canal, which encircled the city of Suez and the entire Third Army. The dangerous scenario now presented itself as a resumption of the war, with the two superpowers being dragged in. The Soviet Union started to deploy 85 ships in the eastern Mediterranean and seven airborne divisions. This could not have hit the administration at a worse time, since the previous day resolutions for Nixon's impeachment had been introduced in congress. The response was calibrated by Kissinger in such a way as to send a clear signal to the Soviets while allowing diplomacy to work. Orders were issued that American forces would have their state of alert increased from DefCon IV and V to DefCon III, the state of maximum readiness without the assumption of the imminence of war. Brezhnev was offered the face-saving device that Soviet and

American personnel could operate under the auspices of the United Nations Truce Supervisory Organisation, something which the Egyptians decided they did not want. Although this had appeared to be one of the most anxious moments of the Cold War, each side had acted with prudence (Kissinger, 1982; Fraser, 1989; Ambrose, 1991).

The war's end ushered in the period of Kissinger's 'step-by-step' diplomacy in the Middle East in which he hoped to nurture trust between the protagonists through a series of carefully measured agreements. The essential first step was to take the pressure off the encircled Third Army whose humiliation he was resolved to prevent. Resentful Israelis were to claim that he had threatened the suspension of military aid. On 11 November, an agreement at Kilometre 101 on the Cairo–Suez road allowed supplies through to Suez and the Third Army. With the immediate crisis behind him, Kissinger convened, with the Soviet Union, the Geneva Peace Conference envisaged in Resolution 338. It was a formal affair which lasted a day, but was significant for the fact that Jordan and Egypt, though not Syria, sat at the same table as the Israelis. It allowed Kissinger to press ahead to disentangle the still volatile situation on the canal and on the Syrian front where an Israeli salient pushed towards Damascus (Fraser, 1989).

The year 1974 saw Kissinger broker two critical agreements. As he carried complex proposals between Jerusalem, Cairo and Damascus, he also introduced the term 'shuttle diplomacy' to the vocabulary. The first agreement, signed between Egypt and Israel on 18 January 1974, stabilised the situation along the Suez Canal. This saw the Israeli forces withdraw from their salient west of the canal and allowed limited Egyptian forces to be stationed along the entire east bank, marking the first return by Israel of territories occupied in 1967. The price was a secret Memorandum of Understanding from the United States, which apparently made a commitment to be responsive to Israel's security needs (Sheehan, 1976; Golan, 1976). The agreement confirmed Kissinger's skill as a negotiator. Negotiations with Syria were a tougher test, since the Israeli army was within 20 miles of Damascus and the disputed territory, the Golan Heights, overlooked northern Israel. Moreover, while Sadat had made positive signals, President Assad had not. While the Syrian leader knew that his demand for the Golan's return could not be met, he could not be seen to have achieved less than Sadat. Negotiations turned on the former provincial capital of Quneitra. On 31 May, Kissinger secured an agreement whereby the Israelis withdrew to a line just west of the town. Assad also gave private assurances that he would not allow the frontier to be violated (Kissinger, 1982). These negotiations were viewed as a tour de force, confirming Kissinger's dominant role in foreign affairs. His achievement in stabilising a highly volatile situation should not be underestimated.

Nixon's Fall

Kissinger was also operating in the death throes of the Nixon administration. Yet even as Watergate was about to engulf him, Nixon made two final forays overseas, as if instinctively realising that his record in foreign affairs might ultimately aid his redemption. On 12 June, he arrived in Cairo to be greeted by Sadat and an ecstatic crowd, followed by visits to Saudi Arabia, Syria, Israel and Jordan. The relationships he opened up with key figures might have enabled him to move a Middle East peace settlement forward from the solid base Kissinger had established, but it was too late for that. But at least he had helped to cement America's new relationship with Arab leaders which others could use to advantage (Fraser, 1989; Ambrose, 1991). Then, on 25 June, he left for Moscow. As before, arms control was at the heart of his mission, but here, too, his domestic problems confounded him. Negotiations for a SALT II agreement had been carrying on for over a year without much progress. Paul Nitze, the

Defense Department's member of the SALT team, had come to the view that the Soviet tactic was to hope that Nixon would make key concessions to save his presidency. Convinced that 'Watergate was destroying the prospects of a sensible and sane SALT II accord', he resigned on 28 May. In a press release, he pointed out that 'it would be illusory to attempt to ignore or wish away the depressing reality of the traumatic events now unfolding in our nation's capital and of the implications of these events in the international arena' (Nitze, 1989). Nitze, of course, was far from alone. In the circumstances, nothing could be hoped for from the third Nixon–Brezhnev summit. The Soviets treated Nixon with great courtesy, but the summit yielded nothing of substance. In his memoirs Nixon recorded his belief that the summit's failure had not been result of Watergate and the impeachment proceedings. Kissinger clearly thought otherwise, the two journeys having convinced him that the erosion of Nixon's authority was threatening to deprive 'our policy of strength and direction and our strategy of credibility' (Nixon, 1978; Kissinger, 1982). He did not have long to fret. On 8 August 1974, Nixon resigned. In his resignation address, he pointed to the openings he had made to China, the moves for peace in the Middle East, the ending of America's longest war, and the limitations on nuclear arms with the Soviet Union (Ambrose, 1991). Nixon might be a disgraced president, but he had not been a negligible one, and even at this moment of humiliation he knew it.

Gerald Ford: The Unelected President

Gerald R. Ford, who took the oath of office the following day, was the nation's first unelected president. His track record on international affairs was unproven. Moreover, he took up office at a time when the economy was badly hit by the severe inflationary spiral generated by the increase in oil prices after the 1973 war in the Middle East. Even so, his reputation for decency ensured him a fair wind from an American people anxious to make a new beginning. But that goodwill began rapidly to dissipate after his announcement on 8 September of a pardon for Nixon, an act of clemency which cost him dear in the 1976 election. While it remained an open question whether Ford would be elected president in his own right, the nature of his succession inevitably marked out his presidency as a caretaker one. His sole asset in foreign affairs was that Kissinger, now regarded as an international celebrity, was his Secretary of State. Not even Kissinger could overcome the temper of the times, which had become profoundly suspicious of the uses of presidential power. Congressional elections in November 1974 returned a large number of young, liberal Democrats anxious to ensure that their concerns over possible foreign involvements were addressed, understandably enough in view of Vietnam and Watergate. Relations between the Ford administration and congress on foreign policy were never easy. Related to this was the increasing intellectual and political assault on détente, which came from both Left and Right. For many liberals, détente was insufficiently idealistic, ignoring human rights abuses inside the Soviet Union. Conservatives, on the other hand, were afraid that it was giving the Soviets too much rope (Isaacson, 1992; Kissinger,1999).

The Pursuit of Détente

The future of détente was at the forefront of the new president's priorities. A Nixon–Brezhnev summit had already been planned for the end of 1974 and Ford was determined to show that progress had not been deflected by American domestic politics. It was clear to both sides that progress on the stalled SALT II negotiations lay at the heart of whether détente would continue. With that in mind, Kissinger returned to Moscow in October. Brezhnev's suggestion that each country should limit itself to 2,400 launchers over a 10-year period seemed to offer the prospect for an agreement. This provided the basis on which, on 23 November 1974, Ford and Kissinger arrived in Vladivostok for the administration's first summit with Brezhnev. The communiqués sought to breath life into détente by confirming that 'the process of improving relations between the US and the USSR will continue without interruption and will become irreversible'. On arms control, the two powers agreed on a ceiling of 2,400 on the total number of ICBMs, SLMs and heavy bombers, of which 1,320 could be armed with MIRVs. This formula proved deceptively simple, fatally so. It took no account of the British and French weapons, of the nuclear delivery systems deployed on America's aircraft carriers, or of the intermediate-range missiles, notably the cruise, then in the course of development. Nor was there a definition of what constituted a 'heavy' bomber, particularly the 'Backfire' the Soviets were building. These ambiguities meant that the Vladivostok agreement was stillborn (Stebbins & Adam, 1977a; Nitze, 1989; Kissinger, 1999).

The Collapse of South Vietnam

As Ford struggled to restore a sense of dignity to American public life, the end for the anti-communist forces came with devastating speed. In his later apologia *No More Vietnams*, published in 1985, Nixon claimed that the United States had won the Vietnam War but lost the peace through congressional irresponsibility (Nixon, 1985). While it was true that Congress denied South Vietnam the level of aid which Nixon and Kissinger had anticipated in 1973, the truth was much more complex. Concerned as they were with America's power and status, most Americans were oblivious to the fact that they were not so much losing the war but that the Communists were determined to win it, and were capable of doing so. While the National Council envisaged in the Paris accords never materialised, the North Vietnamese steadily reinforced their troops in the South. In Cambodia, the Khmer Rouge did the same. On 1 January 1975, the Khmer Rouge went on to the offensive. A week later, communist forces in South Vietnam followed suit. Faced with a fast deteriorating military situation, on 28 January Ford requested $300 million in supplemental aid for South Vietnam and $222 million for Cambodia. Knowing that the American public was weary of the whole involvement, and suspicious that Ford was casting them in the role of villain, congressmen were not inclined to oblige. On 12 March, the House Democratic caucus voted 189–49 against military aid to Cambodia, while the following day the Senate Democratic caucus opposed aid to Cambodia by 38–5 and South Vietnam by 34–6. On 10 April, Ford made a request for an additional $722 million in emergency aid to South Vietnam, but this was rejected by the Armed Services Committees of both House and Senate (Stebbins & Adam, 1977b; Kissinger, 1999).

Ford's request was, in any case, far too late to change the situation. On 17 April, the Cambodian capital of Phnom Penh fell to the Communists. Government members and officials were executed, together with their families. Lon Nol had already left. The caretaker leader, Sirik Matak, shot in the stomach, apparently took three days to die. A short time previously, he had sent a note to the Americans, refusing their offer of evacuation, and concluding 'I have only committed this mistake of believing in you' (Kissinger, 1999). This was a miserable prelude to the fall of South Vietnam. By the time of Ford's request to Congress, all that really mattered was when and how to evacuate the remaining 6,000 Americans and key Vietnamese allies. On 21 April, President Thieu resigned with a bitter final broadside at the Americans for their failure to assist his government. On 29 April, the fall of Saigon was signalled by an attack on Tan Son Nhut airport, where thousands of Vietnamese and Americans were awaiting evacuation. The following day, as communist tanks approached the city centre, the final evacuation by helicopter from the Air France building in Saigon took place. The scenes of mayhem as marines fended panic-stricken Vietnamese away from the helicopters seemed to say it all. Vietnam and Cambodia were now communist states. Only Laos now remained. On 23 August, communist forces there took the capital, completing the transformation of South-east Asia. The 58,156 names inscribed on Washington's Vietnam memorial testified to the failure to contain communism in South-east Asia, first thought of under Eisenhower. The Americans had lost their first war (Isaacson, 1992; Kissinger, 1999).

Reassessment in the Middle East

As these historic events were unfolding, Kissinger had returned to his search for a Middle East peace settlement. The fall of Cambodia and South Vietnam raised obvious questions about American credibility, not least over possible guarantees in the event of Israel pulling out of key defensive positions in the Sinai desert, the Mitla and Gidi passes. What was at issue was an Israeli withdrawal east of the passes in return for Egyptian assurances that they would not use force. The latter proved too imprecise for an Israeli government still smarting over the events of 1973. On 22 March 1975, with negotiations with the Israelis at an impasse, Kissinger announced a period of 'reassessment' in Middle East policy. What was at stake was how the $2.5-billion aid package for Israel about to be submitted to Congress could be used to exert pressure. The implied threat cast an interesting light on the way Israel could mobilise political muscle in Washington. A letter to Ford signed by 76 senators – 51 Democrats and 25 Republicans – urged that his aid recommendations should 'be responsive to Israel's urgent military and economic needs'. In fact, it seems that Kissinger kept up his pressure on the

Israeli government, if less publicly (Golan, 1976; Fraser, 1989; Kissinger, 1999).

On 21 August, Kissinger began his final Middle East mission. Israel had already agreed to pull her forces east of the passes and to return the small oilfield at Abu Rudeis which supplied 55 per cent of her needs. All that Israel appeared to have gained in return appeared to be public confirmation from Sadat that Israeli cargoes would be allowed through the Suez Canal. On this basis the second Sinai agreement was initialled on 1 September 1975. It was clear to all that the next step would be a total Israeli withdrawal from the Sinai. Israel's agreement was secured by a number of American guarantees, linking the two countries in key areas. The United States provided secret guarantees to secure Israel's energy needs over the next five years. Moreover, the United States was to be 'fully responsive' to Israel's 'military equipment and other defence requirements'. Finally, Kissinger assured the Israelis that the Americans would 'not recognize or negotiate with the Palestine Liberation Organization' (PLO) until the PLO recognised Israel's right to exist and accepted Security Council Resolutions 242 and 338 (Fraser, 1989). No one pretended that anything like an overall Middle East settlement had been brought about, but Kissinger had patiently brought Egypt and Israel to a position where a full peace between them seemed within measurable distance. The missing element, as his Democratic critics were to point out, was that nothing had yet been done about the central Israeli–Palestinian issue. In fact, in 1974 Kissinger had begun negotiations with a view to seeing a Jordanian presence reestablished on the West Bank, but these had foundered on Israel's reluctance to move forward, followed by the decision of the Rabat Arab summit in October 1974 that the PLO was 'the sole legitimate representative of the Palestine people' (Ball, 1976; Kissinger, 1999). Progress on this issue proved to be one of the most tenacious obstacles American policymakers had to face.

The Helsinki Agreements

By the summer of 1975, the future of détente was already problematic. One reason for this was the declining health of one of its principal architects: Brezhnev had suffered a stroke immediately after the Vladivostok summit. Even so, both he and Ford travelled to Helsinki for the conclusion of the Conference on Security and Cooperation in Europe (CSCE) on 30 July–1 August 1975. On one level, the Helsinki agreements represented something that the Soviet Union had been working for since Stalin's time, formal confirmation of the boundaries established by the Red Army's victories in 1945, the participating states regarding 'as inviolable all one another's frontiers as well as the frontiers of all States in Europe'. While many American conservatives denounced this as the west's final abandonment of eastern Europe, a new Yalta, in fact Helsinki proved to be one of the defining agreements of the Cold War, since the final text also enshrined principles of human rights. The participating states bound themselves to 'respect human rights and fundamental freedoms, including the freedom of thought, conscience, religion or belief, for all without distinction as to race, sex, language or religion' (Stebbins & Adam, 1977b). Although western statesmen who signed up to these ideals had modest expectations of them, the principles set out were within a few years to be taken up by men and women of courage in eastern Europe and the Soviet Union, with fateful consequences.

8

CARTER: A NEW BEGINNING?

The passion for freedom is on the rise. Tapping this new spirit, there can be no nobler nor more ambitious task for America to undertake on this day of a new beginning than to help shape a just and peaceful world that is truly humane.

Jimmy Carter, Inaugural, 20 January 1977

There is no doubt that Jimmy Carter set out to chart a new course for a country still trying to heal the scars of Watergate and Vietnam. Few doubted that Ford had tried his best, but his pardon of Nixon had handicapped him almost from the start. In a presidential race always likely to favour the Democrats, Carter emerged from relative obscurity to challenge Ford. A former career naval officer who had retired early to run his family's peanut business, his political career had been confined to his native state of Georgia, first as a state senator and then, from 1971 to 1975, as Governor. It was precisely his remoteness from a discredited Washington, combined with his strongly held Christian faith, which appealed to many Americans in 1976. Even so, his plurality over Ford, 40,830,736 to 39,147,793, did not indicate an overwhelming mandate.

The New Administration

Carter brought to his task admirable qualities of personal integrity, a penetrating intelligence and a highly-trained mind. His Achilles heel, frankly admitted in his memoirs, was his determination to maintain his distance from the established Washington elite, both political and in the press. In a city where networking is of the essence, he believed that doing a good job would in itself guarantee the support of those who mattered (Carter, 1982). It did not. Failure to secure congressional support for key elements in his domestic programme, though lying beyond the scope of this volume, helps explain some of the frustrations he encountered in foreign policy. Moreover, he was heir to the severe economic problems which flowed from the 1973 oil crisis. His attempts to meet the energy crisis ran up against the Americans' long-standing love affair with the internal combustion engine, earning him public disfavour rather than the plaudits which should have been his due. When an energy measure ultimately passed, it was significantly watered down in congress (Dumbrell, 1995).

He resembled Richard Nixon in at one respect at least, a determination that the final decisions on foreign policy would be his own (Carter, 1982). His choice as Secretary of State was the New York lawyer, Cyrus Vance. Although out of the political mainstream during the years of Republican hegemony, Vance came to the position with solid experience, having served in the Defense Department in the 1960s and taken part in the Paris peace negotiations. He had thought seriously about foreign affairs, being convinced that the lesson of recent years was that a successful foreign policy had to have a firm base of domestic support. Vance was to lead the Department of State in a highly professional manner (Carter, 1982; Vance, 1983). Like Nixon, Carter decided on an activist National Security Advisor who was both foreign-born, in this case in Poland, and an academic. Zbigniew Brzezinski was a student of the Soviet Union and eastern Europe who had provided Carter with position papers on foreign policy during his bid for the presidency. His immediate task was to help the newly-elected president formulate his basic foreign policy objectives (Carter, 1982; Brzezinski, 1983).

Human Rights

The pursuit and defence of human rights lay at the core of Carter's agenda. He had made this abundantly clear from the date, in December 1974, when he announced his candidacy. The depth of his conviction reflected his deeply felt religious faith, and it was central to both his domestic and foreign agendas (Brzezinski, 1983; Dumbrell, 1995). Carter believed that under his immediate predecessors the country had moved too far from the idealistic and moral basis which ought to drive her foreign policy. The overriding priority of anti-communism had led to American support for repressive regimes, irrespective of their domestic record. In addition, he sensed that the pursuit of human rights would be the 'wave of the future' and that the United States had to be associated with it. But concern for human rights abuses in countries like South Africa and in Latin America was one thing. The real test would come with the Soviet Union, where the treatment of dissidents was regarded as an internal affair, and where the raising of such issues might run against other foreign policy objectives. During the 1976 campaign, Carter made it clear that he would not shy away from this. With that in mind, while welcoming Carter into office Brezhnev pointedly referred to non-interference in each other's affairs. The Soviet leader's response to Carter's raising of human rights cases was that this was a frivolous abuse of his power. But resentment was mixed with fear. Soon after Carter's inauguration, the CIA obtained a report from a Hungarian leader that Brezhnev and his colleagues regarded the adoption of human rights as a deliberate strategy designed to overthrow them (Carter, 1982; Gromyko, 1989; Gates, 1996).

A New Agenda?

Carter enjoyed an asset denied to his immediate predecessors, the absence of war in South-east Asia, even though he could never ignore the legacies of Vietnam (Dumbrell, 1995). He could, moreover, hope to capitalise on the openings made to the Soviet Union and China under Nixon, Ford and Kissinger. Carter, Vance and Brzezinski were pretty much at one on the priorities the new administration should follow. Their thoughts were summed up in a substantial analysis submitted to Carter by the National Security Council on 30 April, which served as a guide to subsequent action. Human rights clearly were an important priority. So, too, were the allied issues of North–South inequality and global development. Collaboration across the industrialised world of the United States, western Europe and Japan was to be strengthened in an attempt to achieve a more stable system. African affairs were to focus on the pursuit of democracy in South Africa, which had just experienced serious rioting, and the transfer to majority rule in the rebellious British colony of Rhodesia. In the Middle East, the objective was to be a comprehensive settlement. In both Africa and the Middle East it was hoped that such policies would lead to the reduction of Soviet influence. Nixon's China initiative was to be followed up by the establishment of full relations by 1979. Relations with the Soviet Union were to concentrate on moving forward from arms limitation talks to arms reduction talks. The objective here was to have a new SALT treaty ratified by 1978 with a view to moving to a Strategic Arms Reduction Treaty by 1980. With hindsight, Brzezinski conceded that, while coherent, this strategy was too ambitious (Brzezinski, 1983). Like most plans, it was also liable to be deflected by events elsewhere.

Carter and the Soviets

SALT soon proved the point. Progress from 1972 had proved stubborn. There had been no real attempt to follow through on the Vladivostok summit, while the SALT agreement was due to lapse on 3 October 1977. The Vladivostok agreement had simply deferred the crucial matters of the Soviet Backfire bomber and the American development of the air-launched cruise missiles (ALCMs). One of Carter's first priorities on assuming office was to inform Brezhnev of his determination to move ahead on the issue. Initial responses were not encouraging, the Soviet leaders confusing Carter's desire for openness in formulating positions with propaganda posturing (Carter, 1982). Conscious of what was at stake, and that his domestic political position was stronger than it would become later in his presidency, Carter's instinct was to attempt a bold move, by putting to the Soviet leaders a proposal for 'deep cuts' in the missile ceilings agreed at Vladivostok, together with limits on the testing of missiles. But when Vance attempted to put these ideas forward at meetings in Moscow in late March 1977, he met with a decided rebuff (Brzezinski, 1983; Vance, 1983).

While it was clear that the new administration was not to enjoy a honeymoon period with the Soviet leadership, it was in the interest of neither party to let such the issue of arms control lie. As the debate continued, its future development was influenced by an important decision on the future of America's bomber fleet. On 30 June 1977, Carter announced the cancellation of the B-1, the bomber which had been developed as the strategic replacement for the B-52. Since large sums had already been invested and four prototypes were already built, it was a hard choice to have to make. Carter's decision was partly influenced by cost – each bomber would cost at least $100 million – and partly because a manned bomber would be highly vulnerable to Soviet air defence. A better alternative would be to equip the existing B-52 fleet with cruise missiles. The B-1 was also to be leapfrogged through the development of 'stealth' technology, which, by the 1990s, would allow a bomber to avoid detection by enemy radar (Carter, 1982). This decision was both courageous and far-sighted, but it came at a high cost. It meant that the cruise missile would inevitably assume greater importance in arms limitation talks. Domestically, it allowed Carter's critics, who could not be told of the highly secret 'stealth' development, to denounce him as soft on defence (Vance, 1983).

In late September 1977, as the SALT agreement was about to lapse, a series of meetings between Carter and Gromyko revived the negotiations. Gromyko accepted that the Vladivostok ceiling of 2,400 launchers could be reduced to 2,250, of which 820 would be land-based. At one level, the meetings marked an advance. But the Americans also hoped that the encounter would inject a new warmth into what so far had been a somewhat frosty relationship. They clearly thought that it had, both Carter and Brzezinski recording this. Gromyko, in contrast, sourly recorded his view that Carter had failed to grasp the most elementary aspects of the Soviet–American relationship (Carter, 1982; Brzezinski, 1983; Gromyko, 1989). Despite the signs of flexibility, progress on SALT proved glacially slow, even though the two sides continued to honour the provisions of the existing treaty beyond its expiry date.

The Panama Canal Treaties

Progress proved quicker on another foreign affairs priority which Carter inherited, though here, too, domestic controversy proved inescapable. This was the future status of the Panama Canal Zone, long a source of irritation between the United States and Latin American sentiment. Under the 1903 treaty between the United States and Panama, concluded in somewhat questionable circumstances, the Americans had full rights over the canal in perpetuity. The canal's strategic value to the United States was never in doubt, proving its worth in the Second World War. In January 1964, tensions over its status led to considerable disturbances and loss of life, leading President Johnson to the conclusion that a new treaty arrangement was needed. Negotiations continued under Nixon and Ford, and in 1974

Kissinger came to the basis of an agreement with the Panamanians, which allowed for a new fixed-term treaty. Domestic opinion was, however, hard to convince. In challenging Ford for the 1976 Republican nomination, Ronald Reagan made great play with the canal's importance to the country's global position. A resolution opposed to ceding American sovereignty over the Canal Zone was sponsored by 38 senators. Since ratification of a treaty could be prevented by 34 senators, the political prospects seemed at best uncertain. Nonetheless, the Carter administration saw a new treaty as fundamental to its relationship with Latin America. It also believed, contrary to much popular sentiment, that the canal's security could best be secured by a friendly Panama and Latin America. Ultimately, it saw a new agreement as a test of whether America was living in a new era or still grounded in imperialism (Carter, 1982; Brzezinski, 1983).

New treaties on the future of the Canal Zone were agreed on 10 August 1977, and signed by Carter and General Omar Torrijos of Panama on 7 September. They provided for the return of most of the Canal Zone to Panama and joint operation of the canal itself. American troops would remain until 31 December 1999, after which they would have the right to return in the event of an external threat to the canal's neutrality. Knowing that public opinion would be hard to convince, and that conservatives would castigate him for 'giving away' the canal, Carter engaged with Republicans who had been involved with the previous negotiations. Gerald Ford was particularly helpful. But Carter's memoirs tell of a long war of attrition in both the House and the Senate to secure the necessary ratification. When the Senate ratified the treaties on 18 April 1978 it was by the uncomfortably narrow margin of 68 to 32; namely, with two votes to spare. There was a political price. The support given by some senators over such a contentious issue meant that they were unlikely to indulge Carter a second time; chiefly, over SALT. Inevitably, too, political opponents would use the treaties to reinforce the perception of Carter as a 'weak' president.

Even so, Carter and Vance believed that the Panama canal treaties were fundamental to the stability of America's wider interests in Latin America, and so they were (Carter, 1982; Vance, 1983).

Towards an Arab–Israeli Settlement

Another key element in Carter's foreign policy was the search for a comprehensive peace settlement in the Middle East. Democratic analysts were critical of Kissinger's approach, believing that it had focused upon tactics rather than strategy. This was summed up by former Under-Secretary of State George Ball's view in 1976 that Kissinger had 'pursued a practice that most medical doctors would deplore; he has sown up part of the wound, leaving a raging infection inside' (Ball, 1976). The new administration's thinking was greatly influenced by a report prepared by the Washington think-tank, the Brookings Institution, in 1975, which argued that the Sinai disengagement agreement of that year had not engaged with the real issues. What the report envisaged was an Israeli return to the 1967 borders, not dissimilar to the Rogers Plan, with agreed modifications. Israeli security would be guaranteed by demilitarised zones under United Nations supervision. At its core was the need for a Palestinian state, either independent or in federation with Jordan, but on the crucial condition that the Palestinians recognised Israel. The idea of a Palestinian state was a bold one, bound to ruffle feathers in Washington's powerful and articulate pro-Israeli lobby (Fraser, 1989).

With characteristic honesty, Carter admitted that since he had brought human rights to the centre of his foreign policy, he could not 'ignore the very serious problems of the West Bank' (Carter, 1982). Once again, given the domestic implications of this, it was essential that he move sooner rather than later. Early meetings with Israeli premier Yitzhak Rabin on 7–8 March 1977 were not encouraging. Days later, at a town meeting in Clinton, Massachusetts, he expressed the view that the Palestinians should have a homeland, and then created shock waves by shaking the hand of the PLO representative to the United Nations at a reception in New York. In contrast with the chill with Jerusalem, on 4 April Carter had his first meeting with President Sadat, creating the basis of a warm relationship. Everything then changed with the Israeli election of May 1977, which, for the first time, brought to power the right-wing Likud, led by Menachem Begin. The new premier was of a different stamp to his pragmatic Labour predecessor, something the Americans were slow to grasp. At the heart of Begin's soul lay a passionate belief that the West Bank, to him Judea and Samaria, were an essential part of the Jewish inheritance. When the two leaders met for the first time on 19–20 July 1977, Begin made clear his opposition to the idea of a Palestinian homeland and made Carter promise to stop using the term (Fraser, 1989).

By the autumn of 1977, secret soundings were being made between the Egyptians and Israelis which were to wrong-foot the Americans. As the result of contacts through King Hassan of Morocco and Romania's President Ceausescu, Sadat concluded that he could move ahead through a bold move of his own. What he had in mind was going to Jerusalem and conducting direct negotiations with the Israelis, which would create the psychological breakthrough for a settlement. His announcement to his People's Assembly on 9 November that he was ready to talk to the Knesset left the Americans stunned (Vance, 1983; Brzezinski, 1983). Although one State Department official referred to Sadat and Begin as two 'unguided missiles', there was little alternative but to hope that the Egyptian leader's initiative would turn out for the best. Sadat's visit to Israel on 19–21 November 1977 provided political drama of the highest order, televised throughout the world. But his plea for an overall settlement which would include the Palestinians met with a low-key response from Begin. Subsequent talks in

Cairo and Ismailia only confirmed to the Americans just how depressingly poor the prospects were. Their problem was that Sadat's initiative was now the only option (Fraser, 1989).

By late January 1978, relations between the Egyptian and Israeli leaders were so poor that the idea of inviting them to a summit at Camp David first surfaced. On 11 March, prospects were further punctuated by a Palestinian raid on the Israeli coast, which led to 35 deaths. The immediate consequence was a full-scale Israeli invasion of southern Lebanon, which threatened to terminate the already fragile peace process. Seeing this as an overreaction, Carter threatened Israel with the ending of military aid (Fraser, 1989). A visit to Washington by Begin on 21–23 March only resulted in a sulphurous encounter between the two leaders. By then, Carter was experiencing the disfavour of the pro-Israeli lobby, with Democratic fund-raising events in New York and Los Angeles in May being postponed through cancellations (Carter, 1982).

Camp David

On 31 July 1978, Carter decided that the only way to move forward was to invite the Egyptian and Israeli leaders to a conference at Camp David in Maryland. The summit, held from 5 to 17 September, proved to be one of the most historic events in the Arab–Israeli conflict. There was no magic formula for success. No rapport had been established between Begin and Sadat. The Israeli position was relatively straightforward. Their aim was a bilateral peace treaty with Egypt which would remove at a stroke their most powerful enemy, rendering powerless any Arab coalition against them. They wanted to do this without surrendering their positions on the West Bank and Gaza. They had little to lose. Sadat, by contrast, had invested too much to see the summit fail. Of course, he needed the return of the Sinai desert, captured by Israel in 1967. But his position in the Arab world demanded that he also achieve something substantial for the Palestinians. Carter, too, needed a success, given the measure of presidential prestige which was being invested (Quandt, 1986).

What emerged after hard bargaining were two 'Frameworks', which, the Americans hoped, would set the Middle East on a new direction. The first outlined a peace treaty under which Israel would return the Sinai desert to Egypt in return for normal diplomatic relations between the two countries. The second set out a timetable for the Israeli-occupied territories:

> for transitional arrangements for the West Bank and Gaza for a period not exceeding five years. In order to provide full autonomy to the inhabitants, under these arrangements the Israeli military government and its administration will be withdrawn as soon as a self-governing authority has been elected by the inhabitants of these areas to replace the existing military government.

Both the Americans and Egyptians believed that at last something significant had been achieved for the Palestinians, but it soon became clear that Begin had his own interpretation of what 'autonomy' implied, which fell short of autonomy for the territories. To the dismay of the other two signatories, Begin stuck rigidly to his view that all he would sanction was autonomy for the 'inhabitants' of the occupied territories. The Palestinians agreed, seeing the Camp David Framework as meaning nothing less than de facto Israeli annexation. Other Arabs rallied in rejection of the Camp David accords (Quandt, 1986; Fraser, 1989).

With the euphoria of Camp David giving way to the hard realities of Middle Eastern politics, Carter was left with no alternative but to invest yet more of his political capital. By November 1978, with the promised Egyptian–Israeli peace treaty still not in sight, he was forced to conclude that, in reality, the Israeli government had not moved from their objective of retaining a free hand in the West Bank and Gaza (Fraser, 1989). By then, the Americans were entering troubled waters on a separate Middle Eastern front, one which would come to torment Carter until the end of his presidency. A successful outcome to the Camp David process was, therefore, all the more imperative. Some of his advisers had come to the depressing conclusion that Israeli strategy was to try to prevent his re-election. Carter himself believed that Begin would do anything to derail the autonomy provisions for the West Bank. It was in an attempt to force the issue that Carter flew to the Middle East in March 1979. To the Americans' intense relief, the peace treaty between Egypt and Israel was signed in Washington on 26 March 1979. The former saw the full restoration of the territory she had lost in 1967, while Israel had at last signed a peace agreement with a major Arab state. In fact, Israel was the clear winner, removing from the military chessboard her most tenacious enemy, while continuing to avoid any real commitments over the West Bank and Gaza. The whole business had absorbed much of the attention of the Carter administration. The peace treaty stood the test of time, surviving even the assassination of Carter's partner, Anwar al-Sadat, by disaffected Islamic militants on 6 October 1981. But any goodwill generated had long been dissipated, and for Egyptians and Israelis it was to be a 'cold peace', far removed from the high hopes Carter and Sadat had once entertained (Fraser, 1989).

Normalisation with China

Carter's tenacious pursuit of a Middle East peace settlement could not be allowed to deflect his administration from its other key foreign policy goals. Normalisation of relations with China was seen as the linchpin of stability in East and South-east Asia, as well as strengthening America's hand in her relations with the Soviet Union. As a boy, the president had been gripped by accounts of the activities of Baptist missionaries in the country, and, then, as a young naval officer in 1949, he had seen something of the dying embers of the civil war as the communist forces prepared to take the port of Tsingtao (Carter, 1982; Brzezinski, 1983). Relations between the two countries had not moved much, if at all, since Nixon's visit in 1972. In 1976, the two men who had inspired the communist movement almost from its inception, Mao and Chou, died, and it seemed obvious that it would take some time for their successors, Deng Xiaoping and Hua Guofeng, to stamp their authority on party and government. As ever, Taiwan was going to prove the potential sticking point in any initiative. Right-wing supporters of Taiwan, wrong-footed in 1972, had regrouped to some effect, and were likely to mobilise support amongst congressmen already hostile to Carter's moves over Panama and SALT. The nature and timing of any initiative would have to take this domestic constituency into account (Carter, 1982; Brzezinski, 1983).

America's future relations with Taiwan were at the centre of recommendations which the National Security Council prepared for Carter in the spring of 1977. Essentially, they reaffirmed Nixon's strategy of pursuing normalisation of relations with Beijing on the basis of a 'one China' policy, rejecting the notion of Taiwanese independence. Provided that he could continue to sell defensive weapons to Taiwan and maintain unofficial relations with her, Carter was ultimately prepared to concede the basic Chinese principles that the defence treaty between Washington and Taipei be ended, that American forces be withdrawn from the island, and that diplomatic relations be established with Beijing. Vance struck a rather different note, warning that the the United States should not 'feel so compelled to establish diplomatic relations with Peking that we jeopardise the wellbeing and security of the people of Taiwan', as well as opposing the ending of the defence agreement (Carter, 1982; Vance, 1983). With the Panama agreements then about to go to the Senate, Vance was also wary of moving too fast. In

August 1977, Vance took to Beijing an offer to normalise relations on the basis that the future of Taiwan would be decided by the Chinese themselves, but that the United States would retain personnel on the island on an unofficial basis. The new Chinese leaders were unimpressed (Vance, 1983).

In the summer of 1978, Carter divided his forces, asking Vance to go to Moscow for the SALT negotiations, while sending Brzezinski to Beijing in pursuit of normalisation. When Brzezinski arrived in China on 20 May 1978, he brought with him the crucial formula that 'the United States has made up its mind'; in short, that the United States was prepared to abrogate the security treaty with Taiwan, terminate relations, and withdraw her military presence from the island. The American conditions were that any resolution of the Taiwan issue must be peaceful and that they could continue to provide the Taiwanese with military supplies for defensive purposes. He was also instructed to convey to the Chinese the common interests of their two countries when faced with the global nature of Soviet power. The visit appeared to convince Deng and Hua of Carter's determination to resolve the remaining differences (Brzezinski, 1983). On 15 December 1978, Carter was able to announce the agreement on normalisation of relations, on the basis of the principles Brzezinski had taken to Beijing the previous May. The new relationship was to come into effect on 1 January 1979, followed by a visit to Washington by Deng later in the month. Thirty years after Mao's triumph, followed by the near-hysteria over the 'fall' of China and the bitterness of the Korean War, Sino-American relations had been brought into a new equilibrium.

SALT II

The moves towards normalisation of relations with China ran somewhat in tandem with a renewal of the SALT negotiations with the Soviet Union. But even as he addressed this key nuclear issue, Carter ran into trouble on another, the proposal to deploy the neutron bomb in western Europe. This weapon, more properly the enhanced radiation weapon, was designed to counter a Soviet invasion through the use of intense radiation. It was an idea which aroused intense opposition in western Europe, and with his key allies Britain and Germany deeply unhappy, Carter felt he had no option but to drop it. Coming as it did in the wake of the B-1 cancellation, this did not strengthen his hand either domestically or in his negotiations with Moscow. Nor was progress on SALT advanced by the growing resentment in Washington over Soviet activism in different parts of the world, notably in Africa. For their part, the Soviet leadership was deeply suspicious of Carter's overtures to Beijing, and, of course, had never liked his stance on human rights. Interestingly, Vance had come round to the view that pressure on the issue was actually becoming counterproductive (Carter, 1982; Vance, 1983).

It comes, then, as no surprise that when Vance and Gromyko resumed the SALT talks in April 1978, and then dragged them through the autumn and winter, progress proved incremental. Critical Soviet concessions were forthcoming, however. In April they accepted the American limits of 2,250 launchers and 1,200 MIRVed launchers, while in July they conceded that each country could proceed with one new type of missile, giving the green light to the American MX. As it happened, the MX proved to be a weapon of mixed fortunes, but at the time its development was felt necessary to the land-based arsenal (Brzezinski, 1983). Nonetheless, highly technical aspects of missile delivery had to be explored and agreed before each side felt ready to move to a final text.

The climax of this process was a Carter–Brezhnev summit held in Vienna from 15 to 18 June 1979. As superpower summits went, it proved a somewhat sober affair, not least because of the transparent decline in the Soviet leader's health. Its real purpose was to sign the SALT II agreement. The new treaty was to run until December 1985, with various limitations to take effect from 1 January 1981. Overall strategic missile delivery systems would be lowered to 2,250, with a sub-limit of 1,320 on the total number of MIRVed ICBMs, SLBMs and aircraft-carried cruise missiles, with a maximum of 1,200 MIRVed ICBMs and SLBMs, a provision which left the Americans at a potential advantage since they alone had air-launched cruise missiles. The treaty did not inhibit the Americans from developing the MX and cruise missiles, while Brezhnev agreed to limit Backfire bomber production to 30 a year. In addition, each side was limited to 820 land-based ICBMs (Carter, 1982; Vance, 1983; Brzezinski, 1983).

The intention was to build upon the treaty to achieve deeper cuts in a SALT III agreement. But the process proved stillborn. Although Carter tried to convince Congress that the treaty had reduced the existing imbalance in favour of the Soviet Union while allowing the United States the possibility of developing new weapons, the prospects for ratification were never good. The bruising legacy of the Panama Canal treaty ratification battle was now felt. Senators were also increasingly restive over the activities of Soviet-backed Cuban forces in Africa. Essential momentum was lost when Senator Frank Church of Idaho, Chairman of the Senate Foreign Relations Committee, revealed the presence of a Soviet army brigade in Cuba, releasing a political storm which raged throughout September 1979. Subsequent investigation revealed that this was actually part of a force which had been in the country, seemingly unnoticed, for years. Such was the degree of concern over the perception of Soviet aggression that on 1 October Carter made a television address in which he assured his listeners that the brigade was no threat to the United States, but argued that the real danger was that of nuclear war and urged that SALT II be ratified. But the episode cost Carter vital time when he could least afford it. Worse still, events were unfolding elsewhere in the world which were to ensure that SALT II was dead in the water (Carter, 1982; Brzezinski, 1983).

Revolution in Iran

So far, it can be said that his Carter and his team had directed foreign policy with steadiness of purpose and could point with conviction to solid achievements on a number of fronts. But in November 1978 worrying signs appeared that America's principal ally in the Middle East, the Shah of Iran, might be in serious trouble. Reza Shah Pahlavi's fate had been bound in with the United States ever since 1953 when the CIA had, in effect, engineered his return to power. It was only really in the early 1970s that the interests of the two countries fully converged. This was partly prompted by the British government's decision to withdraw from its military presence east of Suez, leaving a security gap in the Persian Gulf at precisely the time when its oil was making the region of unique strategic importance. By a westward extension of the Nixon Doctrine, Iran could be seen as filling the gap. In May 1972, Nixon and Kissinger concluded an agreement with the Shah that in return for protecting western interests Iran would have access to some of America's advanced military equipment, though not to nuclear weapons. Fortified by the dramatic escalation of oil revenues after 1973, the Shah could fully indulge his ambition, ordering $9 billion dollars' worth of American arms by 1976. Not everyone in the Defense Department was convinced of the wisdom of this, nor of the investment of so much of the west's security on a single individual. Although aware of serious human rights abuses, the Carter administration felt it had no alternative but to follow existing policy towards Iran. In a visit to Tehran at the end of 1977, Carter, in words which would later haunt him, referred to Iran as 'an island of stability in a turbulent corner of the world'. Within days, the Iranian revolution had begun (Sick, 1985).

Like every other revolution, Iran's was a complex mix of long- and short-term factors. What the Shah's drive to make his country into the regional superpower amounted to was an attempt to bolt an ultra-sophisticated military structure on to a political and economic structure which could not sustain it. With inflation running at some 30 per cent, widespread rumours of corruption, and an ever-increasing gap between the mass of the population and the minority who were the beneficiaries of the oil revenues and arms contracts, Iran showed all the classic signs of a pre-revolutionary society. All of this was grist to the mill of the Shah's long-standing opponents, the country's Shi'a clergy, who had smarted under his westernising policies and growing American influence. Their inspiration was Ayatollah Khomeini, an exile for 14 years whose taped messages helped nurture the spirit of resistance, not least amongst junior officers and conscript soldiers in the armed forces (Saikal, 1980). A week after Carter's visit, on 9 January 1978, demonstrations broke out in the holy city of Qom after the publication of a government article scorning Khomeini. This was the catalyst for a mounting wave of discontent which climaxed in a massacre of demonstrators in Tehran's Jaleh Square in September, the event which probably made revolution irreversible. Faced with a fast-deteriorating situation in the streets, the Shah, already ill with cancer, faltered.

From Carter's perspective the timing of these events could not have been worse, coming as they did at precisely the point when he was trying to push ahead with three key foreign policy objectives; namely, normalisation with China, SALT II and the Camp David accords. His administration was ill-placed to respond to the crisis. American links were almost exclusively with the elite surrounding the Shah, cutting them off from those who were shaking the regime to its foundations. If direct intervention in Iran was not an option, and it never was, how was Washington to react? Policy formation was made no easier by a clear difference which emerged between the State Department and the

National Security Council on how to advise the Shah. State Department officials were increasingly of the view that Shah's days as an autocratic ruler were numbered, that reliance on the military was unrealistic, and that American advice should be to reach out to the secular opposition. The perspective from the National Security Council was that the existing opposition was too weak to confront the Islamic zealots driving the revolution, and that the only viable policy was to strengthen the Shah's resolve (Brzezinski, 1983; Vance, 1983; Sick, 1985). In late October, Ambassador William Sullivan, already doubtful about the regime's prospects, informed Washington that the Shah might either abdicate or install a military government. Sullivan, it seems, had already advised the Shah against this. On 2 November, the NSC prepared a response, endorsed by Carter, that the Shah be informed that the United States supported him 'without reservation', that he needed to show 'decisive action and leadership', and that he would be supported whether he went for a coalition or a military government. On 6 November, the Shah announced the formation of a military government, but it was a gesture of despair rather than of strength. Three days later, in a despatch 'Thinking the Unthinkable', Sullivan speculated that in the absence of the Shah, Kohmeini and the army might preside over a pro-western Islamic republic, which would provide the stability America needed (Sullivan, 1981).

The reality was that the situation could not be influenced from Washington. On 26 December, the Shah discussed with Sullivan the possibility of a regency, asking if the United States was advising him to use an 'iron fist'. The latter prospect appalled Vance and the State Department, while Brzezinski and others argued for stronger support for the Shah. The result was a four-part message to Sullivan that the Shah be advised to end the 'continued uncertainty', that a moderate civilian government was the preferred option, that if this was not a possibility then he should appoint a 'firm military government which would end disorder, violence and bloodshed', and if all else failed appoint a regency council. The Shah's response was that a military government could not end the bloodshed and that the logic of a regency council was that he leave the country (Bzrezinski, 1983; Vance, 1983; Sick, 1985). On the 29th, he appointed Shahpour Bakhtiar, experienced in opposition but without obvious popular support, as head of a civilian government. Since Bakhtiar was clear that his chances of success rested on the Shah leaving, and Khomeini confirming from his Paris exile that he could not support anyone loyal to the Shah, Washington's options were foreclosing fast. Vance, Sullivan and the State Department now advocated opening a direct dialogue with Khomeini, but Carter believed this would split the military and undermine Bakhtiar's prospects. The most he would authorise was contact through a French intermediary (Carter, 1982; Vance, 1983). On 16 January 1979, the Shah left Tehran for exile. Had he gone direct to the United States, where arrangements were in place to receive him, subsequent events might have taken a different turn, but he preferred Egypt. On 1 February, Khomeini returned to a tumultuous welcome. Ignoring Bakhtiar, he appointed Mehdi Bazargan as acting premier. As Bakhtiar went into hiding and army units disintegrated or proclaimed their loyalty to the new regime, the collapse of America's principal ally in the Middle East could not have been more complete. Despite arguments, powerfully put by Bzrezinski, that America should support a military government, Carter had been clear throughout that he could not take decisions on the Shah's behalf (Sick, 1985). It was only to be expected that there would be tension between those who believed Washington should stick with its ally and those for whom prudence dictated there should be open lines to whatever new regime emerged. Not all options were foreclosed by February 1979. (Carter, 1982). If the fall of the Shah was a significant setback, it was not yet a disaster. That was to come later.

The Hostage Crisis

But even in exile the Shah remained the ghost at the feast, moving from Egypt to Morocco, then to the Bahamas, and finally Mexico. He still had powerful friends who were advocating that he be admitted to the United States, but Carter and Vance were now opposed, believing that this would be seen in Iran as support for a restoration and might lead to Americans being taken hostage. On 28 September, however, the administration was informed that the Shah had been diagnosed with a serious illness, soon confirmed as malignant lymphoma, and urgently needed medical treatment in the United States. Caught between the moral imperative to respond and the likely reaction in Tehran, Carter sought to reassure Bazargan's government that the Shah's admission into the United States would be on a temporary basis and that he would undertake no political activity. In the belief that the response in Tehran was containable, the Shah was admitted on 22 October. On 30 October, the Iranian government demanded the Shah's extradition, while Khomeini appealed to students to put pressure on the Americans to do so. Street protests culminated on 4 November when the embassy compound in Tehran was overrun. Sixty-three Americans were held at the embassy, while chargé d'affaires Bruce Laingen and two others were seized at the Foreign Ministry. They had become, in effect, hostages for the Shah's repatriation. Their fate would dominate the rest of the Carter presidency (Carter, 1982; Vance, 1983).

The Soviet Invasion of Afghanistan

Only six weeks later, another international crisis hit the administration, this time in Afghanistan, an independent country but one long judged to be within Moscow's sphere of influence. From April 1978, a series of bloody coups erupted in Kabul, culminating in September the following year when the pro-Soviet President Nur Mohammed Taraki was killed and replaced by Hafizullah Amin. But Amin failed to get on top of a loose coalition of anti-Soviet and Islamic rebels. On 25 December 1979, the Soviet army invaded the country, in the course of which Amin, too, was killed. The administration believed that Brezhnev and his advisers had been prompted by a desire to prevent the spread of Islamic fervour into their own Muslim provinces. Carter feared that if the Soviets could secure a hold in the country, it would place their forces dangerously close to key areas of the Middle East, already destabilised as a result of the events in Iran (Vance, 1983). With the benefit of hindsight, of course, what the Soviet leadership had done was cut a rod for their own backs. Totally misjudging the terrain and the strength of Islamic assistance, they were embarking on a campaign which would ultimately demoralise their armed forces and contribute to the collapse of the communist system. But at the time, Washington's perspective was that this was a 'brutal' extension of Soviet power, which needed to be countered. Overt sanctions were the imposition of an embargo on grain sales to the Soviet Union and withdrawal from the 1980 Moscow Olympic Games, the latter particularly bruising since the Soviets had spent a fortune preparing for them. Carter did not want to link the invasion to the prospects for SALT II, but realistically he knew that the last prospects for ratification had gone. His fears over Soviet intentions in the Middle East could not have been more powerfully expressed than in his State of the Union message, delivered on 23 January 1980, when he announced that: 'An attempt by any outside force to gain control of the Persian Gulf region will be regarded as an assault on the vital interests of the United States of America, and such an assault will be repelled by any means necessary including military force' (Carter, 1982). The so-called Carter Doctrine, with its clear warning to the Soviet leadership, has been seen, correctly, as marking an end to deténte (Dumbrell, 1995). Ultimately more significant than his public castigation was Carter's recourse to covert action in behalf of the Afghan resistance. The CIA was not unprepared, having been predicting some kind of Soviet intervention since the previous spring. Carter sanctioned the supply of Soviet-made weapons to the Mujahedin, as the Afghan fighters became known (Andrew, 1996; Gates, 1996). Such covert aid could do nothing for his electoral stock at a time when he was being vigorously challenged for the Democratic nomination by Senator Edward Kennedy, and then for the presidency by Ronald Reagan.

'Desert One'

This was the depressing situation which presented Carter as he entered election year. Everything now hinged on a resolution of the hostage situation. Early attempts at mediation through the good offices of the Vatican and the PLO were unpromising, though the latter seem to have secured the release of 13 black and female hostages. With Carter freezing the substantial Iranian assets held in the United States or in overseas American banks, any immediate resolution of the crisis seemed remote. By the beginning of April 1980, all American negotiating options appeared to have run out, leading inevitably to the triggering of a military rescue mission which had been maturing since the start of the crisis. This called for an operation of considerable audacity and daunting complexity. It involved eight RH-53D helicopters and eight C-130 transports flying in darkness under Iranian radar cover to a secret airstrip, 'Desert One'. The following night, special forces from a second base, 'Desert Two', would drive into Tehran for a rescue mission, transfer the hostages to waiting helicopters, and fly them out of the country in the transport aircraft. The operation, launched on 24 April, ended in disaster almost before it had begun. With three of his helicopters out of action through technical malfunctions, the commander at 'Desert One' ordered the mission terminated. As they withdrew, one the helicopters collided with a C-130, with the death of eight crew members. All the remaining helicopters had to be abandoned. A further casualty of the operation was Cyrus Vance, who had opposed it and submitted his resignation in advance (Vance, 1983; Sick, 1985).

With the photographs of the smouldering remains of 'Desert One' circulated by the triumphant Iranians, the blow to American prestige could not have been more stunning, not least because of the Americans' self-image as the world's most technically advanced society. Moreover, Carter no longer had the military option, and the prospects for diplomacy seemed dim until the Shah's death from cancer in Cairo on 27 July removed the ostensible cause of the crisis. It was not until early September that German intermediaries passed on the information that Iran would release the hostages provided that Iranian assets were unfrozen, that there would be no further American military or political intervention in the country, and that the assets of the former imperial family be returned. Further pressure on Iran came from an unexpected source when on 22 September President Saddam Hussein of Iraq invaded the oil province of Khuzestan. The Iran–Iraq conflict was to develop into a long and bitter war of attrition, and the Iranians were soon pointing out that their assets in the United States included military equipment ordered by the Shah.

All of these moves were coming too late for Carter as he battled to retain his presidency against the combative challenge of Reagan, who understandably focused on the perceived shortcomings of his foreign and domestic policies. On 4 November, Reagan won an emphatic victory, recording 43,904,153 votes to Carter's 35,483,883. A final agreement was brokered, not without great difficulty, by the Algerian government. Concluded on 19 January, $7.933 billion were transferred from the United States into Iranian accounts. The following day, two hours after Carter had left office, the hostages left Tehran (Carter, 1982; Sick, 1985).

Carter had embarked on a fresh foreign policy agenda, which he pursued with vigour and imagination. Unlike his predecessors, he was willing and able to grasp the nettle of the Panama Canal, despite the domestic froth this was likely to stir. In his pursuit of normalisation of relations with China and of SALT II, he was prepared to build upon the foundations prepared by Nixon, Ford and Kissinger. His human rights initiatives attempted to move foreign policy on to a more imaginative agenda. It was not welcome in Moscow. His search for an overall peace settlement in the Middle East provided what was perhaps the highlight of his presidency, the Camp David summit. While the subsequent Egyptian–Israeli peace treaty was a milestone for two countries which had fought four wars, a settlement of the Palestinian issue remained beyond his reach. The Soviet invasion of Afghanistan was a harsh reminder of what the British had once called the 'Great Game' in central Asia. Iran he inherited, but the situation there proved to be beyond American control. It ought to have been a salutary lesson to Americans that Islam long predated communism as an ideal which was capable of inspiring great emotions. An activist president, Carter carried this into his 'retirement', pursuing his ideals for world peace through the work of the Carter Center in Atlanta. Few former chief executives have earned as much respect.

9

REAGAN: THE COLD WAR REVIVED

As for the enemies of freedom, those who are potential adversaries, they will be reminded that peace is the highest aspiration of the American people. We will negotiate for it, sacrifice for it; we will not surrender for it – now or ever.

Ronald Reagan, Inaugural, 20 January 1981

Like his predecessor, Ronald Reagan came to the presidency as an outsider. He, too, had made his political reputation as a state governor rather than as a congressman or senator. There the comparison with Carter ended. Whereas Carter's naval training had taught him the value of the mastery of detail, Reagan's mind focussed on what he believed to be certain core issues which he saw as vital to the country's future. These ideas he could convey to the broad American public with all the force and effectiveness of an experienced actor. There is no doubt that his skills as a communicator helped him on his way to the presidency. But those who dismissed him as a politically naive movie actor seriously misunderstood a serious and adept politician who, for eight years, had successfully governed the state of California, one of the richest and most dynamic entities on earth. As someone from small-town Illinois who, through his own efforts, had made a reputation in Hollywood, Reagan could express and embody the American dream that anything could be attained through a free society, 'the freedom', he recorded, 'to reach out and make our dreams come true'. This conviction made him a strong anti-communist, convinced that a free society would ultimately defeat one which was not. His sense of mission was probably reinforced when, only weeks into his presidency, he was lucky to survive a serious wound in an assassination attempt (Reagan, 1990; Shultz, 1993).

The Reagan Agenda

What Reagan challenged in the 1980 presidential campaign was not simply the record of the Carter administration, but also by implication the legacies of his two Republican predecessors, indeed, the whole concept of détente over which they had presided. Détente he castigated as a one-way street in favour of the Soviet Union, allowing them to pursue policies of expansion and subversion. The Soviet Union, he believed, had been engaged for over sixty years, except for the 'brief time-out' of the Second World War, in a campaign to destroy democracy and impose communism (Reagan, 1990). Central to his message was the current weakness, or perception of weakness, of America in relation to the Soviets. In a speech in 1984 he castigated the 1970s as 'a decade of neglect that took a severe toll on our defense capabilities'. During this time, he argued, the Soviet Union had been engaging 'in the most massive military build-up in history' (*Realism*, 6 April 1984). As a result, the United States had come to be perceived as a weak and unreliable ally. The pudding was notably over-egged, to the extent that many of the new weapons of the 1980s and 1990s owed their development to the 1970s, notably cruise missiles, stealth aircraft and new submarines and aircraft carriers, but the fact remained that a time when the United States had doubled its missile potential, the Soviet Union was believed to have pushed ahead with a twentyfold increase (Gates, 1996). Reagan and his advisers believed that it was this accession of military strength, as well as the debilitating backwash from Vietnam, which had encouraged the Soviet leadership into pursuing a more aggressive foreign policy in areas like

Afghanistan, Ethiopia and Angola. 'Perhaps the most degrading symbol of this dismal situation', Reagan noted in 1983, 'was the spectacle of Iranian terrorists seizing American hostages and humiliating them and our country for more than a year.' Opposition to 'terrorism' was also to be a theme of the Reagan administration's foreign policy, and was in time to contribute to its most embarrassing lapse. Along with this came an end to the Carter policy of raising human rights matters with countries, like Argentina, deemed friendly to the United States (Haig, 1984).

Reagan's team reflected these priorities, with a distinctly military tinge. Vice-President George Bush had been a combat flyer in the Second World War. Secretary of State Alexander Haig was a career soldier who had been NATO Supreme Commander. He had worked closely with Nixon and Kissinger, but his tenure of the position proved to be short-lived, Reagan resenting his desire to set the foreign policy agenda (Reagan, 1990). Caspar Weinberger, another Second World War officer, and admirer of Churchill's stance against appeasement, became Defense Secretary. William Casey, a veteran of the wartime OSS, went to the CIA with the intention of using it more effectively against the Soviet Union (Gates, 1996). Weinberger's priority, and Reagan's, was a substantial five-year rearmament programme designed to improve the morale of the armed forces and restore the country's offensive capacity as the means by which the Soviet Union could be deterred. Since key elements in the strategic arsenal, like the B-52 bomber, were still based on 1950s technology, Weinberger pressed ahead with the development of the B-1 and Stealth bombers, the MX strategic missile, and a new submarine-launched missile. In an indication of how the country saw its global role, the navy establishment was increased from 455 ships with 12 aircraft carrier-task groups to 600 ships with 15 carrier-task groups. Four Second World War battleships were also recommissioned and converted to platforms for cruise missiles, seemingly a curious piece of nostalgia but one which was to prove useful in the Gulf War.

Overall, defence spending increased by 40 per cent in the Reagan administration, with obvious budgetary implications. By the time Reagan left office, he had built up a debt of $3 trillion. His defenders pointed to the continuing growth in welfare entitlements and the need to cut taxes, but the financial impact of the military programme can hardly be ignored (Spanier, 1985, Weinberger, 1990, Schmertz, Datlof & Ugrinsky, 1997). Rearmament spoke volumes for the administration's world-view. So, too, did Haig's analysis of the American–Soviet relationship. Essentially a restatement of containment, it was that in areas, like parts of Africa or central America, where American policy was weak, the Soviets would try to exploit the situation. The American response, he believed, should be a 'credible show of will and strength' (Haig, 1984). Reinforcing Reagan's analysis was the familiar, if by now somewhat threadbare, analogy of the 1930s. 'They're the same kind of talk', he claimed in a televised address in March 1983, 'that led the democracies to neglect their defenses in the 1930s and invited the tragedy of World War II. We must not let that grim chapter of history repeat itself through apathy or neglect' (Haig, 1984; Melanson, 1996).

The State of the Soviet System

The reality, as Reagan quickly became aware from his NSC briefings, was that the Soviet Union and its alliance system were in much worse shape than the United States (Reagan, 1990). Part of the reason for this was the crippling price of their very military build-up. This was compounded by the costs, human as well as fiscal, of the war in Afghanistan, which proved to be a blunder of historic proportions; not for nothing was it referred to as 'Russia's Vietnam'. The anti-Soviet guerrillas, the Mujahedin, proved to be a tenacious enemy, the more so once sophisticated western weapons began to reach them. Perhaps nothing pointed up the contrast between the United States and the Soviet Union so much as their respective leaders. Although almost 70 at the time of his inauguration, Reagan managed to project an image of vigour which belied his years, even after the assassination attempt. By contrast, the 75-year-old Leonid Brezhnev, by then only with difficulty kept alive, presided over a ageing, incompetent and corrupt Soviet regime. When he died in November 1882, he was succeeded by Yuri Andropov, who was almost an exact contemporary of Reagan's. Andropov, a long-time head of the KGB, realised the need to reinvigorate Soviet society, but his health steadily gave way. His period in office saw a low point in relations with the United States. He died in February 1984, only to be followed by the even older Konstanin Chernenko. Chernenko, who managed to last 13 months, was in no condition to achieve anything (Pearson, 2002). Under their stewardship the Soviet Union's deep-seated problems remained largely unaddressed.

Their eastern European allies were faring no better. If living standards in parts of eastern Europe were better than those in the Soviet Union, this was only because their governments had sought to stave off internal discontent through loans from the West, which they were unable to repay. The most intractable situation was that of Poland, the country considered to be the key to Soviet security. Just as Poland's fiscal problems were about to touch crisis point, her sense of national pride, and independence, were heightened by the election in October 1978 of Karol Wojtyla as Pope John Paul II. The emotional reception when he visited the country in June 1979 laid bare the claims of the Communist Party to national leadership (Crampton, 1994). In 1980, attempts by the government to address their financial problems through price rises were behind the rise of the free trade union Solidarity, led by the Gdansk shipyard worker Lech Walesa. In 1981, the new government of General Wojciech Jaruzelski moved against Solidarity through the use of martial law, but in doing so simply confirmed the repressive nature of communist rule in eastern Europe (Pearson, 1998). Reagan was convinced that these pressures were generating a profound crisis in the Soviet system. 'It may not be easy to see', he advised the British Houses of Parliament on 8 June 1982,

> but I believe we live now at a turning point. In an ironic sense Karl Marx was right. We are witnessing today a great revolutionary crisis – a crisis where the demands of the economic order are conflicting directly with those of the political order. But the crisis is happening not in the free, non-Marxist West but in the home of Marxism–Leninism, the Soviet Union. It is the Soviet Union that runs against the tide of history by denying human freedom and human dignity to its citizens. It is also in deep economic difficulty. (*Realism*, 8 June 1982)

This conviction that the enemy could be beaten, delivered in the home of his closest ally, the equally devoted free-marketeer Margaret Thatcher, underpinned much of what Reagan sought to achieve in his foreign policy.

The Israeli Invasion of Lebanon

In the Middle East it seemed that the Reagan administration had a different agenda to its predecessor. While the Camp David process was not abandoned, it was inevitable that some of the impetus was lost with the defeat of Carter. During the 1980 campaign, Reagan had stressed his commitment to Israel and was rewarded with 39 per cent of the Jewish vote, a record for a Republican candidate. Israel's strategic position in the eastern Mediterranean was attractive to the administration, since this was an area where NATO was in disarray because of the hostility of Greece and Turkey over Cyprus. What the administration hoped to foster in the region was a strategic consensus, which might include Israel,

Egypt, Saudi Arabia, Oman, Somalia and Kenya, but a tour by Haig in April 1981 was not encouraging. What did attract the Americans was a strategic arrangement with Israel. On 30 November 1981, this was confirmed at a ceremony in Washington. It proved short-lived. Weinberger had opposed it from the start, and when on 14 December the Knesset voted for the de facto annexation of the Golan Heights, the agreement on cooperation with Israel was suspended. Tensions also emerged in 1981 over the Defense Department's plan to provide five airborne warning and control systems (AWACs) to Saudi Arabia. Seeing this as a threat to Israeli security, AIPAC directed a major campaign in the Senate to thwart the deal. It was only through Reagan's personal intervention that the sale was approved by 52 votes to 48, after an eight-month campaign (Fraser, 1989).

These events proved to be something of a testing ground for the events which unfolded in the following spring. Part of the background was the tense situation along Israel's border with Lebanon which the previous year had been attacked by PLO rockets. In July 1981, the American diplomat Philip Habib brokered a ceasefire, which was observed, even though tensions remained. Pressure grew in Israel to address the problem of the PLO armed presence in Lebanon. There was also the fact that on 25 April 1982 Israel finally withdrew from the Sinai, completing a key phase of the Camp David process. This would inevitably be followed by calls for progress on the West Bank and Gaza. Rumours surfaced of the possibility of an Israeli move into Lebanon, which would have as its purposes the breaking of PLO power and the establishment in Beirut of a government which would sign a peace treaty. The Reagan administration signalled its opposition to such a move, but not, it seems, strongly enough to deflect the Israelis (Haig, 1984). What neither Washington nor Jerusalem could have foreseen was the attempted assassination of the Israeli ambassador to London on 3 June 1982. Although both British and

American intelligence reported that this was the work of Palestinians opposed to PLO Chairman Yasser Arafat, on 6 June Israeli armed forces began an invasion of Lebanon. 'Operation Peace for Galilee' proclaimed as its purpose the creation of a 40-kilometre security zone in southern Lebanon. The initial American response did not seem hostile to what Israel was doing. Reagan said nothing, as other western leaders condemned the invasion. At the United Nations, the United States vetoed a Security Council resolution which condemned Israel's non-compliance with an earlier resolution demanding withdrawal. But the Israeli army did not stop at the 40-kilometre limit; by 10 June its spearheads were on the outskirts of Beirut, thousands had been killed or wounded or were refugees, and air battles had developed with Syria, which had a treaty of friendship with the Soviet Union. The prospect opened up of street fighting in Beirut between the Israeli army and the much smaller, but well entrenched, PLO fighters. This was an international crisis of the first magnitude, which would take America's diplomatic skills to help resolve.

The administration was divided in its response, though the tone was increasingly hostile to the Israeli advance. While Habib went to the Middle East to negotiate, Bush and Weinberger were reportedly in favour of taking a tough line with Israel, and Haig argued that the scale of Israel's victory could be used to secure a Syrian and PLO evacuation of Lebanon (Haig, 1984). Haig, the administration's most vigorous supporter of the Israeli position, was becoming increasingly isolated, with key figures like the Republican Senator Charles Percy, Chairman of the Senate Foreign Relations Committee, publicly critical. At a 'blunt' meeting with Reagan on 21 June, Begin suggested the deployment of American troops, something which Weinberger and his Chiefs of Staff opposed. On 25 June, complaining of lack of discipline in the administration, Haig resigned (Haig, 1984). In his place, Reagan nominated George Shultz, Second World War marine, trained economist and Secretary of the

Treasury in the Nixon administration. Shultz was to emerge as one the most significant figures in the formation of post-war American foreign policy. The situation in Lebanon was set to test his mettle from the start.

The Multinational Force

Because of the need for a Senate confirmation hearing, Shultz could not be sworn in until 17 July, during which time Habib was faced with an increasingly unstable situation. The essential elements in his negotiating position were the evacuation of the PLO from Beirut supervised by a multinational force, which, at the Israelis' insistence, would include Americans. PLO suspicions of the Americans were counterbalanced by French and Italian offers to take part. With no actual agreement in sight, on 1 August the Israelis began a full bombardment of Muslim west Beirut, flying 127 air sorties. Despite Reagan publicly declaring his loss of patience with the Israelis, 12 days of sustained attacks on the city followed. On 12 August, as Habib informed Washington that Beirut was being destroyed – some 220 sorties were flown and 44,000 shells were fired that day alone – Reagan's patience finally broke. Cabling Begin that he found Israeli military actions 'incomprehensible and unacceptable', he informed the prime minister that what was happening was a 'holocaust', a term which was meant to sting, and did (Reagan, 1990; Shultz, 1993; Fraser, 1989). A divided Israeli cabinet voted for a ceasefire, while on 13 August the PLO submitted a list of their guerrillas who would be evacuated by land and sea. Arafat, whose principal concern was for the safety of the Palestinians who would be left behind in the refugee camps, was given assurances by Habib that every precaution would be taken and that the Israeli army would not enter the city (Weinberger, 1990; Shultz, 1993). On 21 August, French Foreign Legionnaires landed at Beirut, to be followed by the Italians and Americans. Under their supervision, some 14,000 PLO fighters were evacuated. As a piece of crisis management the Multinational Force was felt to have been effective, notwithstanding the delays in putting it in place.

The Reagan Plan and MNF II

Conscious that the Israeli invasion of Lebanon had imperilled the overall Arab–Israeli peace process, Shultz began work on a new initiative which would develop in tandem with the evacuation plan. Since the key elements in the plan, broadcast by Reagan on 1 September 1982, had been divulged in advance, a bleak response by the Begin government was anticipated. While assuring Israel of his personal 'iron-clad' commitment to her security, he looked forward to Palestinians running their own affairs. The United States did not support an independent Palestinian state on the West Bank and Gaza, but neither would she support further Israeli settlements or 'annexation or permanent control by Israel', thus countering something long close to the heart of the Israeli right. The key to the future, he said, was 'that self-government by the Palestinians of the West Bank and Gaza in association with Jordan offers the best chance for a durable, just and lasting peace' (*Realism*, 1 September 1982). Arguing that the plan was a serious deviation from the Camp David Framework, Begin's government angrily rejected it, as did the Knesset, but the Americans had expected that.

Any hopes that the plan might be given a fair wind in the Arab world were immediately dispelled by the murderous realities of Middle East politics. On 14 September, Lebanon's president elect, Bashir Gemayel, a Christian in whom Israel had placed her hopes for a peace treaty, was assassinated in Beirut. In response, the Israeli army occupied the west of the city, precisely the outcome Arafat had feared. Christian gunmen entered the Palestinian refugee camps of Sabra and Shatila, committing a massacre of elderly men, women and children which shocked the world. Reagan, reportedly 'aghast' at what had happened, insisted that the Israeli army evacuate Beirut. The Italians, believing that the Multinational Force had been withdrawn too hastily, now pressed for its return. It now did so, but as a hasty response to tragic events rather than with a clearly-defined mandate. Announcing this on 20 September, Reagan said the force would enable the Lebanese government to resume its sovereignty over its capital, but the effect of this was to identify the Multinational Force with the government, itself little more than the representative of one faction in a murderously divided country. Reagan later rather artlessly conceded that the situation in Beirut was more difficult and complex than had been thought (Reagan, 1990). The section assigned to the American marines in south Beirut controlled the airport, but was perilously vulnerable to attack from the radicalised Shi'ite areas of the city, where opposition to the government was at its most intense.

On 18 April 1983, a car bomb exploded at the American embassy in Beirut, killing 63 people. Among the dead were the CIA's chief Middle East analyst and key policy adviser, Robert C. Ames, as well as the station chief in Beirut and seven other operatives. Such was the depressing turn of events that on 25 April Shultz left for the Middle East in an attempt to negotiate troop withdrawals from Lebanon. The agreement he brokered between Israel and Lebanon on 17 May provided for an Israeli withdrawal in return for a security zone in southern Lebanon. But since Israel's withdrawal was dependent on a similar move by the Syrians, and Shultz had been unable to secure this, it was unclear exactly what the agreement amounted to. It left the Multinational Force's mission in further political doubt and increasingly a target for various Lebanese factions.

Disaster in Beirut

On 3 September, the Israelis pulled out to the south of the city, exposing the American marine positions to artillery fire from the Chouf mountains. As the marines were, in effect, confined to their compound and began to take casualties, their mission came increasingly into question. The climax came on 23 October, when suicide car bombs were driven into the base and the French headquarters. In one of the greatest disasters in their military history, 241 Americans were killed, as well as 58 French troops. While Reagan predictably maintained that the United States would not be driven out by terrorism, the reality was otherwise. American public opinion barely grasped why their forces were in Beirut, Weinberger and his Defense Department had never liked the assignment, and Vice-President Bush saw no point in continuing the mission. Democratic presidential hopefuls predictably joined in the chorus for withdrawal, but more ominously, so did influential Republicans. On 7 February 1984, Reagan announced that the marines would be 'redeployed' to ships offshore, introducing a new concept into the military thesaurus. The result, as Shultz conceded, was a rout. The Italians, French, and the small British contingent which had joined them, had no alternative but to follow. As if to make a point, the French remained until the end of March, leaving with their flags flying and band playing. By then, the Lebanese government had abrogated their agreement with Israel. Her credibility gone, America's reputation in the Middle East had suffered a blow from which it would take years to recover (Fraser, 1989; Weinberger, 1990; Shultz, 1993). The events of 23 October 1983 were a chilling indication of the power of the suicide bomber.

The 'Evil Empire' and the Strategic Defense Initiative

One thing was clear. The unfolding events in the Middle East, sparked by Israel's ill-starred Lebanese adventure, had taken up much of the administration's attention, perhaps too much, certainly dominating Shultz's first year as Secretary of State (Shultz, 1993). But the Middle East was not the administration's main concern, which still turned on the nature of its relationship with the Soviet Union and the communist world. Central to the administration's approach was the Soviet development of a new intermediate-range ballistic missile (IRBM), the SS-20, which it began to deploy in 1977; by 1979, it was estimated that 140 missiles with a total of 420 warheads were in place. The Soviets had, in addition, SS-4 and SS-5 missiles. The SS-20 had a number of features which promised to change the nature of the relationship between the two alliance systems. The missile itself was mobile, making it difficult to locate, and was sufficiently accurate to destroy hardened military targets. But its real significance lay in the fact that it was specifically targeted on western Europe, and, later, Japan. Its strategic purpose appeared to be to prise the countries of western Europe away from the United States (Weinberger, 1990; Shultz, 1993). In 1979, NATO chiefs agreed to counter the SS-20 with the deployment of 464 cruise missiles in Germany, Britain, Italy, Belgium and the Netherlands, and 108 Pershing II missiles in Germany. This proposal stimulated widespread anti-nuclear protests in Europe, notably in Germany and Britain, which had a potential impact on the stability of the Alliance, not least because they threatened the unity of the German Left. Always staunch in their support for NATO, the Social Democrats saw themselves challenged by the rise of the Green Party, which was opposed to nuclear weapons. NATO leaders also agreed that the United States would negotiate for a reduction of INF.

Aware of the febrile state of public opinion in western Europe, the Americans knew that they had to be seen to be engaged in serious negotiation with the Soviets. Their gambit, worked out between Weinberger and Reagan in the autumn of 1981, was what came to be known as the 'zero option' (Weinberger, 1990). 'The United States', Reagan announced at the National Press Club in Washington on 18 November 1981, 'is prepared to cancel its deployment of Pershing II and ground-launched cruise missiles if the Soviets will dismantle their SS-20, SS-4, and SS-5 missiles. This would be an historic step. With Soviet agreement, we could together substantially reduce the dread threat of a nuclear war which hangs over the people of Europe.' In addition, he proposed new Strategic Arms Reduction Talks (START) 'to negotiate substantial reductions in nuclear arms' (*Realism*, 18 November 1981). The official Soviet response was that the 'zero option' was simply propaganda. It was, of course, asking the Soviet Union to disarm its existing INF arsenal on the promise that the United States would not deploy its own, hardly an enticing prospect for the Soviet military. Even so, negotiations began in Geneva between Paul Nitze and Yuli Kvitsinskiy. On 16 July 1982, they attempted a compromise formula which recognised that the 'zero option' was not acceptable to the Soviet Union. Its essence was that in return for the United States not deploying Pershing II missiles, the Soviet Union would restrict the number and targeting of its SS-20s. It did not find favour either in Moscow or in the Pentagon (Nitze, 1989). Failure to make progress on this key issue set the context for a particularly fraught year in American–Soviet relations, so serious that Andropov apparently believed that Reagan might be contemplating a nuclear first strike (Andrew, 1996).

The tone was set by Reagan in a speech on 8 March 1983 to the National Association of Evangelicals in which he counselled his listeners to resist the temptation of 'blithely declaring yourselves above it all and label both sides equally at fault, to ignore the facts of history and the impulses of an evil empire, to simply call the arms race a giant misunderstanding and thereby remove yourself from the struggle between right and wrong and good and evil'. To a world used to the niceties of diplomatic discourse, the term 'evil empire' conjured up all sorts of images. It was not the language of détente. More significantly, Reagan and some key advisers had been rethinking the nature of the strategic nuclear relationship, which since the 1972 ABM treaty had been based upon the principle of mutual assured destruction. MAD itself rested on the premise of mutual vulnerability to nuclear attack, but since weapons technologies were moving ahead it was inevitable that some new thinking would come forward. What Reagan unveiled in a televised address on 23 March 1983 was nothing less than the reversal of the established relationship. The prospect he offered was

> that we embark on a program to counter the awesome Soviet missile threat with measures that are defensive. . . . What if free people could live secure in the knowledge that their security did not rest upon the threat of instant U.S. retaliation to deter a Soviet attack, that we could intercept and destroy strategic missiles before they reached our own soil and those of our allies?. (*Realism*, 23 March 1983)

What this envisaged, though the speech did not spell it out, was a system of satellites which would warn of an attack and a space-based system of lasers which would destroy incoming missiles. With the 'evil empire' speech in mind, the concept was rapidly termed 'Star Wars'. Although the realisation of such complex technology lay many years in the future, if ever, the fact that the president was announcing its launch put the superpower relationship on a new trajectory. For the Soviet leadership, far from being a defensive system, the Strategic Defense Initiative (SDI) would become a shield from behind which the United States could launch a first strike. They argued that its development would be a breach of the 1972 ABM treaty. Nor were European leaders entirely happy with the proposal, questioning its implication for their defence. But the genie was out of the bottle and SDI was to colour arms negotiations between Washington and Moscow over succeeding years. Research on the programme added further pressure to the Reagan budget deficits (Nitze, 1989; Shultz, 1993; Schmertz, Datlof & Ugrinsky, 1997).

Relations between Washington and Moscow, already sour, touched a new low on 1 September 1983 when a Soviet fighter shot down Korean Airlines Flight KAL 007, flying from New York to Seoul. The pilot had strayed over the militarily sensitive Sakhalin Island. This resulted in the deaths of 269 people, 61 of them Americans, one of them a congressman. American opinion was outraged, but beyond a sulphurous meeting between Shultz and Foreign Minister Andrei Gromyko, which the latter described as the sharpest exchange he had ever had with a Secretary of State, nothing could be done (Shultz, 1993; Gromyko, 1989). For many Americans the incident came as a post hoc vindication of what Reagan had said about the Soviets earlier in the year.

Intervention in Grenada

The sense of crisis continued the following month with the intervention in Grenada, a tiny former British colony in the eastern Caribbean whose politics had been characterised by a bloody power struggle between radical groups. Under the premiership of Maurice Bishop close ties were developed with Cuba, whose construction workers arrived to build a new airport. On 23 March 1983, Reagan reported his concern to the American people that this airport constituted a potential threat to their lines of communication. Then, on 19 October, Bishop and four of his ministers were murdered in a coup engineered by his deputy. Complicating the picture was the presence on the island of some eight hundred American medical students, whom it was deemed desirable to rescue from the unfolding chaos. On 22 October the Organisation of Eastern Caribbean States agreed to intervene in Grenada if the United States would also take part. This was the trigger the administration needed, even though, to Reagan's dismay, the British government strongly opposed military intervention in the affairs of a sovereign Commonwealth country. On 25 October, American troops and marines landed on the island; 45 Grenadans, 24 Cubans and 18 Americans were killed. If many viewed it as one of the more unequal contests in military history, the administration claimed that the Brezhnev Doctrine could now be challenged. Gromyko denounced it as a terrorist act (Reagan, 1990; Weinberger, 1990; Shultz, 1993).

Reagan and Gorbachev

The year ended with the two protagonists seemingly far apart. In mid-November, the first cruise missiles were delivered to Britain and Italy, but the Soviets chose to make the Bundestag vote on deployment on 22 November 1983 the focal point of their diplomatic counter-offensive. Given German sensitivities on the nuclear issue and the vexed history of relations between the two countries, it seemed the obvious point where the alliance's unity might be challenged. But on 22 November, German deputies voted to accept the missiles. The following day, Kvitsinskiy announced the INF negotiations at an end. The START negotiations and talks on conventional arms reductions were also halted. With no dialogue between the two sides on arms control, the Cold War seemed to have set in once again (Nitze, 1989; Shultz, 1993).

The year 1984 saw little essential change, since Andropov's death made way for the hapless Chernenko, while Reagan moved to his triumphant re-election in November. Reagan entered his second term with a strong mandate, endorsed by 49 states. Presiding as he did over a rearmed country and western alliance, he had the potential to negotiate with the Soviet Union from a position of strength. Just as American power and self-confidence were increasing, Chernenko's death in March 1985 abruptly changed the nature of the

Soviet leadership. On 11 March, the 54-year-old Mikhail Gorbachev, a protégé of Andropov, became General Secretary. A trained economist aware of the intractable nature of his economic inheritance, Gorbachev believed that by setting in hand new measures he could overhaul the Soviet system to make it work effectively. The two key elements in his policy came to be defined as a greater openness, *glasnost*, combined with a restructuring of the machinery of government, *perestroika*. Given the powerful vested interests in the party, the military and the bureaucracy, the latter demanded the full measure of toughness and flexibility. An early clue that Gorbachev was looking for new openings in foreign policy came in May, with the 79-year-old Gromyko's elevation to the dignity of Chairman of the Praesidium and his replacement with Eduard Shevardnaze, who proved to a flexible and imaginative negotiator (Pearson, 2002).

On 19–21 November 1985, Reagan met Gorbachev at Geneva, his first meeting with a Soviet leader. Gorbachev was concerned to impress upon the Americans that they could not bankrupt the Soviet Union through their level of defence spending. While SDI was a major preoccupation, Gorbachev had to concede the depth of Reagan's commitment to the concept. Even so, this initial encounter between the two leaders ended on a positive note, with agreement that a nuclear war must never be fought, that the countries should work towards a 50 per cent reduction in strategic weapons, and that there should be early progress towards an interim INF agreement. Just as important, it was clear that the two men had established the basis of a relationship. So, too, had Shultz and Shevardnadze (Shultz, 1993). In fact, it was becoming increasingly clear that the only way in which Gorbachev could find the resources to address his country's economic and social needs would be to tackle the level of defence spending.

Signs of Gorbachev's new thinking came on 15 January 1986 with an offer to the Americans that their countries should move to the abolition of nuclear weapons and ballistic missiles by 2000. This would be done in three stages, the first involving INF in Europe. This was close enough to the original American INF 'zero option' for Reagan's advisers to be able to work on the proposal, though Gorbachev had predictably made any arms reductions conditional on America abandoning the SDI. Even so, members of the administration were undecided as to how to respond to what might be little more than a propaganda move on Gorbachev's part, designed to put pressure on the SDI. Nitze, a veteran of arms negotiation, believed that the Soviets had invested too much in their ballistic missile system for elimination to be a realistic possibility (Nitze, 1989). It was increasingly clear that the Soviet Union's claim to be a superpower rested on the strength of her ballistic missile arsenal and the size, and assumed effectiveness, of her conventional armed forces. Nothing highlighted the true state of affairs in the country as much as the devastating explosion at the Chernobyl nuclear reactor in the Ukraine on 26 April 1986, cruelly exposing the tenuous nature of its technical base (Pearson, 2002).

The two leaders explored the complex issues of arms reduction at a second summit held at Reykjavik on 11–12 October 1986. Gorbachev's offer was for the 'zero option' on INF in Europe, a 50 per cent reduction in strategic offensive missiles, and for the United States to continue to adhere to the ABM treaty for a 10-year period, and, crucially, agreeing to limit the SDI to laboratory work. The Americans did not want to confine the INF ban to European-based missiles, on the ground that SS-20s based in Soviet Asia could quickly be moved west. The Soviet negotiators conceded that their INF based in Asia would confined to 100, matched be a similar number in the continental United States, in effect Alaska. The two sides also agreed that they would work towards a limit of 6,000 warheads on their strategic nuclear missiles rather than a 50 per cent reduction. But at a final meeting, Gorbachev insisted that all the Soviet concessions rested on

America's willingness to restrict the SDI to the laboratory. An irate Reagan refused to budge, and the summit ended on a sour note. For a system that was still at best speculative, the SDI was proving to be a major Soviet preoccupation. If Gorbachev had come to Reykjavik hoping to choke it off, then he had failed, but in the process he had revealed how far he was prepared to move on other fronts. If the summit had not matched expectations, the Americans could still claim a tactical victory of sorts. It was clear that substantial progress on nuclear disarmament had at last entered the realm of possibility (Nitze, 1989; Reagan, 1990; Shultz, 1993).

The Iran-Contra Affair

But every administration, it seems, is vulnerable to what the British Prime Minister Harold Macmillan once called 'events', and before that progress could be made Reagan's authority was sapped by what came to be known as the 'Iran-Contra affair'. As an episode in American foreign policy it had little lasting importance, but it did illustrate in the most telling manner the dangers inherent in the system of semi-independent government agencies which had come into being. As a piece of Grand Guignol, it inevitably gripped political and public attention, diverting attention from matters of greater substance, though the consequences for some of those involved were serious enough. The Reykjavik summit was barely over when the public unravelling of the two separate, but related, scandals began. On 3 November, a magazine in Beirut claimed that Robert McFarlane, the former National Security Advisor, had been in Tehran; later that day the speaker of the Iranian parliament further claimed that in September 1986 McFarlane and four other Americans had travelled to Iran on Irish passports on a plane carrying arms. The Irish government, which had no knowledge of this, naturally protested vigorously, to Shultz's embarrassment (Shultz, 1993). What was emerging was an operation, first suggested by the Israelis, to supply Iran with TOW anti-tank missiles and Hawk anti-aircraft missiles in return for assistance in securing the release of Americans held hostage in Lebanon. This ran counter to the administration's repeated rhetoric of not making deals with terrorists. Nevertheless, over the opposition of Shultz and Weinberger, Reagan gave the green light to the initiative (Reagan, 1990).

Then, on 25 November, the affair took a dramatic new twist when Reagan announced on television the reassignment of National Security Advisor Admiral John Poindexter and marine Lieutenant-Colonel Oliver North of the NSC staff. He was followed by Attorney-General Ed Meese with the startling information that between $10 and $30 million paid by Iran for the missiles had been diverted to the Contras, the anti-Sandinista rebels in Nicaragua. Reagan had a passionate personal attachment to the Contras, whom he saw as standing in the way of a communist takeover of the region. In the early stages of his administration, the CIA had provided them with assistance, but Congress had voted to end this with effect from October 1984. Believing that the Sandinista government posed a continuing threat to American interests in central America, key members of the NSC staff had seen the Iranian money as the way to keep funding the Contras. Although both the Iranian and Nicaraguan ends of the operation were brought to a stop, the damage to Reagan and his administration had really only begun, as Americans awaited the workings of the Joint Congressional Committee on the Iran-Contra Affair set for the summer of 1987. Unlike Watergate, there was no public or political will to pull down the administration. The reality was that in allowing the CIA and NSC to extend their reach into foreign policy, successive administrations had created the conditions in which an episode like the Iran-Contra Affair had been an accident waiting to happen, especially under a president whose day-to-day control was famously relaxed (Reagan, 1990; Schmertz, Datlof & Ugrinsky, 1997).

The INF Treaty

There is no doubt that the president's authority had been undermined by this trail of revelations, but this was nothing compared with the pressures bearing upon Gorbachev, who badly needed a foreign policy success. The Afghan war was proving an insupportable burden. In 1984, the Americans and Saudis agreed a substantially increased aid package to the Mujahedin, so that when a major Soviet offensive began in the following spring the mechanisms were already in hand to challenge it. In March 1985 a new presidential directive authorised a major effort to drive the Soviets out of the country, as the result of which heavy machine-guns, anti-aircraft weapons, food and clothing were delivered to the Mujahedin on a massive scale. The Afghan fighters were also reinforced by dedicated Muslim volunteers from throughout the Middle East, determined to rid the country of the enemies of their faith. In order to counter Soviet helicopter gunships, in April 1986 Reagan approved the supply of 400 Stinger anti-aircraft missiles over the head of Pentagon fears of their technology falling into Russian hands. So effective did they prove that the Soviets had to abandon close air support for their troops for ineffective high-level bombing (Andrew, 1996; Gates, 1996). Faced with an unwinnable and unpopular war, in September 1987 Shevarnadve privately informed Shultz that the Soviets intended to pull out.

Other signals were not long in coming. When Shultz went to Moscow the following month, Gorbachev indicated his belief that an INF agreement could not be long delayed. He had already publicly indicated that he was no longer insisting on his Reykjavik stipulation of retaining 100 INF missiles in Asia (Nitze, 1989; Shultz, 1993). On 8 December, Gorbachev and Reagan signed the INF treaty in Washington.

Setting out the conditions for the elimination of this cate-
gory of nuclear weapons, totalling 1,752 Soviet and 859
American missiles, Reagan saw the treaty as the justification
for his 1981 'zero option'. An essential element in the operation of the agreement was verification by American and
Soviet inspectors. On the vexed question of SDI, the summit
agreed the delphic formula which committed 'the sides to
observe the ABM Treaty, as signed in 1972, while conducting
their research, development and testing as required, which
are permitted by the ABM Treaty'. This enabled the
Americans to claim that they could test as required, while the
Soviets fastened on the qualification 'permitted by the ABM
Treaty' (Nitze, 1989). Overall, the signing of the treaty
reflected a growing trust in the Soviet leader and his intentions, certainly a changed atmosphere from the tensions of
1983. Breaking with his security, Gorbachev managed to
establish a warm rapport with Washingtonians. While helping with his domestic position, this was also a dramatic
change of tone. The great imponderable for the Americans
was, of course, the stability of Gorbachev's hold on power,
not entirely without justification, as events were to confirm.

Libya and the Middle East

As the Reagan presidency moved into its final phase, the
affairs of the Middle East once again came into focus. On 14
April 1986, American aircraft flying from bases in England
and carriers in the Mediterranean bombed Libya. The
Americans had a long-running, some thought almost obses-
sive, quarrel with President Muammar Gadaffi. This focused
on the Libyan leader's claim that the whole of the Gulf of
Sidra between Benghazi and Tripoli lay in Libyan waters, but
the Americans also believed that the country was inspiring
acts of terrorism, something the administration had pledged
to confront. Rejecting the Libyan claim to territorial waters,
the Americans flew patrols over the Gulf from their aircraft

carriers. On 18 August 1981, two Libyan fighters were shot down. To assert that these were international waters, the American Sixth Fleet continued to hold exercises in the Gulf. In 1986, Gadaffi proclaimed the Gulf a 'zone of death' within which American ships and planes would be attacked. On 24–25 March, hostilities broke out between the Libyans and the Sixth Fleet in which three Libyan patrol boats were sunk and missile sites were attacked. These events were followed on 5 April by a bomb explosion in West Berlin, which American intelligence blamed on Libyans. The raids of 14 April were the American response. Notably, while Britain allowed the Americans the use of their bases, other European countries were less enthusiastic, both France and Spain refusing permission for the fighters to fly over their airspace (Weinberger, 1990; Shultz, 1993; Gates, 1996). The perils of the Middle East were also brought home to Americans on 17 May 1987, when the *USS Stark*, on patrol in the Persian Gulf, was hit by missiles from an Iraqi plane, killing 37 of her crew. The Americans accepted President Saddam Hussein's admission that this had been an error.

The year 1987 also saw the administration turn once again to the Arab–Israeli conflict. It was none too soon. The palpable lack of diplomatic progress, combined with a seemingly unstoppable expansion of Israeli settlements on the West Bank and Gaza Strip, had built up a barely suppressed head of resentment among the Palestinians of the occupied territories. In the course of 1987, Shultz and his diplomats pursued a fruitless quest for an international conference, but no agreement could be reached before the Palestinians transformed the situation by taking their fate into their own hands. The Intifada, or uprising, which broke out on 8 December 1987 was not planned, but soon spread across the Gaza Strip and West Bank. As Israeli security forces confronted rioters with live ammunition, casualties mounted alarmingly. Voices both from Europe and the Middle East urged the Americans to use their undoubted influence. The PLO, in reality somewhat sidelined by the Intifada, held the key to progress. But PLO involvement, as Shultz well knew, depended upon acceptance of Resolution 242 with its recognition of Israel. On 15 November 1988, Arafat proclaimed an independent state on the West Bank and Gaza, carrying with it an implicit recognition of Israel. 'Back-channel' negotiations promised 'substantive dialogue' if the PLO renounced violence and accepted the existence of Israel. On 12 December, Swedish mediators informed Shultz that Arafat was prepared to announce that the PLO would negotiate with Israel on the basis of Resolutions 242 and 338, would respect Israel's right to exist within recognised borders, and would condemn terrorism. Arafat's speech to the United Nations in Geneva the following day seemed to the Americans to fall short of this. Swedish intervention resulted in Arafat giving a press conference on 14 December, the nature of which allowed Shultz to announce that the 'substantive dialogue' could begin. In the final days of the Reagan presidency both the Americans and the PLO seemed to have broken free from the constraints which had kept them at arm's length since 1975 (Fraser, 1989; Shultz, 1993).

On 8 February 1988, Gorbachev announced his intention to withdraw his troops from Afghanistan within 10 months, beginning on 15 May. An inevitable decision, in retrospect it can be seen as signalling the beginning of an imperial retreat. Few foresaw this at the time, but Gorbachev's action was viewed, not least in eastern Europe, as marking a clear departure from the Brezhnev Doctrine.

While the Soviet evacuation marked a key point in the Cold War, the travails of Afghanistan did not end. It was not until 1991, in the Soviet Union's dying weeks, that Washington and Moscow agreed to stop military aid to their allies. Scant thought was given to the state of a country awash with arms or to the passions which had been aroused. Civil war continued until the success of the Muslim fudamentalist Taliban movement in 1996. Some Americans were aware that new threats might come, the CIA's Robert Gates conceding that: 'We expected post-Soviet Afghanistan to be ugly, but never considered that it would become a haven for terrorists worldwide' (Gates, 1996). Reagan speculated: 'I don't think you can overstate the importance that the rise of Islamic fundamentalism will have to the rest of the world in the century ahead – especially if, as seems possible, its most fanatical elements get their hands on nuclear and chemical weapons and the means to deliver them against their enemies' (Reagan, 1990).

The Soviet withdrawal coincided almost exactly with one of the last acts of the Reagan presidency. On 29 May, Reagan arrived in Moscow for what Shultz later termed the last of the superpower summits, notable for tone rather than substance. Reagan and Gorbachev walked amiably round Red Square, a prospect which few could have anticipated in 1981. In a speech at Moscow State University, Reagan spoke of the hopeful times the country was going through and appealed for the removal of the Berlin Wall. It was not quite a valedictory. On 7 December, as Reagan was awaiting the succession of the recently elected George Bush, Gorbachev came to New York to address the United Nations. His message continued to be one of conciliation and arms reduction, announcing that within two years 500,000 men and 10,000 tanks would be taken out of service, and that 6 tank divisions would be withdrawn from the German Democratic Republic. The end of the Reagan era in American foreign policy could not have been more markedly different to its beginning. The Soviet Union was clearly undergoing profound change, the ultimate results of which could only be speculative. When Reagan left office in January 1989, the Cold War had not come to an end, many in Washington believing in the threat a communist Soviet Union revived and reformed by Gorbachev might present, but the military and strategic balance had finally tilted America's way. This advantage had been brought at price which the American people had yet to pay.

10

BUSH: A WORLD REORDERED

The totalitarian era is passing, its old ideas blown away like leaves
from an ancient, lifeless tree. A new breeze is blowing, and a nation
refreshed by freedom stands ready to push on. There is new ground
to be broken, and new action to be taken. There are times when the
future seems thick as a fog; you sit and wait, hoping the mists will lift
and reveal the right path. But this is a time when the future seems a
door you can walk right through into a room called tomorrow.

George Bush, Inaugural, 20 January 1989

While on one level prophetic, on another George Bush's
assessment of the international situation could not have
been wider of the mark. The year 1989 proved to be the most
significant of the post-war era, the point at which all the
apparent certainities of the East–West relationship began to
unravel in a matter of weeks. But this was not foreseen. 'I
know of *no one*', recorded Robert Gates, Bush's Deputy
National Security Advisor, 'in or out of government who
predicted early in 1989 that before the next presidential
election Eastern Europe would be free, Germany unified in
NATO, and the Soviet Union an artifact of history' (Gates,
1996). No president since Truman had to respond to such
fast-moving events as Bush, something which anyone
tempted to see his presidency as something of an interlude
between those of his ideologically driven predecessor and
his flamboyant successor should remember. Bush won the
1988 election by the comfortable margin of 48,886,097 votes
to 41,809,074 over Michael Dukakis. Higher than Reagan's
1980 total, it was well short of the 54,455,075 who had voted

for the Republican team in 1984. One major problem Bush had to face was that his message of a 'kinder, gentler America' did not sit well with the right-wing ideologues of his own party, who preferred the certainties of Ronald Reagan. The other was that he had no interest in the kind of rhetorical flourishes with his predecessor had captured the public imagination. This was ultimately to cost him dear in terms of political support (Cyr, 1997). The domestic agenda was ultimately to prove his Achilles heel, but on foreign policy few presidents had come into office with wider experience. A combat hero from the Second World War, congressman, de facto ambassador to Beijing, Director of the CIA, ambassador to the United Nations and vice-president for eight years, Bush brought a range of insights which few could have hoped to match. If he could not have predicted the course of events, he had the confidence to respond as someone who knew the dynamics of the international system, and many of its leaders. Personal telephone diplomacy became the hallmark of his incumbency. He was backed by a strong team. His Secretary of State, James Baker, was a long-standing friend from Texas, while his National Security Advisor was a cerebral veteran from the days of Nixon and Ford, Brent Scowcroft. Scowcroft brought in to the National Security Council talented young advisers from outside (Bush & Scowcroft, 1998).

Bush and Gorbachev: The Beginning of a Partnership

The new administration knew that it priority was to define its policies towards Gorbachev, but that was less straightforward than might be imagined. Bush admitted that he felt more positively towards the Soviet leader than some in his administration, believing him to be sincere in his pursuit of better relations with the United States; indeed, that he liked him. Others, like Scowcroft, were more sceptical. For them, Gorbachev was engaged in an exercise to revitalise the Soviet

Union after the sterile years of Brezhnev, Andropov and Chernenko, the end result of which could only be a more powerful opponent. In the sense that Gorbachev never pretended to be other than a dedicated Communist, their wariness was understandable. There was also an uneasy feeling that Gorbachev was having too much of an appeal to America's European allies (Gates, 1996; Bush and Scowcroft, 1998). The truth was that Gorbachev was struggling to reform the unreformable. His attempts at economic change did nothing to reduce the country's endemic problems of production and distribution. His recourse was to attack the Communist Party, which was the basis of his power. In June 1988, he denounced the party's incompetence. Leading Communists were then defeated in elections in March 1989. The problem was that it was by no means clear what future direction politics would take, everything being so dependent on the communist apparatus and its functionaries. Critically, he was taking the element of fear and coercion out of the Soviet system, and nowhere was this to be of greater importance than in eastern Europe, where communism had never shed its legacy of having been imposed from outside. Almost as Bush was being inaugurated, historic decisions were being taken in Warsaw and Budapest. On 18 January 1989, the Polish Communists agreed to begin discussions on restoring the trade union Solidarity. This was done on 5 April, with the Catholic Church also being given full legal status. But it was the Hungarians, with their bitter memories of 1956, who really set the pace. In January, the government announced that it was going to set up an enquiry into the events of 1956, directly questioning the legitimacy of the communist position. This was followed by sanction for a multi-party system. Events then followed in rapid succession, reaching their climax on 16 June 1989, when hundreds of thousands lined the streets of Budapest for the reburial of Imre Nagy and four of his executed colleagues from 1956 (Crampton, 1994). But by then the Hungarians had made one of the most far-reaching moves in the history of Europe's post-war division, since in May they had begun to dismantle their section of the Iron Curtain along the border with Austria, a gesture which was to trigger the unravelling of the Soviet system.

These events, especially the 5 April agreement in Poland, set the scene for Bush's first major foreign policy address at Hamtramck, Michigan, chosen for its large population of Polish extraction, on 17 April 1989. This set out the principle that progress in eastern Europe depended on political and economic liberalisation. Such liberalisation would attract western help, and Bush set out measures such as tariff relief and support through the IMF. While Moscow Radio retorted that this smacked too much of a return to the old notion of 'roll-back', the Poles and Hungarians signalled their approval. At a second speech, at Texas A&M University on 12 May, Bush refined his position towards the Soviet Union itself. It was still set within Cold War parameters. While the United States would welcome the Soviet Union into the community of nations, Bush said, it would have to be on the basis of positive actions, including self-determination for eastern Europe and conventional force reduction. Finally, in a speech on 24 May he spelled out his thoughts on arms reduction, appealing to the Soviets to remove the Warsaw Pact's offensive role (Bush & Scowcroft, 1998).

The Tiananmen Square Massacre

Even as Bush was making this series of speeches, tragic events were developing in Beijing. As an old 'China hand', Bush saw good relations as a key priority, but the Americans were worried what a projected state visit by Gorbachev, the first by a Soviet leader since the Sino-Soviet split, might entail. Bush's chance to explore the possible implications came with the death of Japan's Emperor Hirohito in February 1989. The funeral presented him with the excuse to make a side trip to Beijing, in the course of which the Chinese leaders reassured him that they were not about to restore their old alliance with Moscow. But China was not immune from the changes which were taking place elsewhere. In the late 1980s, the leadership, led by Deng Xiaoping, began to liberalise the country's economic system, but this set up stresses within the system which were hard to contain. In April 1989, large numbers of students began to congregate in Tiananmen Square in the centre of Beijing, demanding, in effect, that this process be extended to the country's political structure. A new dynamic seemed to be under way. Gorbachev's state visit between 15 and 18 May encouraged hundreds of thousands more demonstrators to assemble, in full view of the world's media. The response of the crowds to what appeared to be official indecision was the erection of a Goddess of Democracy, but on 3 June the government brought in troops from outside the city and brutally dispersed them, in what became known as the 'Tiananmen Square Massacre'. The Chinese later admitted to 310 deaths; the Americans believed the real total was in the thousands. The administration was caught between its distaste over what happened and its knowledge of how resentful the Chinese were over interference from outside. Bush's response was a finely calibrated one of imposing sanctions, especially over weapons supplies, which would signal American disapproval, while not imperilling the relationship which had been developing since 1972. To those who felt this was too flaccid a response, it was argued that the United States was the first country to impose sanctions. The truth was that, faced with the Chinese government's repression, there was little to be done beyond public disapproval and private diplomacy. The extent of the violence in Tiananmen Square may well have helped convince Gorbachev of the need to avoid any such outcome in eastern Europe, though he did not denounce the massacre (Bush & Scowcroft, 1998; Pearson, 2002).

The Year of Revolution in Eastern Europe

In the summer of 1989, the two world leaders criss-crossed each other as Gorbachev toured Germany and France, while Bush visited Warsaw, Gdansk and Budapest. Gorbachev was carrying mixed signals to the west Europeans, talking positively of a 'common European home', indicating that he would not intervene in Poland and Hungary, but insisting that eastern Europe's future would be socialist. Bush's purpose was to show his solidarity with the reformers in Poland and Hungary, while urging them to tread warily. The nagging fear was that the pace of reform might lead to Gorbachev's overthrow by hardliners in the party or military, or both. Even so, Bush would have been less than human had he not been stirred by what he saw. At an emotional meeting at the Lenin Shipyard in Gdansk, home to Solidarity, he declaimed that this was Poland's time of destiny. In Budapest, he was presented as a souvenir with part of the Iron Curtain. A further sign of how eastern Europe was stirring came with growing demands for independence in the three Baltic states of Latvia, Lithuania and Estonia, grabbed by Stalin in 1940. In their case, Gorbachev growled, as well he might, since their independence would question the very existence of the Soviet Union (Bush & Scowcroft, 1998).

Perhaps the most decisive event in the unravelling of Moscow's empire came on 10 September 1989 when the Hungarians opened their border with Austria. East Germans, who needed no visa to travel through Czechoslovakia and Hungary, saw their chance, travelling across Europe in their thousands, to be welcomed by the Austrians. It was a repetition of the events of 1961 which had led to the construction of the Berlin Wall. All that the East German government of Erich Honecker could think of was to close their borders, triggering mass demonstrations in Leipzig, Dresden and Berlin. Anticipating such a challenge, the government had been preparing for their own version of Tiananmen Square, the so-called 'Chinese solution'. With their strong security apparatus backed by the 19 Red Army divisions in the country, there could only have been one outcome, but for Gorbachev deploying his troops as the instrument of repression across East Germany, Poland and Hungary was simply no longer an option. Honecker was informed that Soviet support would not be forthcoming. Had the people on the streets but known it, this was the green light for revolution.

The implications of this historic decision soon became clear. When Hungary declared herself a sovereign republic on 23 October, the Soviet Union immediately made clear there would be no objection. Two days later in Helsinki, Gorbachev repudiated the Brezhnev Doctrine. Honecker's replacement by the more emollient Egon Krenz brought no relief to the embattled government in East Berlin. Then, on 9 November, came a somewhat muddled announcement that border controls with West Germany would be relaxed. As crowds converged on the Berlin Wall, confused border guards let them cross. The ultimate symbol of the Cold War in Europe had been breached, for ever, as it happened. No one who witnessed the events of that evening could ever forget the sight of people freely crossing a border where so many had been shot dead. Other east Europeans now rushed to follow the path the Hungarians and east Germans had set. In quick succession, Bulgaria, Czechoslovakia and Romania shed their communist rulers. In Prague, the 'velvet revolution' brought to power the poet Vaclav Havel as president and Alexander Dubcek, who had tried to tread the same ground in 1968, as chairman of the assembly. Only in Romania, whose dismal rulers Nicolae and Elena Ceausescu were executed, was there violence. Few lamented them. Stalin's empire in eastern Europe stood revealed for what it always was. Exactly what might replace it was quite another matter (Pearson, 2002).

When Bush and Gorbachev met for their first summit at Malta in early December 1989, the revolutions in eastern Europe were still unfolding. The real lesson of the Malta meeting was one of mutual reassurance in the face of fast-changing events. So far, the policies of the Bush administration had been almost entirely reactive, welcoming change while avoiding any impression of triumphalism which might trigger moves against Gorbachev. Diplomatically, this made sense, but it did not serve him well in terms of public perception. The one thing which seemed clear to Bush was that the United States should put her influence behind German reunification. In doing so, he was riding ahead of his allies in western Europe, where Britain's Margaret Thatcher was famously unenthusiastic. He was also challenging the basic Soviet fear of a resurgent Germany, entirely understandable in the light of 1941–45. In a meeting with West Germany's Helmut Kohl on his return from Malta, Bush indicated his support for a policy of reunification. While the fast-disintegrating political structures in East Germany were already pointing to that outcome, America's blessing would be a key element in its realisation (Bush & Scowcroft, 1998).

Intervention in Panama

As this situation developed, the Americans decided to lance a problem which they had seen festering for months, deteriorating relations with Panama's ruler, General Manuel Noriega. Noriega was a controversial figure, who had been indicted by two Grand Juries in the United States on drugs offences, while being alleged by some of having enjoyed links with Washington. By 1989, he was seen as a major embarrassment, not least through his nullification of election results in May. Former president Carter denounced the election as a fraud. Panama was, however, a sovereign nation and it was not the only country in the region where the drugs trade was a concern. On 20 December 1989, American troops intervened in the country in massive force. Noriega surrendered to the Americans, but not before over 500

Panamanians and 23 American servicemen had been killed. It was to be expected that the Soviet leadership would denounce what they saw as the double standard of the United States by intervening in the affairs of a sovereign state. In the light of Gorbachev's decisions in eastern Europe, they had a point, confirmed by the United Nations General Assembly, which voted that the United States had violated international law. Whisked to Florida, Noriega was convicted of manufacturing and distributing cocaine, receiving a 40-year prison term (Woodward, 1991; Hurst, 1999).

The Future of Germany

Germany was not the only issue affecting relations with Moscow, but its future lay at the heart of East–West relations. The revolutions in eastern Europe meant an effective end for the Warsaw Pact, raising the obvious issue of the withdrawal of Soviet troops to the homeland after over four decades. How would the Red Army react to the prospect? Even less predictable were the clear signals that change was not being arrested at the Soviet border. As 1990 began, the republics of Armenia and Azerbaijan were at war, requiring Moscow's military intervention. Elections in March produced majorities for independence in the Baltic states and in Moldova, prompting the Lithuanians to break from the Soviet Union. Gorbachev's riposte was to put an economic embargo on Lithuania. Perhaps as surprising as these expressions of nationalism was what was happening to the communist apparatus, the glue which had held the Soviet Union together. In May 1990, the communist reformer Boris Yeltsin was elected president of the Russian Parliament. The following month, the Parliament declared that its laws took precedence over those of the Soviet Union, and the Russian Communist Party broke away from the Communist Party of the Soviet Union (Pearson, 2002). Throughout all of this, American hopes remained pinned on Gorbachev, but they had to be tempered by the agonising question of long he could survive.

On the critical issue of Germany, the Soviet leaders were insisting that the price of unity would be a neutral country outside NATO. Bush and Kohl thought differently, seeing a Germany fully tied in with the western system as the guarantee of stability. At a meeting in Camp David in late February they agreed that a united Germany integrated into NATO, but with sensitivity over troop deployments in the east, was the way to entice the Soviets. Elections in East Germany saw the Christian Democrats emerge as the strongest party. Unity was now unstoppable, but still needed agreement between Washington and Moscow. Germany inevitably dominated the agenda when Gorbachev arrived in Washington on 31 May, but was linked to continuing tensions over Lithuania and the Soviet leader's hopes for western aid to prop up his faltering economy. No final agreement was reached on Germany. The closest the two leaders came was Gorbachev's apparent concession that a united Germany could join NATO should she choose to do so, but this caused such consternation amongst his colleagues that the Americans could not be quite sure where they stood. Trade and grain concessions, Most Favored Nation (MFN) status, would be granted subject to Soviet concessions on Jewish emigration. Secretly, the Americans insisted that the request for MFN would not be sent to Congress until Gorbachev lifted the economic pressures on Lithuania. The real significance of the summit was that Gorbachev was signalling the end of Soviet opposition to a united Germany inside NATO (Korchilov, 1997; Bush & Scowcroft, 1998). Kohl was now free to conclude the process, which he did with the aid of financial concessions. On 12 September 1990, the four wartime allies and the two Germanies signed a treaty in Moscow whereby Germany was reunited, permitted to choose her alliances, recognised the Oder–Neisse frontier with Poland, and the four former allied powers surrendered their rights. The new country came into being on 3 October. It was less than a year since

247

the Wall had fallen. While the essential dynamic had come from Germany, America's participation had been the clue to ensuring that the process remained on track.

Crisis in Kuwait

It is poignant, in a way, that this peaceful end to one of the post-war world's most intractable problems, the division of Germany, would be overshadowed by a crisis of a very different order, but it was. As had happened with so many administrations, affairs in the Middle East claimed priority. During the eight years of the Iran–Iraq war, the United States had not been ill-disposed towards Iraqi president Saddam Hussein. Given what had happened in Iran, this should not give cause for surprise. The Americans were still wrestling with the security of western interests in the oil-rich Gulf in the light of Britain's withdrawal and the Shah's collapse. Despite Iraq's long-standing links with the Soviet Union, diplomatic relations, severed since the 1967 Middle East war, were restored in 1984. The war had left Saddam with massive problems, the most acute of which was how to pay for it. His war effort had been supported in the Arab world, notably by Saudi Arabia and Kuwait, but it had left him with substantial debts, $30 billion being owed to Kuwait alone. He was also irritated by the actions of certain oil-producing states in increasing production, hence forcing down prices. Here, too, his anger focused on Kuwait, with which, in any case, Iraq had long-standing border disputes. By mid-July 1990, with growing rhetoric against Kuwait and the movement of two divisions to the border, it seemed that a dangerous crisis might be developing. Nevertheless, diplomacy, led by President Mubarak of Egypt and Jordan's King Hussein, appeared to be working. On 25 July, OPEC announced new pricing levels, agreed to by Kuwait, which went far in meeting Iraq's case. The same day, Saddam met the American ambassador, April Glaspie. He seemed to reassure her that he was cooperating with Arab diplomacy, while she made it clear that the United States would only condone the resolution of disputes by peaceful means, and repeated the State Department formula that the United States did 'not take a stand on territorial disputes' (Woodward, 1991; Bush & Scowcroft, 1998). On 2 August, the Iraqi army crossed the Kuwaiti border, occupying the country in a matter of hours.

Operation Desert Shield

American thinking immediately turned to the economic, diplomatic and military options. The first was relatively straightforward. Bush signed an order freezing all Iraqi and Kuwaiti assets in the United States. Other economic options, especially with regard to Iraqi and Kuwaiti oil, were urgently examined. On the diplomatic front two things were going on, fortuitously as it happened. Bush was due to meet Margaret Thatcher in Colorado. She was quick to point to the moral of the 1930s, expressing the view that if Saddam were to make a move on Saudi Arabia he would control 65 per cent of the world's oil reserves. British solidarity with Bush was clear and would be consistent (Thatcher, 1993). Secondly, James Baker was in the Soviet Union, where he secured a joint statement condemning the Iraqi action (Gates, 1996). But pivotal to how events subsequently developed was the vote in the United Nations Security Council, with only Yemen abstaining, condemning the invasion, demanding an Iraqi withdrawal, and negotiations to resolve the dispute. Subsequent resolutions mandated economic sanctions against Iraq. There were clear echoes of Korea in 1950, though on this occasion the Soviet Union was in support (Bush & Scowcroft, 1998).

Any military riposte was the responsibility of Central Command, headed by General Norman Schwarzkopf. On 4 August, the general explained the military position to Bush and his principal advisers. The Iraqi army, he reported, had

900,000 men organised in 63 divisions, well equipped with tanks, artillery and missiles, as well as a modern air force. If his mission were to defend Saudi Arabia, then he could instantly deploy a brigade of the 82nd airborne division, reinforced within two weeks by a marine brigade and more paratroopers, but all lightly armed forces with which to confront Iraqi armour. Air support could be quickly sent. It would take a month to mass the heavily armoured forces needed to repel an attack, and three months to be absolutely certain of doing so. If the objective were to expel the Iraqi army from Kuwait, then six divisions with full logistical support would be needed, and this would take between eight and ten months (Schwarzkopf, 1992). These hard military realities lay behind all subsequent planning. Everything would turn on Saudi Arabia's willingness to see American forces deployed on her territory, and initial soundings with Riyadh had not yet given a positive reply. Despite this, on 5 August Bush seemed to nail his colours to the mast when he announced: 'This will not stand, this aggression against Kuwait', even though no decision for military action had yet been taken (Bush & Scowcroft, 1998). Critics inevitably fastened on oil supplies as the driving force behind American actions, but others have argued that this was not the issue, pointing to the fact that the safe course would have been to have defended Saudi Arabia and the Gulf states, while buying oil from Saddam Hussein on the world market. There is, in fact, no reason to doubt that the international coalition which assembled did so in the belief that Iraq's action was in clear violation of Article 51 of the United Nations Charter (Hurd, 1997).

Bush's statement was followed by the critical information that King Fahd of Saudi Arabia was willing to allow American troops on his territory. In order to avert any pre-emptive invasion by Iraq, Bush did not announce this until after the first paratroops had arrived. His broadcast on 8 August drew the inevitable comparison with Hitler in the 1930s, before demanding the 'immediate, unconditional and complete withdrawal of all Iraqi forces from Kuwait'. The assistance of British forces was announced the next day. France quickly followed, but it was vital that any military build-up should amount to more than the Americans and their European allies. Arab participation, in particular, was of the essence if what was now being called operation Desert Shield were to have any credibility in the region. Saddam Hussein was already drawing comparisons between the situation in Kuwait and the Israeli occupation of the West Bank and Gaza, something which he knew would find a strong echo across the region, as it did. Bush informed Egypt that he would recommend to Congress that her entire debt to the United States be written off, not an undertaking lightly given in view of mounting criticism in the legislature over the likely costs, financial and human, of confronting Iraq. The former was in part met by indications from Japan and Germany that they would contribute financially to the coalition the Americans were assembling (Hurst, 1999). It was at this point that a new phrase began to enter Bush's vocabulary, that of a 'new world order' in which the United States and the Soviet Union would unite against aggression. To that end, he suggested a special summit with Gorbachev, which was held in Helsinki on 9 September. The Americans' main purpose was to ensure Gorbachev's acquiescence in the fact that force might have to be used. The best they could get was a Soviet reaffirmation of support for the United Nations' resolutions. Gorbachev was clearly irked that he had not been consulted on the American decision to send troops. What the summit really revealed was that if there were a new world order, then the Soviets were the junior partner in it (Bush & Scowcroft, 1998).

From Desert Shield to Desert Storm

Two critical meetings in Washington on 30 October confirmed the conflicting pressures bearing down on Bush.

In the first, Speaker Tom Foley and Senate Majority Leader George Mitchell conveyed the concern of many Democrats in Congress that the military deployment was shifting from a defensive to an offensive posture. In a clear reference to the 1973 War Powers Resolution, they were insisting that Bush get a declaration of war from Congress before launching offensive action. The same day, Bush and his key advisers were on a different tack. Convinced that sanctions were proving ineffective, the Pentagon was authorised to continue its military build-up to a level which would permit offensive action should diplomacy fail. The recommendation from the National Security Council was that there should be a new United Nations Security Council resolution authorising all necessary means to secure an Iraqi withdrawal from Kuwait. Saddam should then be presented with an ultimatum to do so. Bush admitted that by imposing such a deadline, they were committing themselves to war, should negotiations fail. The military's favoured date was 15 January. On 29 November, after intensive American diplomacy, the Security Council passed Resolution 678, stating that unless Iraq withdrew from Kuwait by 15 January 'all necessary means' could be used (Bush & Scowcroft, 1998).

The administration's strategy in securing Resolution 678 was twofold; it would help cement the coalition, especially its Arab members, and consolidate support in a still sceptical Congress. Congressional opposition did not die away, with leading Democrats continuing to voice deep reservations, not least on the possible scale of American casualties. On 12 January 1991, the two houses voted on a joint resolution authorising the use of force under the terms of the United Nations resolutions. The House vote was 250–183, but the Senate margin, 52–47, reflected a greater degree of concern (Hurst, 1999). Bush later recorded that he would have acted anyway. On the expiration of the deadline on 15 January, the aerial bombardment of Iraq, now called Desert Storm, began (Bush & Scowcroft, 1998; Schwarzkopf, 1992).

Two days later, Saddam made what the Americans had

long known would be his obvious move to disrupt the coalition, which included Saudi, Egyptian and Syrian forces, by firing Scud missiles into Israel. Israel had long made it plain that she would retaliate against attacks on her territory, and her feisty premier Yitzhak Shamir's instincts were to mount air strikes. American Patriot missiles were deployed in Israel, American and British special forces were sent to destroy missile bases, and 30 per cent of allied air strikes had to be used against the missile sites, but, crucially, the Israelis did not intervene (Bush & Scowcroft, 1998; Shamir, 1994). On 24 February, after efforts by Gorbachev to secure a mediated settlement had failed, the American-led ground attack on Iraqi positions began. Three days later, with the Iraqi army in retreat from Kuwait, Bush announced the campaign at an end. By then much of the Iraqi army, though not certain key formations, was in ruins.

In achieving its declared purpose, restoring the independence of Kuwait, the campaign had been a triumph, and Bush's approval ratings with the American public soared to unprecedented levels. Once the Iraqi army had collapsed in Kuwait, there was no alternative but to stop. That is exactly what was sanctioned under the Security Council resolutions, and if the Americans had attempted to carry their campaign into Iraq the coalition would have dissolved. An advance on Baghdad was never an option (Hurd, 1997). There was, nevertheless, a nagging sense of a mission only partly fulfilled. The clear hope had been that defeat would lead to Saddam's overthrow, either through an army mutiny or a popular uprising. The latter did take place, but only in the Kurdish north and the Shi'a south, which had long sat uneasily under the country's dominant Sunnis. It can be argued that a basic American misconception throughout the crisis was to underestimate the degree of support for Saddam in the Sunni heartland, and in the army. To demonise him as a brutal ruler was one thing, but he was also a skilled and determined politician. His linking of the crisis with the Palestinian issue was keenly judged, since the war left many in the Middle East contrasting America's readiness to act over Kuwait with the glacial progress on the Arab–Israeli conflict. Moreover, Bush conceded that it was not in America's interests to see the disintegration of Iraq, which would only further destabilise the region. For the United States to have advanced into Iraq would, of course, have negated the very principle for which the coalition had fought. What the crisis seemingly demonstrated was the reality of American power. American military, naval and air forces dominated the coalition, even though the British, French and Saudis made substantial contributions. Cooperation with the Soviet Union had been vital in securing the support of the Security Council, but the imbalance in their relationship had been embarrassingly obvious. Bush and Scowcroft later conceded that while it was important to reach out to the rest of the world, even more important had been to keep control firmly in American hands (Bush & Scowcroft, 1998).

The Collapse of the Soviet Union

Bush's hopes for a new world order harked back to the days before 1945, to the notion that the United States and the Soviet Union would cooperate to keep the peace, but this was confounded by the latter's terminal state of collapse. On 13 January, Soviet troops opened fire in Vilnius, the Lithuanian capital, killing 15, and then in Riga, the capital of Latvia, killing 4. Gorbachev claimed this had been done without his knowledge. Even so, Bush sent the Soviet leader a private letter threatening to end American aid unless such actions stopped (Gates, 1996). It was not a good omen. Yeltsin, now president of Russia, openly gave his support to the Baltic states. As the Americans struggled over what financial aid they could give Gorbachev, on 20 June they received information of the possibility of a coup against him. On 29 July, Bush arrived in Moscow for what was to be his last formal summit with the man he had come to regard as a partner. Its purpose was to sign the Strategic Arms Reduction Treaty (START), which had been maturing since 1982. What might once have been hailed as a major event in superpower relations now seemed almost irrelevant. On 19 August, the Americans' fears were realised when a group of communist hardliners seized control in Moscow, isolating Gorbachev at his vacation residence in the Crimea. Possibly the most dramatic event in the Soviet Union's history, it lasted just two days before foundering on the resistance of ordinary Muscovites, divisions in the army, and the vigorous reaction of Yeltsin. Beyond making clear to Yeltsin that he had his support, there was little Bush could do to influence the situation (Bush & Scowcroft, 1998).

The coup shattered the Communist Party, which was banned, and Gorbachev himself. The Baltic states seized their chance for independence. On 24 and 25 August, the Ukraine, and then Belarus, also voted for independence. When the Russian Supreme Soviet met on 23 August, it was clear that Yeltsin held the ascendancy over Gorbachev. Yeltsin, it soon appeared, had little interest in trying to breathe life into the Soviet Union. In all of this, the Americans were simply bystanders. Their worry was the future of the Soviet nuclear arsenal if, as seemed likely, Russia, Ukraine, Belarus and Kazakhstan, were to go their separate ways (Gates, 1996). On 21 December, all the former Soviet republics, except Georgia and the Baltic states, joined the Commonwealth of Independent States (CIS). Four days later, Gorbachev resigned as President of the Soviet Union, transferring control of the nuclear arsenal to Yeltsin as President of the Russian Federation. The Soviet Union was a historical memory.

Final Initiatives

The year 1992 was election year and conventional wisdom had it that with the Gulf War behind him Bush would secure a second term. Despite the political pressures, several developments did take place that year. Bush and Baker knew they had to use America's position of strength in the Middle East to work towards an Israeli–Palestinian peace settlement. Baker's diplomacy resulted in the opening of the Madrid Conference, under the joint auspices of Bush and Gorbachev, on 30 October 1991. It was noteworthy in that Syria and Lebanon were directly negotiating with Israel, and for the fact that the Israelis accepted a joint Jordanian–Palestinian delegation. The Shamir government's unwillingness to make concessions at Madrid provoked Bush into threatening to veto $10 billion in loan guarantees to Israel. The electoral success of Yitzhak Rabin and the Labour Party in June 1992 was partly the result of Israeli electorate's unease over relations with Washington. With Rabin pledged to work for a peace settlement, Bush placed the loan guarantees before Congress. Such pressure on Israel was a bold move to make in an election year, unusual for any president since Eisenhower (Fraser, 1995). Interest was also taken in the deteriorating situation in Bosnia, the result of the disintegration of Yugoslavia, and troops were sent to Somalia. In the case of the latter, where a combination of drought and the disintegration of central authority had produced famine, the judgement was that only the United States had the logistical strength to assist the United Nations to distribute the necessary aid. The administration tried to move ahead on strategic nuclear weapons by negotiating a START II treaty with Yeltsin's Russia. This was signed in January 1993, just as Bush was about to hand over power to his successful rival for the presidency, Bill Clinton (Bush & Scowcroft, 1998; Hurst, 1999). When Bush left office, Clinton inherited the world's only superpower. It remained to be seen what he would do with it.

11

CLINTON: WHY, THIS ISN'T
KANSAS: CONFRONTING A BRAVE
NEW WORLD

Today, a generation raised in the shadows of the cold war assumes new
responsibilities in a world warmed by the sunshine of freedom . . . .
Our hopes, our hearts and our hands are with those on every continent who are building democracy and freedom. Their cause is
America's cause.

Bill Clinton, Inaugural, 20 January 1993

At 46, William Jefferson Clinton was the second youngest
man elected president and the first of the 'baby-boomer'
generation touched not by the Second World War but by
Vietnam. Arguably the most controversial president of recent
times and certainly the most perplexing, Bill Clinton's
tenure was dogged by rumours followed by revelations of
scandal of the most salacious nature, culminating in
impeachment, making him the first elected president to
befall such a fate.

His slick election campaign, that combined the optimum
use of modern communications technology with an engaging and charismatic personality, secured him an election
victory of 44,909,326 popular votes to George Bush's
39,103,882 and an electoral college landslide of 370 to 168.
The Democrats now controlled the executive and legislative
branches of government. As president, Clinton displayed
political skills of the highest order (including, some would

say, those of his wife Hillary Rodham Clinton), which would ensure a presidency of two terms, the first Democratic one since Franklin D. Roosevelt.

Clinton came to the White House promising an end to the era of drift and deadlock resulting from a decade of Republican economic mismanagement that had produced the largest budget deficit ever seen and left the national economy weakened and in recession. His campaign pledge to 'get the country moving again' was summed up in a handwritten sign that had been tacked up in Clinton's campaign headquarters: '*Change vs. More of the Same; The economy, stupid; Don't forget health care*' (Stephanopoulos, 2000). Clinton outlined an aggressive dual strategy that focused on lifting the economy through increased public and private investment while at the same time cutting the Federal deficit by some $500 billion. He also targeted the high unemployment rate, promised health-care reform, tax increases for the wealthy and tax cuts for the middle class.

On foreign policy Clinton was less prescriptive, choosing to focus criticism on the Bush administration's coddling of 'dictators from Baghdad to Beijing', and its failure to respond positively to the opportunities offered by the disintegration of the Soviet Union (Dumbrell, 1997). It was this emphasis on 'new opportunities', as opposed to Bush's espousal of the status quo, that seemed to portend a new direction in international affairs. In suggesting that foreign and domestic policy were inseparable, Clinton hinted at a foreign policy driven by economic considerations designed to protect and advance America's primacy in the world. Added to this were commitments to pursue a new brand of liberal internationalism crafted to promote human rights and environmental issues, and a pledge to review the country's defence spending, while increasing military preparedness by developing rapid deployment capabilities and better intelligence. A few specific promises on Haiti (no forced repatriation of refugees), Bosnia (he would bomb the Serbs and lift the arms embargo) and Iraq completed his platform (Shawcross, 2001).

Clinton came to office at a unique time in American and world politics that witnessed changes that were totally inconceivable even a decade earlier. With the end of the Cold War less than a year before, he became the first post-Cold War president and leader of the world's only remaining superpower. Even in the short time between the collapse of the former Soviet Union and his election, the world had changed a great deal. The repercussions of these momentous events could scarcely be comprehended, let alone coolly analysed, not least because of the speed with which they had occurred. For 50 years the conflict between the two superpowers had dominated and dictated policy. Without the Cold War to define foreign and domestic politics in the United States, the country was immediately and without warning catapulted into a strange and unfamiliar New World that was, Clinton aptly noted, 'more free but less stable' (Drew, 1994). Alongside the complexities and uncertainties that accompanied this shift came new possibilities. Without the omnipresence of the Cold War, 'real issues' such as health care began to emerge as political objectives in their own right, rather than as problems viewed through the distorted lens of Cold War politics that had competed constantly for attention with foreign policy and national security issues. This sense of change and challenge was not restricted to domestic politics; America's role in the world was also up for redefinition as politicians and the public wrestled with the question of how and when America should become involved in problems far from her shores. Central to Clinton's strategy was the assumption that economics would replace politics as the dominant factor in international relations. In this he was wrong.

With less foreign policy experience than all his post-war predecessors save perhaps Harry S. Truman, Clinton was, arguably, poorly placed to meet the numerous and difficult crises that broke with unrelenting rapidity from the earliest days of his first term. His foreign policy team comprised, for the large part, officials who had cut their teeth during the

Carter administration. Passing over the weighty, senior figures such as Vance and Brzezinski, he chose instead their deputies and assistants such as Warren Christopher as Secretary of State, Anthony Lake as National Security Advisor and Madeline Albright, who was appointed Ambassador to the UN. Clinton's friend and Russia expert, Strobe Talbott, took on the role as Special Ambassador before becoming Deputy Secretary of State; Congressman Les Aspin became Clinton's first Defense Secretary before being replaced a year later by William Perry. James Woolsey was appointed Director of Central Intelligence and, in one of the few holdovers from the previous administration, Colin Powell briefly stayed on as Chairman of the Joint Chiefs of Staff. In addition, a keen commitment to national and international economic development demanded a strong economic team. This was led by Commerce Secretary Ron Brown, Trade Representative Mickey Kantor, and Robert Rubin, who headed the newly created National Economic Council (established to coordinate domestic and foreign economic policy) before taking over at Treasury and being replaced by Laura D'Andrea Tyson. The Christopher–Lake–Albright team brought two main shared assumptions about the character of the foreign policy to be pursued by the new administration. First, the US should conduct her international relations guided by a nobler goal than traditional geopolitical concerns. This implied, and supported, the use of force not limited to the pursuit of traditionally defined 'vital interests' but predicated on the desire to further moral principles. Secondly, unilateral action was replaced by a desire to secure both domestic and international support. It appeared as if 'the era of multilateral foreign policy and collective security, centered on the UN, had finally dawned' (Hyland, 1999). These general principles aside, Lake and Christopher, in particular, had quite different views about the substance of Clinton's foreign policy. Lake promoted a strategy of 'enlargement' based on democratisation and the expansion of market economies, whereas Christopher proposed a strategy of 'active engagement' that emphasised key geographic regions such as Russia, Western Europe, East Asia and the Middle East (Hyland,1999). These views, together with Albright's emphasis on collective security, were synthesised in Clinton's first comprehensive strategy document, *A National Security Strategy of Engagement and Enlargement*, released in July 1994. Although the basic tenets of this policy remained largely unchanged during Clinton's two terms in office, a new emphasis on the use of military force as a vital component of US foreign policy was added, together with numerous case-by-case presidential directives designed to respond to individual crises. Committed to promoting both a neo-Wilsonian agenda and economic liberalism on a global scale, the administration was attempting to pursue, as Talbott suggested, 'idealpolitik as well as realpolitik'. The difficulties involved, coupled with an almost schizophrenic movement between unilateral action and multilateralism, hinted at major problems on the horizon. Moreover, Clinton's decision to prioritise domestic affairs while allowing his foreign policy team to manage foreign matters, compounded the problem and frequently resulted in confusing contradictions, policy U-turns and charges of incompetence.

In 1996, Clinton ran a formidable election campaign that secured an impressive 379 electoral college votes to challenger Robert Dole's 159. It was a handsome win that testified to the resilience and indeed the ingenuity of the 'comeback kid'. In Clinton's second term, several key figures from the first remained in different roles, including Madeline Albright, who became the first woman to hold the office of Secretary of State when she replaced Christopher. Lake's deputy, Sandy Berger, became Clinton's National Security Advisor and, after bitter confirmation hearings, Lake, who had been chosen to head the CIA, withdrew, and was replaced by George Tenet. Finally, retiring Republican Senator William Cohen took over from Perry. Clinton's second term saw a wiser and stronger president, more understanding of both the limitations of power and his own ability to exercise it. The Republican-dominated Congress elected in 1994 (the first since 1952) certainly affected his foreign policy initiatives, but in his second term, Clinton strove hard to prevent their conservative agenda (deeply hostile to the UN and critical of international interventions) from dominating his programme. Inevitably, however, he was forced to move more to the right and, as a result, his foreign policy, increasingly divested of the neo-Wilsonianism that had underpinned his first term, revealed a much more pragmatic core.

Somalia

Operation Restore Hope marked the beginning of US intervention in Somalia. Here years of war and anarchy had created a legacy of famine and extreme political instability, heightened after 1991 by the civil war precipitated by the overthrow of Said Barre's brutal 22-year dictatorship. Largely in response to intense media pressure and because his advisers saw less chance of a quagmire developing in Africa as opposed to Bosnia, George Bush took the unprecedented step of involving the United States in her first humanitarian peacekeeping mission; he had received neither a local invitation nor the backing of congress (Shawcross, 2001). Airlifts of foodstuffs in August 1992 were followed by the arrival of some 28,000 American troops after the UN approved the establishment of 'a secure environment for humanitarian relief' in Somalia and approved military intervention. Mandated to guarantee access by aid workers, the multilateral military-backed food distribution effort succeeded in preventing mass starvation. In early 1993, Congress officially approved Bush's actions, and by June the mission had been scaled down to about 4,000 troops and placed under the command of the UN (Hyland, 1999). Although hailed in many quarters as a model of humanitarian intervention, concurrent increases in tribal warfare and spiralling crises manifested in the almost complete breakdown of law and order had compelled an expansion of the peacekeeper's role in Somalia. Unwilling and increasingly unable to effectively continue to address the symptoms of the problem, the UN Secretary-General, Boutros Boutros-Ghali, insisted on confronting its roots – chronic instability perpetuated by internecine warfare. In March 1993 the UN passed Resolution 814, which extended the humanitarian mission to include the rehabilitation and reconstruction of the country (Rubinstein, Shayevich & Zlotnikov, 2000). This policy of nation-building (virgin territory for the UN) was strongly supported by the new Clinton administration, which regarded it as a fitting implementation of the president's post-inaugural commitment to 'assertive multilateralism'.

The resultant 'mission creep' driven by UN demands that those responsible for perpetuating the crisis be arrested, tried and punished provoked little immediate anxiety and no high-level discussion in Washington. It was the targeting of one such figure – Mohammed Farah Aideed – that provided a sobering reminder of the grave dangers associated with such a strategy. The pursuit of Aideed saw US troops caught up in one of the bloodiest exchanges since the Vietnam War. On 3 October, a US Rangers/Delta Force team descended on the Olympic Hotel in Mogadishu, where intelligence reports suggested the Somali warlord was meeting with his advisers. Expecting minimal resistance, the team came under heavy attack in a 17-hour battle that left 18 American soldiers dead and 75 wounded. Aideed's evasion of captivity was embarrassing for both civilian and military leaders. The television images of a dead American Ranger being dragged through the streets of Mogadishu cheered by scores of Somalis proved unbearable. Faced with a firestorm in Congress in the aftermath of the failed raid, Clinton rejected calls for immediate withdrawal on the grounds that this would only add further damage to American prestige and worsen his relations with a military already deeply critical of attempts to force the controversial issue of gays in their ranks. Although he had been growing increasingly uncomfortable with his administration's strong commitment to nation-building, the president was reluctant to allow events in Mogadishu to force the US to 'cut and run' as Reagan had done in Lebanon. Instead, Clinton authorised a plan that sent 5,000 more troops to protect the mission in Somalia; drew up a timetable for the withdrawal of all US troops by March 1994, and approved the establishment of contact with Aideed. The following spring a peace agreement effectively returned him to power. American troops pulled out on schedule.

Rwanda: A Line in the Sand

Somalia was, according to Samuel Berger, 'the low point' of Clinton's eight years in office. It ensured that a reappraisal of peacekeeping operations resulted in a decision seriously to curtail future involvement. Presidential Decision Directive 25 (PDD 25), completed in May 1994, advocated extreme caution, selective and less costly intervention. Strongly reminiscent of the Weinberger–Powell (non-intervention) Doctrine, it reflected, in part, the administration's reluctance to regularly confront congress on this issue; moreover, it represented a complete reversal of Clinton's earlier commitment to 'assertive multilateralism' (MacKinnon, 2000). One of its first applications was in Rwanda.

One of the tragedies of the perceived failure of American intervention in Somalia was the deep reluctance to expose the US to a similar situation. Still reeling from the images of impotence and charges of disastrous mismanagement, the Clinton administration had little interest in involving American forces in the deepening crisis in the ethnically divided Central African country of Rwanda. Here a wave of carefully planned and sustained ethno-political violence beginning on 6 April eventually resulted in the murder of up to one million Tutsis and moderate Hutus. Although the slaughter rate was five times that achieved by the Nazis, the international community, preoccupied by the dimensions of the civil war in the country, recoiled from contemplating intervention (Melvern, 2000). They had a mandate – the 1948 Genocide Convention – established to prevent another Final Solution. What they lacked was the will. Not before early May did the UN describe the mass murder as genocide. The US government held out longer, labelling the killings as 'acts of genocide'. The administration's argument that America and the world could do nothing to halt the terrible bloodshed sounded both defeatist and brutally machiavellian. Tragically, investigations some months later concluded that a relatively small intervention force deployed during the first two weeks of the genocide could have saved up to half a million lives (Melvern, 2000). Political, military and financial considerations had taken precedence over the lives of hundreds of thousands of men, women and children butchered in the most appalling way. Although the horror of the Rwandan genocide did prompt Clinton to contribute several thousand US troops to take part in a multinational military force to deal with the refugee crisis in eastern Zaire, this did little to deflect criticisms of his handling of the catastrophe or his attempts to mitigate America's inactivity by speaking of genocide some 11 times during a visit to Kigali 4 years later (Halberstam, 2001). Nor did it point to a new-found commitment to Africa. Before his administration ended, an enormous refugee problem precipitated by events in Rwanda and neighbouring Burundi, and war in Zaire and Congo which eventually engulfed some 14 African countries, had caused death and destruction vastly more substantial than that experienced in Europe during the same period. It was a damning indictment of American and Western indifference towards the people and politics of the Dark Continent.

Haiti

The administration's early infatuation with assertive multi-lateralism saw the policy being applied to address problems in Haiti highlighted by Clinton during the presidential election campaign. Vowing to take a more aggressive stance, he had committed his government to reversing the 1991 military coup that had removed democratically elected President Jean-Bertrand Aristide and promised to grant refuge to the Haitians fleeing amidst the political terror. Once elected, the administration chose to continue the forced repatriation of the refugees, deciding instead that economic pressure (in the form of a complete embargo and the freezing of Haitian assets) would produce a more satisfactory result. The UN-brokered Governors Island Accord, which provided for the return of Aristide, paved the way for a relaxation of the embargo, raising hopes that the combined application of economic and diplomatic pressure and the threat of force had resolved the matter. Political assassinations and widespread terror proved within weeks that the Haitian military leader, General Raul Cedras, was less than committed to the peaceful handing over of power. The arrival in early October of UN personnel tasked with preparing for the implementation of the Governors Island Agreement led to angry protests, culminating on 11 October with a ship full of American and Canadian military personnel being prevented from docking by a violent mob in the Haitian capital Port-au-Prince shouting 'Somalia! Somalia!' (Shacochis,1999; Shawcross, 2001). Anxious not to invite more trouble in the aftermath of the Somali debacle, the administration ordered the *USS Harlan County* to return to Guantanamo Naval Base. With the agreement clearly in tatters, the UN responded by tightening the embargo and naval blockade and introducing sanctions. Coming as it did a mere week after the Somali debacle, Clinton's humiliation was profound. As veteran commentator David Halberstam noted, 'rarely had the United States looked so impotent, its mighty military driven away from a banana republic by a pip-squeak dictator and a hired mob' (Halberstam, 2001). By May 1994 a 'comprehensive review' of Clinton's Haiti policy produced a 'new emphasis' on the enforcement of sanctions. As for the mechanism by which America's stated aim of returning Aristide to power would be achieved, this was less evident. The administration was split between hawks such as Strobe Talbott, who favoured an invasion (authorised by the UN in early May), and Warren Christopher, who favoured more diplomacy. The debate continued until Clinton issued an ultimatum on 15 September warning the Haitian regime 'Your time is up. Leave now or we will force you from power' (Stephanopoulos, 2000). In a nod to his negotiation-minded advisers, he also approved a last-minute mission, headed by Jimmy Carter, designed to persuade Cedras to step down voluntarily. Against the backdrop of a firm invasion deadline, the talks succeeded, allowing the unopposed arrival of American troops and the restoration of Aristide. Chastened by Somalia, the Clinton administration quickly announced an exit strategy that outlined the reduction and eventual removal of the 20,000-strong US effort by April 1996.

Bosnia

The disappearance of the strong, centralised, authoritarian regimes characteristic of the Cold War left a vacuum in parts of Europe in which the long-suppressed sentiments of ethnic nationalism began to remerge more intensely, perhaps as a result of the speed with which they achieved their release. In the Balkans, the disintegration of the former Yugoslavia following the declaration of independence by four of its six constituent republics – Bosnia-Herzegovina, Slovenia, Croatia and Macedonia – prompted the rapid and violent ignition of these old hostilities and renewed fears of a wider conflagration involving NATO allies Greece and Turkey, as well as neighbouring Albania and Bulgaria and the traditional protector of the Slavs, Russia. Having initiated hostilities against Slovenia and Croatia, the Federal Republic of Yugoslavia (comprising the remaining two republics of Serbia and Montenegro) moved, in the spring of 1992, to annex Bosnia-Herzegovina in a bid to reconstruct a greater Serbia. The international response to this catastrophe which saw, in the years 1991 to 1995, the deaths of some 300,000 people was, according to Assistant Secretary of State Richard Holbrooke, 'at best uncertain and at worst appalling' (Holbrooke, 1999). Early recognition of the breakaway republics by members of the EU, led by Germany, and a reluctant United States, removed any lingering hope that the separation could be contained within a federal framework. Although unhappy with the mechanics of the European-led response, the Bush administration had little inclination to intervene.

Committed to a multi-ethnic, multi-religious, democratic Bosnia, the Clinton administration was less content to follow the plan devised by the European allies to resolve the Balkan war. Refusing to endorse the Vance–Owen plan that effectively partitioned Bosnia into three separate ethnically constituted Muslim, Croat and Serb states, because it rewarded Serbian aggression, Clinton chose instead in early February to propose an alternative. This involved the renegotiation of the Vance–Owen plan, the appointment of a new American special envoy, stronger sanctions, enforcement of a 'no-fly zone' and the establishment of an international war crimes tribunal. Unwilling to consider either bombing or military intervention, the strategy was crafted to buy the new administration some time. Unfortunately for Clinton, the situation on the ground was deteriorating too rapidly to allow him this luxury. Three months later the president changed tactics and put forward a plan around which some degree of consensus had emerged. The half-hearted 'Lift and Strike' proposal that Christopher tried to sell to the Europeans in May 1993 envisaged the removal of the UN arms embargo against Bosnia, combined with the threat of air strikes against Serbian forces. Unconvinced by the plan and concerned by Clinton's apparent lack of confidence in it (suggestions that he had put his presidency on the line and predictions of deeper escalation appeared to have weakened his resolve), the Allies had little difficulty in rejecting his efforts (Hyland, 1999). It was, for the new administration, an embarrassing condemnation of their attempt to assert leadership. Having acted hesitantly and with little comprehension of the procedural norms of great-power politics, Clinton, who looked weak and inexperienced, retreated, citing NATO Alliance unity rather than the war in Bosnia as America's main priority.

Later that month, working on the basis of an Anglo-French proposal, UN resolution 836 declared Sarajevo and other Muslim enclaves 'safe havens' under its protection. The situation worsened as the fragile Croat–Muslim alliance deteriorated and evidence of ethnic cleansing and mass murder became a sickening feature of the bloody conflict. Insecure and deeply divided about how to proceed, the administration procrastinated, keeping one eye on public opinion and the media and the other on Congress for some sense of direction. Official policy focused on preserving unity among the NATO allies. By the spring of 1995 the tide had apparently begun to turn in favour of intervention. Opinion polls suggested that the frequent atrocities had lessened resistance to the involvement of American troops. This was certainly welcome news for Clinton, who learned that a Serb victory would require the use of American troops to extricate the lightly armed UN forces from the region (Rubinstein, Shayevich & Zlotnikov, 2000; Shawcross, 2001). After nearly two years of vacillation the administration adopted a number of measures designed to mitigate the gains made by the Serbs, such as training the Croatian army and allowing weapons to reach both them and the Bosnian Muslims. The catalyst for action came when the Serbs brutally invaded and then ethnically cleansed the long-besieged UN-safe areas of Srebrenica and Zepa in the early summer, killing more than 6,000 Muslim males of military age. These attacks (which took place over a period of weeks) unfolded almost in slow motion as the West watched, impotent and derided by accusations of cowardice and betrayal. The Serbs' blatant disregard for the forces ranged against them, which was almost as shocking as the calculated and systematic way in which they realised their goals, provoked NATO into pledging to respond with massive air strikes in the event of further attacks on UN-protected areas. In Washington, Congress voted to lift the arms embargo. In August, the Croats launched an offensive that saw them retaking a sizeable part of Croatia (ethnically cleansing more than 250,000 Serbs from the region). A combination of the Croat advances, Congressional attempts to steer the course of American foreign policy, the outcry that accompanied the destruction of the UN 'safe havens' and Clinton's desire to make progress on Bosnia before the 1996 presidential election, prompted a major new initiative involving discussions with Russia and the European allies and intensive negotiations led by Holbrooke (Drew, 1996). As this mission got under way another attack, this time on a crowded marketplace in Sarajevo, galvanised NATO. Advancing a combined diplomacy and overt force approach, Clinton approved US involvement in Operation Deliberate Force, the largest bombing campaign in NATO's history, against Serbian positions and opened up negotiations with Yugoslavia's president Milosevic.

This was followed by peace talks hosted by America, the EU and Russia in Dayton, Ohio. On 21 November 1995, Holbrooke's efforts produced an agreement. The three main sides agreed that Bosnia would remain a single state with her present borders, as a federation comprising two 'entities' – a Bosnian Federation of Muslims and Croats (occupying 51 per cent of the territory) and a Serb Republic (holding the remaining 49 per cent). More than two years after the first suggestion that Bosnia be divided the country was, in fact, partitioned in kind. For the Bosnian Muslims, in particular, this was a substantially less favourable outcome than the arrangement proposed in the Vance–Owen plan, which gave the Serbs only 43 per cent. Bolstered by American assurances, they had rejected this deal only to find that their position had not improved. They felt betrayed.

Excluding UN involvement, Dayton provided for a NATO-dominated International Implementation Force (IFOR) made up of some 60,000 heavily armed troops, one-third of whom would be American. Conscious of the fact that public opposition to the deployment of US forces was running at about 70 per cent, Clinton announced that the American contribution would be a short-term commitment lasting not more than 18 months. 'It was', according to Holbrooke, 'the single most unpopular action of President Clinton's entire first term' (Holbrooke, 1999). Shortly after his re-election one year later, he suggested that deep divisions and tensions in the region demanded that the NATO force remain for some time longer. By late 1997, a less buoyant president admitted that it was impossible to predict an end to US involvement in Bosnia. The Dayton agreement had fashioned a fragile arrangement that showed few signs of blossoming into a more deep-rooted and permanent peace in the region. Although the conflict in the Balkans also placed an enormous strain on relations between Europe, the United States and Russia, defining new post-Cold War relationships that lacked much of the cohesion and warmth characteristic of the period past, Clinton's efforts, even if belated, seemed to presage a reinvigorated, more assertive American foreign policy.

Trade Expansion

The North American Free Trade Agreement (NAFTA) between the United States, Canada and Mexico had been negotiated and signed by Bush in 1992. A concept that had long been favoured by the United States, economic reforms in Mexico that had begun in the early 1980s had made the proposal a reality a decade later. Once signed, however, its passage was far from assured. The rocky road to ratification was strewn with numerous obstacles, including the intense politicking surrounding the 1992 presidential election, strong pressure-group interests and growing obduracy on the part of the legislative branch. Congressional intransigence centred on an unwillingness to permit presidential use of the 'fast-track' powers that had traditionally allowed him to negotiate a treaty in consultation with Congress rather than being faced with congressional disapproval and amendments after completion of the deal. Clinton supported the agreement (with a few adjustments to protect the environment and labour), believing that it 'advanced the interests of ordinary Americans more than it undermined them'. Once elected, his administration launched a formidable vote-gathering campaign that resulted in the ratification of the Agreement in the autumn of 1993. One of the more remarkable features of the outcome was the bipartisan nature of the vote; in fact, more Republicans than Democrats approved its passage. Given the poisonous atmosphere that dominated Executive–Legislative relations increasingly after the 1994 Republican victories in both houses of Congress, this became an isolated and anomalous example of political cooperation. Having facilitated the successful ratification of the Agreement, the administration began planning for its expansion. Although expert opinion held that NAFTA's contribution to the economic wealth of the country would be a modest one, the pitched battle that accompanied its ratification heightened expectations that would almost certainly come back to haunt the administration in the absence of future economic miracles. The clouds on the horizon began gathering sooner than many predicted. Having just overtaken Japan as the number two consumer of American exports, the Mexican currency crisis broke in December 1994 and threatened the country with economic implosion. Growing political stability now further exacerbated by economic turmoil abruptly cast doubt on the future of the Free Trade Agreement. The administration responded by putting together a rescue package amounting to $20 billion. Strong congressional disapproval of the president's handling of the Mexico crisis had implications for Clinton's unsuccessful efforts to gain new fast-track authority and frustrated his administration's attempts to negotiate the expansion of NAFTA and, in particular, the accession of Chile.

In another area of trade expansion, the successful completion of the Uruguay Round of GATT talks and the creation of the World Trade Organization (WTO) both reinforced Clinton's commitment to pursing a significant economic foreign policy agenda, and brought additional headaches to the administration when talks collapsed in Seattle in December 1999 amidst violent protests from groups opposed to the organisation (*New York Times*, 4 December 1999).

Asia

During the 1992 election campaign, Clinton aggressively attacked Bush's China policy, accusing him of putting trade ahead of human rights and democracy, and having turned a blind eye to China's export of missile components to Pakistan and North Korea. When he entered office, Clinton, pointing out that the US no longer needed to cultivate Beijing as a counterweight to Moscow, initially embarked upon a policy of linking improvements in China's human rights record to expanded trade with the US. In May 1993, the president sidestepped a major congressional assault on his decision to renew China's MNF status by making it conditional on progress on human rights. Christopher's criticisms before and during his March 1994 visit to China, where he found his hosts to be 'rough, somber, sometimes bordering on the insolent', symbolised the last serious effort by the administration to use the 'economic club' (Christopher, 2001). In May, after 15 months of no visible progress, Clinton announced that 'We are developing a broader engagement with the People's Republic of China that will encompass both our economic and strategic interests. That policy is best reflected in our decision to delink China's Most-Favoured-Nation status from its record on human rights.' This policy of engagement and enlargement was, however, complicated by strong congressional criticism of China and renewed tensions between China and Taiwan.

Clinton supported Taiwan's cause in international organisations such as the WTO and APEC and in June 1995 he reversed his earlier position and acceded to congressional pressure to allow the Taiwanese president, Lee Teng-hui, to visit the United States. What Taiwan read as a diplomatic breakthrough, China predictably regarded as a sign of bad faith. Tensions rose as China called off dialogues with the US and Taiwan, began conducting missile tests off her northern coast and warned that 'a Taiwan move toward de jure independence would lead to a PRC invasion of Taiwan and a protracted Cold War with the United States' (Rubinstein, Shayevich & Zlotnikov, 2000). Talk of independence from both front-runners in the Taiwan presidential elections prompted China to mount major military exercises (including missile tests over Taipei) in March 1996, further raising tensions in the region. Clinton responded by dispatching two aircraft carrier-task force groups before the re-election of President Lee, who quickly backed away from talk of independence, calmed Chinese fears and allowed the resumption of bilateral negotiations.

Elsewhere in Asia, a severe financial and economic crisis beginning in the autumn of 1997 overtook Thailand, Malaysia, the Philippines, South Korea and Japan. What the administration initially viewed as a temporary glitch in the international system rapidly developed into a global crisis, requiring a massive bail-out plan that eventually cost the

United States more than $100 billion. The Clinton team's inability to comprehend the gravity of the problem, combined with the tardiness of their response, contradicted a much-articulated commitment to Asian and, indeed, international economic growth and stability.

Increasingly unable to convince a Japan mired in recession to address the widening trade deficit, the administration, whose only significant victory in this ongoing argument came in June 1995 when Japan agreed to allow expanded US access to her car market, appeared more preoccupied with redefining a relationship with China. Clinton continued to advocate engagement, claiming that economic reform would beget political reform in China, a position underscored in 1998, by the administration's decision to drop the annual US-sponsored attempt to condemn China's human rights record in the UN. By the time of Clinton's visit to China in June 1998, his policy of 'constructive strategic partnership' found him supporting the very policy he had attacked in 1992, confronted by a Congress that had adopted the very same criticisms that he had made. This role reversal was complete. Relations, however, continued to be strained in 1999 by revelations of nuclear espionage, human rights abuses, a growing trade deficit, the Kosovo crisis and the accidental bombing of the Chinese embassy in Belgrade. In addition, the administration's failure to close a deal on WTO membership for China reinforced the myriad of problems besetting relations (*Foreign Affairs*, 78, 1999). In Clinton's last year in office, successful negotiations produced an agreement on WTO entry and the extension of permanent MNF status for China (giving the president his biggest legislative victory in the foreign policy arena since the passage of NAFTA) (*New York Times*, 20 September 2000). Although debates about the best strategy for engaging the Asian behemoth continued, some consensus, at least, had been reached. Clinton ended his Asian adventure on a positive note, heavy with symbolism. His three-day trip to Vietnam in November brought home the president-elect's promise in 1992 to put national and international economic development at the heart of his administration and made him the first US president to visit the country since the Vietnam War.

The Russian Federation and NATO Expansion

The foreign policy goals of the Clinton administration consistently focused on promoting economic improvement around the world. Underpinning the administration's policy towards Russia was a firm belief in the need to promote economic reform and political stability in order to prevent the destabilisation of the country. This required a delicate balancing act that involved encouraging reform and reformers, managing the perceived and real differences between the two glaringly unequal 'strategic partners', and supporting President Yeltsin as he struggled to head off challenges from the extremists emerging on all sides and at times appeared himself to be embracing a more hardline attitude. During the first US–Russian summit meeting in April 1993 the two leaders struck a deal that linked progress towards democracy to economic assistance, forging what Clinton termed 'a strategic alliance with Russian reform' (Hyland, 1999). Pursing a policy that closely linked this reform to Boris Yeltsin committed Clinton to supporting the Russian leader as he exercised an increasingly precarious hold on power. The first major test of this support came in late September 1993 when a two-week stand-off developed between Yeltsin and the Russian Congress (which had occupied the Parliament building and impeached the president) that ended only after the army took Yeltsin's part by attacking the 'rebels'. During the crisis Clinton remained supportive and publicly critical of anti-democratic forces in Russia. The subsequent elections for a new Parliament, however, produced something of a mixed bag: although the extremists won the majority of the popular vote (with the radical, right-wing party led by Vladimir Zhirinovsky polling a stunning 32 per cent of the vote) these events were somewhat obscured by the passage of a new constitution that formed the legal basis for a system of government comprising a strong president with a weakened Parliament. Three months later, Clinton met with a significantly stronger Yeltsin and reaffirmed America's commitment to Russia, saying, 'Our ability to put people first at home requires that we put Russia and its neighbors first on our agenda abroad' (Rubinstein, Shayevich & Zlotnikov, 2000).

The disintegration of the Soviet Union and the end of the Cold War raised difficult questions not only about how to construct a relationship with the new Russia, but about the nature of the very alliance that had faced off against the world's second superpower for almost 50 years – NATO. With its original rationale gone, the future of the organisation became hotly debated. Calls for enlarging the alliance and redefining its purpose largely drowned out those who suggested disbanding NATO or simply maintaining the status quo. Among the most committed advocates of change were the former central and eastern European countries and the Baltic states, which craved some measure of assurance now that they had moved out of the Soviet sphere. Of the two routes theoretically open to these newly emerging democracies, the economic path via membership of the EU appeared, at least in the short term, the most complex option, primarily because of the reluctance of core member states to admit quickly countries debilitated by crippling economic problems and political instability. Admission to NATO seemed both more doable and attractive to western governments, and in particular the United States. Clinton was motivated by a number of factors, including congressional and public interest-group concerns about the implications of failed democracy in Russia, pressure from the 10 countries wanting admission and calls for a redefinition of NATO's future from fellow members. Reluctant, however, according to Strobe Talbott, to 'draw a new line' between

East and West that suggested a band of 'neocontainment' extending to the border of Russia itself, the administration instead proposed a 'Partnership for Peace' (PFP). Announcing the plan in January 1994, Clinton remarked, 'With the Cold War over, we must confront the destabilising consequences of the unfreezing of history which the end of the Cold War has wrought. The best strategy against this threat is to integrate the former communist states into our fabric of liberal democracy, economic prosperity, and military operation.' This was an open-ended arrangement that invited prospective new members (including Russia and other republics from the former USSR) to meet a number of conditions such as respect for human rights, the consolidation of democratic institutions and a demonstrable commitment to sustaining economic reform, before being granted full entry.

Clinton's January summit meeting in Moscow produced renewed commitments from both sides to promote reform and democratisation and an announcement that from 30 May, Russian and American ICBMs would no longer be targeted against one another. Perhaps most significantly, however, Yeltsin (having told Christopher that the plan was 'a stroke of genius') reacted positively to the idea of NATO enlargement, suggesting that Russia might consider joining (Christopher, 2001). In June 1994, Russian Foreign Minister Andrei Kozyrev signed the PFP Framework Document in Brussels. Some months later the Clinton administration adopted a schedule for formal membership. By this time, Yeltsin, who was under pressure from hardliners, felt compelled to react angrily, warning delegates at the CSCE that Europe was in danger of plunging into a 'cold peace'. Despite this outburst, by the end of 1995 those participating in the PFP included all of the old Warsaw Pact countries, the former USSR (excluding Tajikistan), Finland, Sweden, Austria and Macedonia. By the end of Clinton's second term membership had grown to 26.

Russia's war with Chechnya (a province within the

Federation with aspirations of autonomy) did little to encourage American sympathy for Russian fears about the direction of NATO expansion. Certainly, by the time the two leaders met in Moscow to celebrate the fiftieth anniversary of the end of the Second World War in May 1995, relations had reached a new low. Unwilling to contemplate any action stronger than words, Clinton channelled his annoyance at the harsh and bloody war in Chechnya by strengthening his support for NATO enlargement. At the end of the year, the Communists had won a clear majority in the parliamentary elections. By early 1996, Clinton's Russia policy looked to be deeply in trouble. Indeed, the only bright spot came in June when policy-makers were relieved to find that Yeltsin did not resort to cancelling or indeed rigging the June presidential elections; the Russian leader's 'American-style' campaign, his adept handling of power politics and a timely ceasefire in Chechnya had all helped him retain his hold on power.

Meanwhile, in a skilful political move aimed both at capturing eastern European-Americans' votes and mitigating congressional pressure, Clinton announced in the last weeks of the presidential election campaign that the first round of NATO enlargement would take place by 1999. Although the president had failed to consult either Congress or indeed his European allies, NATO approval came less than two months later (Rubinstein, Shayevich & Zlotnikov, 2000). By this time relations between the US and Russia had improved to the extent that Secretary of State Madeline Albright was claiming that they were 'on the same side'. The Russian—NATO Founding Act was signed in Paris in May 1997, which essentially gave Russia 'a voice but not a veto' in the Alliance's affairs. In early July, agreement was reached on formally inviting Poland, the Czech Republic and Hungary to join NATO.

Congress ratified NATO expansion in the spring of 1998, amidst growing economic and political turmoil in Russia that saw Yeltsin fire his entire Cabinet twice before appointing the conservative Yevgeny Primakov in a move widely interpreted as indicative of his growing weakness. In March 1999, Hungary, the Czech Republic and Poland joined NATO. The surprise departure of Yeltsin from the political scene in December 1999 and his replacement by the unknown former KGB man, Vladimir Putin, provoked no significant change in Clinton's Russia policy, which continued to promote the concept of 'cooperative engagement' (I. Sigov, *The World Today*, April 2001). The souring of relations over Kosovo, a second war in Chechnya and Putin's predilection for a more hardline approach, combined with the deepening economic problems crippling the country (the Russian budget in 2000 was slightly larger than that of Illinois), growing regionalism and political fragmentation, ensured close monitoring of the unstable region until the end of Clinton's term (S. Nunn & A. N. Stulberg, *Foreign Affairs*, March/April 2000).

Weapons of Mass Destruction

Aside from attempting to promote democratisation and economic reform in Russia, the Clinton administration had a second goal relating to weapons of mass destruction (WMD). This involved dismantling the Soviet military machine and nuclear arsenal by persuading the former Soviet states of Belarus, Kazakhstan and Ukraine to give up their nuclear weapons, thus preventing 'vertical' nuclear proliferation in Russia and 'horizontal' proliferation elsewhere. This was complemented by a wider aim of meeting the threat posed by chemical, biological and bacteriological weapons.

Much of the groundwork had been done by Bush, whose assistance to the three former Soviet states meant that Russia alone possessed a nuclear capability, and although much of her stockpile remained vulnerable, recent fears of mass proliferation resulting from the break-up of the Soviet Union proved to be exaggerated. Nuclear proliferation was, however, still a major concern. The 1970 Non-Proliferation Treaty (NPT, eventually signed in 1992 by a reluctant China and France) had heralded, at least in theory, a period of nuclear non-dissemination. As it approached the end of its 25-year lifespan, the Treaty appeared to be under some threat by the actions of countries such as North Korea, India and Pakistan.

North Korea had signed the NPT in 1985 and, by the early 1990s, appeared to be attempting to re-enter the international community. In 1991 the two Koreas signed a non-aggression accord and the following year, after the US withdrew her nuclear forces from the South, North Korea permitted international inspection of her nuclear facilities. Somewhat shaken by the rapid disintegration of the Cold War world, North Korea, had, by 1993, reversed this earlier decision to cooperate, refusing to entertain inspection teams, tested her first nuclear-capable missile and was threatening to pull out of the NPT (which she did in 1994). The American response was to propose economic sanctions while mounting a large-scale military build-up in East Asia. A 'private' intervention in June 1994 by former president Jimmy Carter produced a tension-defusing agreement that permitted the restoration of inspections. Further negotiations after the death of Kim Il Sung in July produced a more permanent agreement. Under the terms of the Agreed Framework signed in October 1994, North Korea agreed to dismantle weapons-grade plutonium-producing nuclear reactors in exchange for light-water reactors (built by the US and largely financed by Japan and South Korea) for the production of nuclear energy for civilian purposes. Follow-up negotiations aimed at neutralising the country's missile threat ended in late 2000 without agreement (*New York Times*, 6 March 2001).

The NPT was renewed indefinitely in 1995 by a unanimous vote after the 174 signatories, upset by the tests conducted by China and France, obtained an agreement from all the nuclear powers to negotiate a Comprehensive

Test-Ban Treaty. Although Clinton signed the Treaty, ratification proved elusive and hampered the administration's efforts to persuade other countries such as India and Pakistan, who both tested nuclear weapons in 1998.

Another rogue state with worrying tendencies towards developing weapons of mass destruction was Iraq. After years of hostility towards UNSCOM inspectors, Saddam Hussein declared once again in February 1998 that 'presidential sites' and 'sensitive areas' were off limits. The immediate crisis that this provoked was defused by an agreement brokered by UN Secretary-General Kofi Annan that allowed for more limited inspections (D. Byman, *Foreign Affairs*, January/February 2000). By the end of the year, however, continued non-cooperation provoked an Anglo-American assault, codenamed Desert Fox, aimed at destroying Iraq's weapons of mass destruction and the ability to threaten neighbouring countries. Buoyed by French, Chinese and Russian dissent in the Security Council, Saddam Hussein refused to allow the return of the UNSCOM teams (Shawcross, 2001). Lacking international consensus and will, Clinton found it virtually impossible to construct an agreed policy for dealing with Iraq. It was a frustrating anticlimax to five years of efforts to force Iraq to comply with the terms agreed to at the end of the Gulf War, and represented the coming of Clinton's policy full circle. At the beginning of April 1993, the administration reacted to a plot to assassinate President Bush by launching military strikes against Iraq. Relations continued to deteriorate as Saddam Hussein turned non-compliance into an art form, periodically provoking crises with the West by threatening to reinvade Kuwait (October 1993), taking action against Iraqi minorities (the northern Kurds in August 1996), and regularly refusing to allow UNSCOM inspectors to operate unhindered. The unsuccessful military action against Saddam Hussein in 1998 confirmed what many policy-makers had struggled with since 1991 – attempts to contain and coerce the Iraqi leadership had produced few (if any) tangible results. The absence of the United Nations inspection teams at the end of Clinton's second term testified to the impotence of this policy, strengthened anti-UN elements in Congress and pointed to problems ahead. Indeed, Iraq's behaviour served as a reminder that so-called 'rogue states' or 'states of concern', as they were renamed in 2000, could not easily be controlled. And, while American ratification of the Chemical Weapons Agreement in 1997 had demonstrated a important step towards reducing the threat posed by these weapons of mass destruction, the threat remained very much alive.

This sense of vulnerability was magnified by the onset of a series of terrorist attacks that punctuated Clinton's eight years in office. Less than five weeks after his inauguration a truck bomb exploded in the garage of the World Trade Center in New York, killing six people, Sheik Abdel-Rahman, the man thought to have planned the destruction of the twin towers and the deadly cyanide attack to have accompanied it, was linked both to CIA operations in Afghanistan, and Osama bin Laden, a veteran of the war against the Soviet Union and founder of the Al Qaeda terrorist organisation. The 1995 and 1996 strikes against US military facilities in Saudi Arabia were followed two years later by the bombing of the American embassies in Kenya and Tanzania. In October 2000 another suicide attack almost sank the *USS Cole* anchored off Yemen. American intelligence linked the assaults to Al Qaeda, which, it was thought, was seeking and possibly had chemical, biological and nuclear capabilities (*New York Times*, 22 January 1999). But even without these weapons of mass destruction, they prophetically warned, highly organised terrorists could inflict tremendous harm simply by hijacking and flying passenger planes into buildings. Moreover, cyber-terrorism, which threatened mass disruption rather than mass destruction, was regarded as extremely probable. This information prompted Clinton to seek more than $10 billion to improve America's defences against the dangers outlined by the intelligence services.

Finally, mindful of the spectre of bin Laden, the president signed a 'lethal finding' which effectively authorised the CIA to eliminate bin Laden (*Newsweek*, 1 October 2001). Although there is no reason to suspect that the agency and others did not endeavour to neutralise what had, by the end of Clinton's presidency, become one of the gravest national security concerns of the administration, as later tragedy would show, they did not succeed.

Kosovo

Identified at the beginning of the 1990s as a conflict epicentre, Kosovo, though ominously quiet during the Bosnian war, was, by the mid-1990s, showing signs of destabilising. Policymakers now familiar with the divisive ethnic, religious and political fault lines criss-crossing the region recognised that a number of fundamental differences between the war just ended and a future conflict in Kosovo presented a much more complex problem than that posed by Bosnia. Significantly, when NATO went to war in 1995 it was to preserve the territorial sovereignty of an independent state. Although distinct in ethnic, cultural and historic terms, Kosovo was, however, officially regarded as part of Serbia. Moreover, the Kosovar Albanians comprised some 90 per cent of the population. Finally, having rescinded the province's autonomy in 1989, Slobodan Milosevic had built a large part of his political reputation and, indeed, career on promoting Serbian nationalism and defending the small Serb minority in the region. The stakes were undeniably higher in Kosovo.

In his last weeks of his presidency, Bush had warned Milosevic not to abuse the human rights of the Albanians in Kosovo. Once elected, Clinton reaffirmed this message. By 1997 a marked deterioration was apparent. Now considerably more heavily armed with weapons acquired during the collapse of the Albanian government, the Kosovo Liberation

Army (KLA) posed a much more serious threat to both Belgrade and the Kosovar Albanians' main political leader, Ibrahim Rugrova (Glenny, 1999). In early 1998, Milosevic began to move against Kosovo. The timing could not have been more unfortunate for an administration deeply distracted by the breaking Monica Lewinsky affair. By the spring, Washington had ruled out unilateral military action, suggesting that a strategy for Kosovo had to be fashioned in concert with NATO. The presence of 20,000 US troops in Bosnia compelled restraint. Although some senior officials like Albright openly supported military intervention, others, including National Security Advisor, Sandy Berger, cautioned against making threats that would imply a military response if ignored. Early attempts to facilitate talks between the Belgrade government and Rugova ended in failure.

In September, after more massacres, NATO approved air strikes but a lack of enthusiasm for bombing in the US (the congressional midterm elections loomed and impeachment proceeding were ongoing) resulted in a mission undertaken by Richard Holbrooke to broker a ceasefire deal that would arrest the crisis and allow the return of the 300,000 Kosovar civilians who had fled their homes. Belgrade agreed to a partial withdrawal of Serb forces and the presence of Organization for Security and Cooperation in Europe (OSCE) observers to monitor the situation. Within weeks the situation began to fall apart as evidence mounted that the Serbs were preparing for a military operation to expel hundreds of thousands of Albanians from Kosovo. In January, OSCE observers arrived at the village of Racak where they saw evidence of mass murder. Rather than pursuing a retaliatory bombing response against a backdrop of questionable alliance unity, a plan for a negotiated political settlement backed by the renewed threat of force and supported by the UN Secretary-General was hatched. The talks held at Rambouillet produced no settlement and were, according to Albright, one of the worst experiences of her career. With an end to the intense political crisis in

Washington that accompanied Clinton's impeachment and subsequent acquittal by the Senate in February, the administration redoubled its efforts to formulate a consensus for forward action against Belgrade. A second round of peace talks in Paris produced an agreement signed only by the KLA. The refusal of the Serbs to sign paved the way for the air strikes, which began on 24 March after one last-ditch diplomatic effort led by Holbrooke.

NATO's decision to engage in military action without the explicit approval of the UN Security Council provoked strong criticism from China and Russia. Operation Allied Force's war aims at the commencement of the 78-day offensive reflected a less than homogenous allied coalition. These were described variously as being designed to force Milosevic to the negotiating table; prevent a humanitarian catastrophe; to degrade and destroy the Yugoslav army; to weaken Milosevic's grip on power; and to stop the spreading of the conflict beyond Kosovo (Glenny, 1999)). Moreover, Clinton's unfortunate assertion prior to the commencement of military action that ground troops would not be used removed a considerable threat and allowed Milosevic to implement a programme of systematic ethnic cleansing that forced hundreds of thousands of refugees into Albania, Macedonia and Montenegro. The flood of 'biblical proportions' that accompanied the NATO bombing threatened to further destabilise the region as the unwilling host countries struggled to come to terms with the massive demographic changes occurring overnight (Glenny, 1999). The human rights abuses perpetuated by Milosevic against his own citizens were judged unlikely by him to provoke military intervention by the West. While his actions were morally reprehensible, unlike in Bosnia and Croatia, he had violated no rules of territorial sovereignty. In a radical and unprecedented development the West chose to invoke a humanitarian rationale for unleashing military action against a sovereign state. This was truly a departure from the accepted morality of the Cold War when human rights, apart from the rhetoric of the Carter administration, never took precedence over power politics (Glenny, 1999). At one level this was the manifestation of perhaps an almost subconscious search for a post-Cold War role for the United States/ NATO/UN, made necessary by the absence of any clear focus or justification. On another level, it represented the emergence, or perhaps more accurately the revival, of a humanitarianism provoked at best by altruism and at worst by vested interests. For Clinton, it was a foreign policy success that saw his approval rating boosted to 60 per cent.

Although Russia had withdrawn from the Permanent Joint Council (a forum for NATO–Russian consultation) and suspended cooperation with NATO in March after the Alliance bombing began, these ties were re-established after Yeltsin helped to broker an agreement to end the air campaign. Moreover, Russian participation in the Kosovo peacekeeping force (KFOR), after a tense couple of weeks that saw Russian troops moving into the region ahead of the main force, demonstrated a degree of international unity welcomed by the United States. In the last year of the twentieth century, Russian and American troops had joined over thirty countries engaged in peacekeeping activities in the Balkans.

In a largely unanticipated but widely welcomed postscript to the Kosovo story, on 6 October 2000, following Milosevic's refusal to acknowledge the results of the Yugoslav elections, protesters seized the Parliament in Belgrade demanding that he comply with the democratic process. After a tense stand-off, Milosevic conceded, allowing Vojislav Kostunica to assume the presidency. Offering words of support but promising no military action, Clinton and the West played a passive role in the peaceful revolt.

The Middle East

In the Middle East, Clinton was fortunate on two counts: first, he inherited a more promising situation than perhaps all of his predecessors; second, the Israeli Labor Party led by Yitzhak Rabin had won power in June 1992. Both Rabin and his Foreign Minister, Shimon Peres, were committed to the concept of land for peace and determined to move the faltering peace process forward. The first major development to take place had no American involvement and arose out of highly secret meetings between Israeli and PLO officials in Norway. These negotiations produced the Oslo Accords. While the United States' help was clearly not required to make the historic breakthrough, American prestige and financial support were needed to facilitate the implementation of the agreement. Thus in a dramatic signing ceremony on the White House lawn on 13 September 1993, Rabin and Arafat shook hands awkwardly, with Clinton hovering closely behind. The president had never seemed so presidential. It was a euphoric moment that prompted Christopher to remark that 'anything, *everything*, seemed possible' (Christopher, 2001).

The content of the Accords signalled a new attempt to reach a lasting agreement by setting out plans for cooperation over a five-year 'interim' period. During this time, Israel would withdraw from Gaza and Jericho, transferring authority to a Civil Administration of Palestinians. In return for a degree of immediate self-rule and the promise of negotiations to make these arrangements permanent, the PLO recognised the existence of the State of Israel. The following year, after reaching agreement in Washington, Jordan and Israel signed a formal peace treaty on 26 October in a ceremony at the Israeli–Jordanian border. Much of Clinton's diplomacy involved offering incentives to encourage the engaged parties to make concessions. For the Palestinians this included financial aid and promise to put pressure on the Israelis to implement the Oslo Accords as rapidly as possible. Economic carrots also featured strongly in the package held out to Israel – a $3 billion a year foreign-aid package, assistance to defray the cost of troop redeployment and access to advanced weapons such as the F-15E aircraft.

Indeed, after the Jordan–Israel agreement this also included the prospect of US troops serving in a peacekeeping capacity in the Golan Heights, should Israel and Syria achieve a similar breakthrough (Rubinstein, Shayevich & Zlotnikov, 2000). By 1995, however, the promising political developments began to unravel as the militants of Hamas and Islamic Jihad stepped up their activities in a series of attacks targeting Israeli military personnel and civilians. On 4 November the peace process was dealt another devastating blow when Rabin was assassinated by an Israeli extremist. In the new elections that followed in May 1996, Shimon Peres narrowly lost out to challenger Benjamin Netanyahu, the leader of the Likud Party.

As Netanyahu was regarded as a hardline conservative, his election promised a new Israeli approach to making peace. Netanyahu was not a man with whom Clinton could easily do business. Talks in Washington in October hosted by the president produced no visible movement until months later, when American pressure and new assurances that America was committed to meeting Israel's security needs resulted in an agreement on the implementation of Israeli withdrawal from Hebron. Having secured a significant mandate in the 1996 presidential election, Clinton turned his attention once more to the Middle East. By the summer of 1997 calls by influential figures like Henry Kissinger for movement towards negotiating a final settlement reintroduced the idea of accelerated talks. Meeting in Washington in January 1998, Clinton presented Netanyahu with a detailed plan for a phased withdrawal from the West Bank, linked to the beginning of final-status talks. This was a compromise between the Israeli desire to avoid further damaging piecemeal concessions and the Oslo process that required small, incremental steps to construct a solid peace process (Hyland, 1999). The initiative, however, soon stalled when both sides refused to agree on crucial details such as the phased withdrawals. At a meeting in London in early May, Albright proposed a summit meeting in Washington conditional upon Netanyahu's acceptance of the American plan (Arafat had endorsed it when it became clear that the Israeli prime minister was opposed). Netanyahu's refusal to participate in the Washington talks was predictable and highlighted what now appeared to be a new American policy of intervening in rather than facilitating the peace process. Faced with domestic pressure and congressional attacks that accused his administration of reneging on an earlier commitment to Israeli security, Clinton, through Albright, patched up differences with Netanyahu.

After months of difficult discussions the administration succeeded in bringing Arafat and Netanyahu together in October at the Wye River Conference Center in Maryland. The basis of the agreement reached was 'land for security' and committed Israel to returning an additional 13 per cent of West Bank territory to the Palestinian Authority, the release of 750 Palestinians from detention and allowing the opening of the Gaza International Airport. In return, the Palestinian Authority promised to outlaw and combat terrorist organisations, prohibit illegal weapons and all forms of incitement to violence and remove the anti-Israeli provisions of the Palestinian National Charter. Clearly, two potential hostages to fortune existed: first, Arafat had to be able to control the Palestinian extremists; second, the agreement made no attempt to tackle the most fundamental and intractable issues such as the status of Jerusalem, Jewish settlements in the West Bank and Gaza, the refugees, water resources and the final boundaries (Rubinstein, Shayevich & Zlotnikov, 2000). On 13 December, Clinton arrived on a three-day visit to set his seal on the agreement. After the collapse of his coalition in early 1999, Netanyahu was forced to call an election in May which he subsequently lost to the new Labor leader Ehud Barak, a highly decorated war hero and former Chief of Staff. Barak gained 56 per cent of the electoral vote and a more secure mandate than any recent Israeli leader to pursue the peace process vigorously. Within four months he had visited Egypt and Jordan, met with

Arafat, opened discussions with Syria, had extensive meetings with Clinton in Washington and promised to withdraw Israeli forces from southern Lebanon. Talks at Camp David in July came tantalisingly close to setting the terms for an overall settlement, but not even Clinton's mediating skills could close the final gaps between Barak and Arafat. In September, renewed negotiations presided over by Albright resulted in an agreement to reach final borders and a settlement for Jerusalem in a year. Talks continued throughout 2000 against a familiar backdrop of violence and crisis. This took on a new dimension at the end of September when the visit by right-wing Likud Party leader Ariel Sharon to the most contested site in Jerusalem, the Temple Mount to the Jews, but the Haram ash-Sharif (the Noble Sanctuary) to the Muslims, triggered a riot that spiralled into widespread violence. Israel appeared to have been transported back to the darkest days of the history of the state. American efforts to reignite the peace process were drowned out amidst the harsh Israeli crackdown and scenes of death and destruction. Over the next 12 months 800 Palestinians and 200 Israelis were killed. Try as they might, the outgoing administration made no progress on achieving a final settlement. Perhaps this illusory prize had never been within his grasp, but Clinton understandably felt that he had been close. It was a deeply personal and political disappointment for the president, one mitigated only by the knowledge that his efforts had helped produce an intact settlement in another part of the world – Northern Ireland.

Northern Ireland

Since 1969, Northern Ireland had been one of Europe's most intractable problems, with a low-level, but vicious conflict, as Protestant unionists held to their British allegiance, while Catholic nationalists looked to a united Ireland. If most of the population despised violence, armed groups on each side had engaged in a campaign which left over 3,000 dead. In deference to their British allies, previous administrations had held back from overt involvement. Clinton felt differently. He visited Northern Ireland three times during his two terms in office, making him the first sitting American president to visit the province. Having committed himself to a measure of involvement during the 1992 presidential election, Clinton joined in the political manoeuvrings by controversially granting a visa to Gerry Adams, the leader of the Republican Party, Sinn Fein, despite intense pressure from within his government. His gamble that the gesture would produce a breakthrough in the peace process proved astute and helped, according to Adams, to create the conditions for the IRA ceasefire that was announced on 31 August 1994 (Wilson, 1995). Spurred by the visa success, the administration remained engaged in Northern Ireland. Clinton's commitment was reinforced by his appointment of retiring Senator George Mitchell, former Speaker of the House, as his special envoy. Initially charged with coordinating economic initiatives, Mitchell quickly took on a more central role as both Chairman of the Arms Decommissioning body and later, Chairman of the political talks set up to determine the political future of Northern Ireland.

After two years of intense debate and discussion, these talks produced the 'Good Friday' Agreement on 10 April 1998, which contained a framework for devolved government with power-sharing between the two communities and mechanisms for cooperation between the two parts of Ireland. On 1 December 1999, after a review of the Agreement also chaired by Mitchell, this was finally implemented. Unlike much of his foreign policy, the president's policy and commitment to Northern Ireland remained thoughtful and constant; although often intangible, the US dimension encouraged, massaged, supported and pressured the politicians involved. Significantly, the president succeeded in winning over a large section of unionism, hitherto deeply suspicious of American involvement because of the assumed partiality of Irish-Americans to the nationalist side. Moreover, Clinton's timely visits provoked a groundswell of goodwill from the war-weary people of Northern Ireland. Of course, involvement did not necessitate ground troops or large financial rescue packages and, apart from staking his personal and political prestige on a positive outcome, Clinton risked little by committing himself to the pursuit of peace. Nevertheless, his efforts and those of his staff played a significant role. His satisfaction was both a personal and a political one. Describing the events in Northern Ireland as 'the first true conflict resolution', it encouraged Clinton to hope that similar successes could be made in other troubled parts of the world. Sadly, this triumph was not to be repeated. At the end of his presidency, Northern Ireland was the only peace process that had not unravelled on Clinton.

12

BUSH: A BAPTISM OF FIRE

The enemies of liberty and our country should make no mistake:
America remains engaged in the world by history and by choice,
shaping a balance of power that favors freedom. We will defend our
allies and our interests. We will show purpose without arrogance.
We will meet aggression and bad faith with resolve and strength.
And to all nations, we will speak for the values that gave our nation
birth.

George W. Bush, Inaugural, 20 January 2001

The divisive 2000 presidential election campaign and its
controversial denouement provided an apt metaphor for
America at the dawn of a new millennium – prosperous and
powerful, adrift, insecure and apathetic; divided about the
past and uncertain about the future. After months of tedious
and often policy-challenged campaigning, the outcome ultimately turned on the candidate perceived least negatively by
the largely unmoved electorate (and several thousand
ballots in Florida). Calling the election first for Gore, the
high-tech media which has, over the last several decades,
become such an integral part of the whole affair, retracted
and named Bush the winner. Finally, after announcing that
this too could not be confirmed, they settled on a 'wait and
see' policy. Hours turned into days and days into weeks as
the lawyers, and, finally, the Supreme Court battled over
voting procedures, counts and ballots. By the time George
W. Bush emerged as the forty-third president of the United
States, exhausted, and not just a little embarrassed, America
breathed a sigh of relief. For the majority of the voting

294

public, Bush may not have been the preferred candidate, but he was the product of a democratic system that had worked in the end, albeit imperfectly. It may not have been pretty, but America proved to the insouciant world that her democratic process was intact.

His commitment to a deeply conservative domestic agenda that included the largest tax cut since the Reagan era compelled Bush to devote his immediate attention to reconstructing a new Republican consensus to replace the traditional cohesion swept away by the end of the Cold War (*New York Times*, 7 May 2001). Perhaps the most positive comment made about Bush's foreign policy instincts was the fact that the man who had been abroad three times in his adult life had the good sense to choose a highly impressive team of experts, all of whom had played significant roles in previous (mainly) Republican administrations. His running mate, Vice-President Dick Cheney, had served as his father's Secretary of Defense. Donald Rumsfeld returned to the Pentagon for a second time as Secretary of Defense and Colin Powell became the first black Secretary of State. Finally, the key position of National Security Advisor went to another former Bush Sr staffer, Condoleezza Rice – the first female to occupy the post. In as much as Bush considered the foreign policy issues facing his administration, it was the rather abstract concern about the country's 'Ugly American' image abroad that seemed to shape the president-elect's outlook (*New York Times*, 18 February 2001). Electoral pledges to withdraw from the Balkans and the development of a National Missile Defense system were among the few policies commonly articulated. Beyond that, what had emerged during the campaign for the White House was a strong indication that under Bush the United States would pursue a much more limited engagement with the rest of the world.

Bush's first 100 days were characterised less by the emergence of a clearly-defined set of policies and more by its anti-Clintonism. His predecessor's engagement with North

Korea, involvement in the Balkans and policies towards Iraq, China, Russia and the Middle East were all unceremoniously rejected, as were a number of international agreements such as the Kyoto Accords. This was hardly surprising given what was ostensibly, at least, a vast political, personal and ideological gulf between the two men. However, in its articulation of Bush's foreign policy the administration made little effort to soften the blows being meted out during this early honeymoon period, prompting the Europeans, in particular, to feel justifiably unnerved by the new president's apparent propensity for unapologetic unilateralism.

By the time Bush made his first major international trip to Europe in June, however, the administration had begun backing away from many of the policy positions articulated in the preceding months (*New York Times*, 18 June 2001). The capture by China of the American spy plane at the beginning of April had been a turning point for the administration and its commander-in-chief, whose instinctive bellicosity quickly gave way to the low-key diplomacy that secured the release of the American military personnel involved. Powell's handling of the crisis strengthened his position, and rescued the Secretary of State from the sidelines where he had been languishing since the rather Clintonesque platform outlined at his confirmation had left him glaringly out of step with some of his colleagues (*Newsweek*, 1 January 2001). Now, his views appeared to be on the ascendant. On Iraq, the policy of recasting the UN sanctions to focus more specifically on military items was adopted. The previously derided Clinton team talks with North Korea were reinstated and the administration's position on the Kyoto protocol was restated to include a commitment to fashion a more amenable treaty. Moreover, far from withdrawing from the Balkans, the American forces, Powell announced, had arrived with her allies and would leave with them (*New York Times*, 27 March 2001). Indeed, a small token force of 200 joined Operation

Essential Harvest, whose job it was to disarm Albanian soldiers in Macedonia. On other issues such as missile defence the administration tempered its approach. A concerted effort was made to allay Russian fears about the proposed shield and the expansion of NATO, another subject which inspired hostility. The Bush team also sought to reintroduce the notion of strategic ambiguity with respect to Taiwan (earlier removed by Bush, who had pledged to defend China's *bête noire* against any attack) and restricted a controversial arms sale to the island. Finally, after observing from afar the steady disintegration of relations between Israel and the Palestinians, Bush sent CIA Director George Tenet to broker a ceasefire in the Middle East.

Although described by the administration as better policy articulation rather than a series of perhaps nuanced U-turns, Bush's foreign affairs agenda bore not just a little resemblance to the highly criticised moves made by his predecessor. Still undeniably central to its world-view, the unilateralism that fuelled the administration's foreign policy plans had become a less blatant and more suppressed feature of American foreign policy.

11 September

On 11 September 2001 two hijacked airliners were flown into the World Trade Center, whose massive twin towers collapsed more than an hour after the impacts. A third hijacked plane hurtled into the Pentagon. A fourth, possibly bound for Washington, DC, crashed in Pennsylvania, apparently forced away from its target by a group of passengers who attempted to overpower the hijackers. More than 3,900 Americans and nationals from dozens of other countries were killed. Destroyed, too, was America's sense of invulnerability. Speculation that Osama bin Laden was behind the atrocity quickly gained credence. Within days, the US government confirmed that they had enough evidence to support this theory.

As America and the world struggled to absorb the unprecedented enormity of the attacks the president began a controversial flight across the country, before returning almost eight hours later to Washington, just in time to salvage his presidency. Faced with the most devastating attack in America's history, the president struggled to find a voice. Initially eclipsed by the commanding Mayor of New York, Rudolph Giuliani, and the charismatic Powell, Bush's unscripted reaction included a grating description of the perpetrators of the horror as 'folks'.

But rather than alienate the American public, Bush's awkward, ineloquent and very public struggle to articulate his feelings endeared him to them. Then, in simple terms and with undeniable emotion, the president began outlining how the United States would cope with this disaster, vowing that he would 'hunt down and punish those responsible for these cowardly acts'. To the surprise of some, the administration rejected any suggestion of immediate retaliation. For any number of reasons this was never really an option anyway. Nevertheless, the period of just under four weeks which elapsed between the attacks and America's reprisal allowed the administration to construct a unique coalition. When the war against Osama bin Laden and his Taliban hosts in Afghanistan came it was backed by a multinational force which included the UN, NATO, the European Union, the OAS, and the Organization of Islamic States. Never an easy alliance to maintain, Operation Enduring Freedom weathered five weeks of war in Afghanistan and remained intact. By late November, the Taliban had been driven out of all but a few remaining parts of the country and talks had begun to form a new representative government for Afghanistan. The undisputed target of America's efforts, however, remained frustratingly elusive. An interim government for Afghanistan headed by Hamid Karzai came into being on 22 December.

Conclusion

The aftermath of '11 September', and the ongoing campaign in Afghanistan, formed the context of Bush's first State of the Union Address delivered before Congress, and in the presence of Hamid Karzai, on 29 January 2002. Few such addresses have been listened to as keenly, not least for clues as to the future direction of Bush's foreign policy. While acknowledging 'Islam's own rich history', and committing America to the reconstruction of Afghanistan, Bush focused on the 'unprecedented dangers' facing the country. His two 'great objectives' were, he explained, to 'shut down terrorist camps, disrupt terrorist plans, and bring terrorists to justice', and to 'prevent the terrorists and regimes who seek chemical, biological or nuclear weapons from threatening the United States and the world'. Three countries, North Korea, Iran, and, in particular, Iraq, which 'has something to hide from the civilized world', posed just such a threat. 'States like these and their terrorist allies', he held, 'constitute an axis of evil, arming to threaten the peace of the world.' The critical lesson for Americans of the 11 September attacks was that they were 'no longer protected by vast oceans'. It was not reassuring, nor, in the circumstances, could it have been.

CONCLUSION

At the end of the Second World War the United States chose to embrace the world rather then return to the isolationism more typical of and familiar to the young nation. The bond was fragile and risked being torn asunder by those opposed to the concept of entangling alliances. Nevertheless, by the late 1940s, developments in international affairs meant that this battle had been all but won.

By the summer of 1947, with the articulation of the Truman Doctrine, the emerging policy of containment, and the implementation of the Marshall Plan, America was fast locking herself into the affairs of Europe and beyond. The Rio Treaty foreshadowed the NATO alliance two years later. The formation of the Cominform confirmed the ideological edge to what was happening. Stalin's desire for a defensive perimeter was understood, but the brutal manner of its achievement was not appreciated. The United States had not gone to war with one European dictator to see another expand his power. The analogy with Munich was ever-present. Most Americans would have agreed with the view of the much-respected Senator George Mitchell in 1999, that they were citizens of 'the most open, the most free, the most just society in human history' (Mitchell, 1999). Commitment to western Europe made moral, as well as political, economic and strategic sense, and, given the collapse of British, French and German power, was probably inevitable. Leadership of the western world led the country into uncharted waters. The National Security Act of 1947, which set in place the National Security Council, Central Intelligence Agency and Department of Defense, created mechanisms for the waging of a new kind of warfare. Given America's towering economic lead over her rival, perhaps there was only ever one likely outcome, but that was not always how it seemed. Rearmament on a vast scale, signposted by NSC 68 and affirmed by the Korean War, characterised the American response. The Cold War was fought on a number of fronts, and in a variety of ways, but fought it was. If that meant that the leader of the 'free world' gave her support to a variety of anti-communist regimes where democracy was little more than a thin veneer, then policymakers were prepared to do so. This was not without its dangers.

Another striking facet of post-Second World War American foreign policy was the failure of successive administrations to realign policy away from Europe. Despite the fact that almost every president recognised the importance of Africa, Asia and Latin America, none proved able or perhaps willing to forego Europe's embrace for the Third World. Several indulged in covert action in a bid to alter the balance of power in countries considered to have strategic value for the United States; many attempted (with varying degrees of success) to bring peace to the Middle East; all pursued proxy wars on each of the three continents and poured assistance of all kinds into key regions such as Southeast Asia, central Africa, the Middle East and the Caribbean. However, as long as Moscow remained the focus, Europe remained the key.

Driven by a fear of communism, the United States fought two wars in Asia – in Korea where, months before, Acheson had identified no strategic interest and in Vietnam, where a civil conflict rooted in anti-colonialism compelled an American commitment in order to prevent the realisation of the Domino Theory. America's experience in Vietnam marked the country and its people in countless ways. Involvement, beginning with aiding the

Vietnamese nationalist leader Ho Chi Minh during the Second World War ended with the re-establishment of trade relations at the end of the 1990s. A bitter, devastating and ultimately unwinnable war filled much of the decades in between. Its legacy was such that presidents such as George Bush Sr felt the need to claim, after the Gulf War, that the 'Vietnam Syndrome' had been defeated once and for all. Few believe this to be the case. Fear of casualties and media-shaped public opinion infused policy-making at its highest levels.

It is interesting that despite the almost pathological fear of communism, the United States never relinquished the idea of a relationship with China – a country traditionally viewed as a possible partner, even after her shocking 'fall' to communism in 1949. After just over 20 years of hostility and proxy confrontation, Nixon reached out again. Not with-standing ideological differences, the lack of democracy and abundant human rights abuses, successive administrations attempted to 'do business' with the populous and closed country during the Cold War and after the collapse of communism in Europe. Unlike China, one of the other last remaining communist enclaves, Cuba, found successive administrations unwilling to stand down after decades of unfettered hostility. Too close, controversial and provoca-tive, Cuba possessed none of the economic attractiveness of China. It was also the stage for the closest the two superpow-ers came to unleashing nuclear war on the world. The Cuban Missile Crisis was, undeniably, adeptly handled by JFK. To what extent was the crisis a self-made one? America's relationship with Cuba often appeared to operate outside the realms of good judgement and, one might argue, basic common sense. Fortunately, few countries got under American leaders' skins as did the tiny Caribbean island.

One of the factors underpinning the desire to seek coop-eration with China was the preoccupation with economic stability and growth. A fundamental part of the Cold War for successive presidents was building and maintaining a healthy economy capable of sustaining the American war effort and outlasting the Soviet Union. Defence spending certainly rose steadily throughout the Cold War, although some presidents such as Eisenhower attempted to keep spending down to levels lower than those approved by his successor. Apart from Johnson's increasingly unpopular Vietnam spending and Reagan's massive increases, however, presidents tended to come in for criticism from all sides on this issue. For many, the amounts allocated for defence were too large, for others, government spending was too conservative.

Perhaps this had something to do with the nature of defence after 1945. Nuclear weapons and the many strategies surrounding their use were complex. Each administration attempted to reconstruct America's defence based on their understanding of how best to employ this force. Likewise, another theme evident throughout the period is that of arms control, disarmament and nuclear proliferation. After the Cold War, the immediate and obvious threat of deliberate nuclear war between the superpowers quickly receded, only to be replaced by new threats such as nuclear strikes unleashed by 'rogue states' or terrorist attacks armed with nuclear, chemical, bacteriological or biological weapons.

The end of the Cold War cannot be charted with certainty or precision. There was no equivalent of General MacArthur on the *USS Missouri* dictating the terms of surrender. Simply put, the United States had outlasted the Soviet Union as some, like Eisenhower, always believed would be the case. The United States and her alliance system had survived over four decades of confrontation, while her rival imploded with unforeseen speed. The Cuban Missile Crisis may be seen as a turning point, since Kennedy's success pushed the Soviet leaders into a drive for nuclear parity which was ultimately unsustainable. By the early 1980s, the Soviet Union could barely meet the costs of supporting her east European allies, maintaining nuclear parity, while conducting war in Afghanistan. Once the Americans gave effective aid to the

Afghan mujahedin, confirming that this had become their Soviet Vietnam, the process of imperial retreat began. That the Americans could even give serious consideration to the Strategic Defense Initiative confirmed that Moscow had lost the arms race. Mikhail Gorbachev drew the obvious conclusions. That he wished to save and revive the Soviet system is not in doubt, and many Americans feared the consequences if he could do so, but it was too late.

With the unexpectedly sudden end of the Cold War came a brief period of heightened expectations, expressed in George Bush Sr's 'New World Order'. Many of the issues such as the environment, poverty, disease and drugs – global problems with implications for all countries that had largely been subsumed by the Cold War – emphasis on national security and defence now moved closer to the top of policy-making concerns. Domestic and foreign policy often seemed indistinguishable. For policy-makers though, the disintegration of a clearly identifiable enemy ushered in a new period of uncertainty, and readjustment. The post-Cold War world was a more dangerous and less predictable place where potential threats were ubiquitous and the rules appeared to have changed. In the 1990s the United States attempted to redefine her place in the world. Politicians, the public and the media questioned the nature of future American involvement, what cost was acceptable (both in terms of financial expenditure and lives lost), and what issues were important.

What made this re-evaluation more complex was the process of realignment in the balance of power between the Legislative and Executive branches. Fuelled by the abrupt disappearance of the rationale that saw Congress largely deferring foreign policy responsibility to the president out of a need for speed and secrecy, Congress, during the Clinton period, reasserted itself to an unprecedented degree, challenging, criticising and blocking presidential decisions and policy. This, too, coincided with a process ongoing since the watershed of the early 1970s which culminated in the emergence of media and interest groups less deferential to the

Chief of State and more inclined to pursue an independent agenda. Presidential power has certainly been constrained by external developments as well as the men who have occupied this position of power. Personality is crucial. The 11 presidents since 1945 shaped and were shaped by the office. Nine faced largely similar threats and fought the Cold War in ways that both reflected their personal views and accommodated the accepted wisdom of their contemporaries. The last president of the twentieth century, William Jefferson Clinton, the first truly post-Cold War president, knew no such reassuring familiarity. Perhaps his ultimate inability to carve out a new, strong, admirable foreign policy for the United States arose because of his failure and that of his team to fully grasp the enormity of the changes, as well as the less visible continuity in the world which he faced. George W. Bush's electoral success in November 2000 won him the right to shape America's foreign policy in the twenty-first century.

Like his predecessor, Harry Truman, George W. Bush took control of the world's sole superpower at a time of great change and uncertainty. Fifty-five years apart, they both identified Asia as America's primary national security threat: Truman used atomic weapons to bring the Second World War to an end there, while Bush feared that China had aspirations of becoming the world's second superpower and 'states of concern', formally 'rogue states', such as North Korea, might be tempted to launch a nuclear strike against the US. Just as Truman placed his trust in the new technology that produced atomic and hydrogen bombs, Bush put his faith in the developmental National Missile Defense System – 'Son of Star Wars' – a space-based nuclear missile umbrella designed to intercept and destroy a strike against the United States. Within a few short years of taking office, Truman was facing a Cold War conflict where issues of national security and cultural and economic supremacy were of paramount importance. Bush, too, entered a war less than eight months after assuming the presidency. America's 'war against terrorism' launched after the attacks of 11 September pitted the deeply shaken country against an enemy as menacing as the communist threat 55 years before. In choosing to confront what they perceived as a fundamental threat to the national security of the United States, Truman and Bush charted a new course for their country, one that deflected, for a time, difficult questions about America's connection to the troubles confronting the nation.

BIBLIOGRAPHY

The authors are conscious of the fact that a bibliography on a subject as important and wide-ranging as post-war American foreign policy can at best be partial. What we have included here are volumes cited in the text, or which have been particularly useful.

Acheson, Dean, *Present at the Creation* (New York, 1969).

Adams, Sherman, *First Hand Report* (London, 1962).

Aldrich, Richard J., *The Hidden Hand. Britain, America and Cold War Secret Intelligence* (London, 2001).

Allison, G. and Zelikow, P., *Essence of Decision: Explaining the Cuban Missile Crisis* (New York, 1999).

Ambrose, Stephen E., *Eisenhower*, Vol. 2: *The President* (New York, 1984).

Ambrose, Stephen E., *Nixon: The Education of a Politician, 1913–1962* (New York, 1987).

Ambrose, Stephen E., *Nixon: The Triumph of a Politician, 1962–1972* (New York, 1989).

Ambrose, Stephen E., *Nixon: Ruin and Recovery, 1973–1990* (New York, 1991).

Andrew, C., *For the President's Eyes Only* (London, 1996).

Anon. (ed.): *Realism, Strength, Negotiation: Key Foreign Policy Statements of the Reagan Administration* (Washington, 1984).

Applemas Williams, W., McCormick, T., Gardner, L. and LaFeber, W. (eds), *America in Vietnam: A Documentary History* (New York, 1985).

Ball, George, *Diplomacy for a Crowded World* (London, 1976).

Beschloss, Michael R., *Kennedy v. Kruschchev: The Crisis Years, 1960–63* (London, 1991).

Beschloss, Michael R., *Taking Charge: The Johnson White House Tapes, 1963–64* (New York, 1997).

Bill, James A., *George Ball: Behind the Scenes in US Foreign Policy* (New Haven, 1997).

Billings-Yun, N., *Decision Against War: Eisenhower and Dien Bien Phu, 1954* (New York, 1988).

Bird, K., *The Color of Truth. McGeorge Bundy and William Bundy: Brothers in Arms* (New York, 1998).

Bischof, G. and Ambrose, S., *Eisenhower: A Centenary Assessment* (Baton Rouge, 1995).

Bissell, R., *Reflections of a Cold Warrior: From Yalta to the Bay of Pigs* (New Haven, 1996).

Blight, James G., *The Shattered Crystal Ball: Fear and Learning in the Cuban Missile Crisis* (Lanham, 1992).

Bohlen, Charles E., *The Transformation of American Foreign Policy* (New York, 1969).

Bose, M., *Shaping and Signalling Presidential Policy: The National Security Decision Making of Eisenhower and Kennedy* (College Station, 1998).

Bowie, R. and Immerman, R. H., *Waging Peace: How Eisenhower Shaped an Enduring Cold War Strategy* (Oxford, 1998).

Brandon, H., *Special Relationships* (London, 1988).

Briggs, Philip J., *Making American Foreign Policy* (Lanham, 1994).

Brogan, H., *Kennedy* (London, 1996).

Brzezinski, Zbigniew, *Power and Principle* (New York, 1983).

Buhite, R. D., *Major Crises in Contemporary American Foreign Policy* (Westport, 1997).

Bundy, William, *A Tangled Web. The Making of Foreign Policy in the Nixon Presidency* (London, 1998).

Burleigh, Michael, *The Third Reich. A New History* (London, 2000).

Burr, William (ed.), *The Kissinger Transcripts* (New York, 1999).

Bush, George and Scowcroft, Brent, *A World Transformed* (New York, 1998).

Byrnes, James F., *Speaking Frankly* (London, 1947).

Calvocoressi, Peter, *Survey of International Affairs 1947–1948* (London, 1952).

Caro, Robert A., *The Years of Lyndon Johnson*, Vol. 2: *Means of Ascent* (New York, 1991).

Carter, Jimmy, *Keeping Faith. Memoirs of a President* (London, 1982).

Chace, James, *Acheson* (New York, 1998).

Bibliography

Chambers II, John Whiteclay, *The Oxford Companion to American Military History* (Oxford, 1999).

Chang, L. and Kornbluth, K. (eds), *The Cuban Missile Crisis 1962. National Security Archive Documents* (New York, 1998).

Christopher, Warren, *Chances of a Lifetime* (New York, 2001).

Clifford, Clark, with Holbrooke, Richard, *Counsel to the President* (New York, 1991).

Clinton, William Jefferson, *Between Hope and History* (New York, 1996).

Clubb, O. Edmund, *Twentieth Century China* (New York, 1964).

Cohen, W. I., *The Cambridge History of American Foreign Relations*, Vol. IV (New York, 1996).

Copeland, Miles, *The Game of Nations* (London, 1969).

Crampton, R. J., *Eastern Europe in the Twentieth Century* (London, 1994).

Crockatt, Richard, *The Fifty Years War. The United States and the Soviet Union in World Politics, 1941–1991* (London, 1995).

Cyr, Arthur I., *After the Cold War* (Basingstoke, 1997).

Dallek, Robert, *Franklin Roosevelt and American Foreign Policy 1932–1945* (Oxford, 1979).

Dallek, Robert, *Flawed Giant: Lyndon Johnson and His Times, 1961–1973* (Oxford, 1998).

Divine, R., *The Sputnik Challenge* (Oxford, 1993).

Divine, R., *The Johnson Years*, Vol. 3, *LBJ at Home and Abroad* (Lawrence, 1994).

Dockrill, S., *Eisenhower's New Look National Security Policy, 1953–1961* (Basingstoke, 1996).

Drew, Elizabeth, *On The Edge. The Clinton Presidency* (New York, 1994).

Drew, Elizabeth, *Show Down: The Struggle between the Gingrich Congress and the Clinton White House* (New York, 1996).

Dumbrell, J., *The Carter Presidency. A Re-evaluation* (Manchester, 1995).

Dumbrell, J., *American Foreign Policy: Carter to Clinton* (London, 1997).

Eisenberg, Carolyn, *Drawing the Line. The American Decision to Divide Germany, 1944–1949* (Cambridge, 1996).

Eisenhower, Dwight D., *Mandate for Change* (New York, 1963).

Eisenhower, Dwight D., *Waging Peace* (New York, 1965).

Feis, Herbert, *From Trust to Terror. The Onset of the Cold War 1945–1950* (London, 1970).

Fraser, T. G., *The USA and the Middle East since World War 2* (London, 1989).

Fraser, T. G., *The Arab–Israeli Conflict* (Basingstoke, 1995).

Freedman, L., *Kennedy's Wars: Berlin, Cuba, Laos and Vietnam* (Oxford, 2000).

Fulbright, J. William, *The Arrogance of Power* (London, 1967).

Fursenko, A. and Naftali, T., *One Hell of a Gamble: Kruschchev, Castro and Kennedy, 1958–1964* (New York, 1997).

Gaddis, John Lewis, *The United States and the Origins of the Cold War* (New York, 1972).

Gaddis, John Lewis, *Strategies of Containment: A Critical Appraisal of Postwar American National Security Policy* (New York, 1982).

Gaddis, John Lewis, *The Long Peace. Inquiries into the History of the Cold War* (New York, 1987).

Gaddis, John Lewis, *We Now Know. Rethinking Cold War History* (Oxford, 1997).

Gardner, Lloyd C., *Pay any Price: Lyndon Johnson and the Wars for Vietnam* (Chicago, 1995).

Gardner, Lloyd C., *Approaching Vietnam: From World War Through Dien Bien Phu* (New York, 1988).

Garthoff, Raymond L., *Reflections on the Cuban Missile Crisis* (Washington, 1989).

Gates, Robert M., *From the Shadows* (New York, 1996).

Glenny, M., *The Balkans 1804–1999: Nationalism, War and the Great Powers* (London, 1999).

Golan, Matti, *The Secret Conversations of Henry Kissinger* (New York, 1976).

Goodwin, Doris Kearns, *Lyndon Johnson and the American Dream* (New York, 1991).

Goold-Adams, R., *The Time of Power: A Reappraisal of John Foster Dulles* (London, 1962).

Greenstein, F., *The Hidden-Handed Presidency: Eisenhower as Leader* (Baltimore, 1994).

Gromyko, Andrei, *Memories. From Stalin to Gorbachev* (London, 1989).

Haig, Alexander M., *Caveat: Realism, Reagan, and Foreign Policy* (New York, 1984).

Halberstam, D., *The Best and the Brightest* (New York, 1992).

Halberstam, D., *War in a Time of Peace* (New York, 2001).

Haldeman, H. R. *The Haldeman Diaries: Inside the Nixon White House* (New York, 1994).

Bibliography

Halle, Louis J., *The Cold War as History* (London, 1967).

Hamby, Alonzo L., *Man of the People. A Life of Harry S. Truman* (Oxford, 1995).

Herring, George C., *The Pentagon Papers* (New York, 1993).

Herring, George C., *LBJ and Vietnam* (Austin, 1995).

Herring, George C., *America's Longest War: the United States and Vietnam, 1950–1975* (New York, 1996).

Higgins, T., *The Perfect Failure: Kennedy, Eisenhower and the CIA at the Bay of Pigs* (New York, 1987).

Holbrooke, Richard, *To End a War* (New York, 1999).

Humphrey, Hubert H., *The Education of a Public Man* (New York, 1976).

Hurd, Douglas, *The Search for Peace* (London, 1997).

Hurst, Steven, *The Foreign Policy of the Bush Administration* (London, 1999).

Hyland, William, *Clinton's World: Remaking American Foreign Policy* (Westport, 1999).

Immerman, R. H., *John Foster Dulles and the Diplomacy of the Cold War* (Princeton, 1990).

Isaacs, J. and Downing, T., *The Cold War* (London, 1998).

Isaacson, Walter, *Kissinger: A Biography* (New York, 1992).

Isaacson, Walter, and Thomas, Evan, *The Wise Men: Six Friends and the World They Made: Acheson, Bohlen, Harriman, Kennan, Lovett, McCloy* (New York, 1986).

Jensen, Kenneth M. (ed.), *Origins of the Cold War. The Novikov, Kennan, and Roberts 'Long Telegrams' of 1946* (Washington, 1993).

Johnson, Loch K., *America as a World Power* (New York, 1995).

Johnson, Lyndon Baines, *The Vantage Point: Perspectives of the Presidency, 1963–69* (New York, 1971).

Kaiser, D., *American Tragedy: Kennedy, Johnson and the Origin of the Vietnam War* (Cambridge, MA, 2000).

Karnow, S., *Vietnam. A History* (London, 1991).

Kearns Godwin, Doris, *Lyndon Johnson and the American Dream* (New York, 1991).

Kennan, George F., *American Diplomacy 1900–1950* (Chicago, 1951).

Kennan, George F., *Memoirs 1925–1950* (Boston, 1967).

Kennan, George F., *Memoirs 1950–1963* (Boston, 1972).

Kennedy, R. F., *13 Days: The Cuban Missile Crisis* (London, 1969).

Bibliography

Kissinger, Henry A., *White House Years* (Boston, 1979).

Kissinger, Henry A., *Years of Upheaval* (Boston, 1982).

Kissinger, Henry A., *Years of Renewal* (London, 1999).

Korchilov, Igor, *Translating History* (London 1997).

Kyle, Keith, *Suez* (London, 1991).

La Feber, Walter, *America, Russia and the Cold War* (New York, 1993).

Leffler, Melvyn P. and Painter, David S. (eds), *Origins of the Cold War. An International History* (London, 1994).

Lowe, Peter, *The Origins of the Korean War* (Harlow, 1997).

Lucas, W. Scott, *Divided we Stand. Britain, the US and the Suez Crisis* (London, 1991).

Lucas, W. Scott, *Freedom's War. The US Crusade against the Soviet Union 1945–56* (Manchester, 1999).

MacKinnon, Michael G., *The Evolution of US Peacekeeping Policy under Clinton* (London, 2000).

McCauley, M. *The Origins of the Cold War, 1941–1949* (Harlow, 1995).

McCormick, T. J., *America's Half-Century* (Baltimore, 1995).

McGee, G., *Envoy to the Middle World: Adventures in Diplomacy* (New York, 1983).

McMaster, R. H., *Dereliction of Duty: Lyndon Johnson, Robert McNamara, the Joint Chiefs of Staff and the Lies that led to Vietnam* (New York, 1998).

McNamara, Robert S., *Argument Without End: In Search of Answers to the Vietnam Tragedy* (New York, 1999).

McNamara, Robert S., with VanDeMark, Brian, *In Retrospect. The Tragedy and Lessons of Vietnam* (New York, 1995).

Mahoney, R. D., *Sons and Brothers: The Days of Jack and Bobby Kennedy* (New York, 1999).

May, Ernest R. (ed.), *American Cold War Strategy. Interpreting NSC 68* (Boston, 1993).

May, Ernest R. and Zelikow, P. (eds), *The Kennedy Tapes* (Cambridge, MA, 1997).

Melanson, R. A., *American Foreign Policy Since The Vietnam War: the Search for Consensus from Nixon to Clinton* (New York, 1996).

Melvern, L. R., *A People Betrayed: The Role of the West in Rwanda's Genocide* (New York, 2000).

Meyer, M. S., *The Eisenhower Presidency and the 1950s* (Boston, 1998).

Millis, Walter (ed.), *The Forrestal Diaries* (New York, 1951).

Miscamble, Wilson D., *George F. Kennan and the Making of American Foreign Policy 1947–1950* (Princeton, 1992).

Mitchell, George, *Making Peace* (London, 1999).

Morris, Dick, *Behind the Oval Office* (New York, 1998).

Murray, Donette, *Kennedy, Macmillan and Nuclear Weapons* (London, 2000).

Nitze, Paul H., *From Hiroshima to Glasnost: At the Center of Decision* (New York, 1989).

Nixon, Richard M., *RN: The Memoirs of Richard Nixon* (New York, 1978).

Nixon, Richard M., *No More Vietnams* (New York, 1985).

O'Cleary, Conor, *The Greening of the White House* (Dublin, 1997).

O'Donnell, K. P. and Powers, D. F., *Johnny, We Hardly Knew Ye* (Boston, 1972).

Oliver, K., *Kennedy, Macmillan and the Nuclear Test-Ban Debate, 1961–1963* (Basingstoke, 1998).

Paterson, T. G. (ed.), *Kennedy's Quest for Victory* (New York, 1989).

Paterson, Thomas G. and McMahon, Robert J., *The Origins of the Cold War* (Lexington, 1991).

Pearson, Raymond, *The Rise and Fall of the Soviet Empire* (Basingstoke, 2002).

Pickett, W.B., *Dwight David Eisenhower and American Power* (Wheeling, 1995).

Quandt, William B., *Camp David. Peacemaking and Politics* (Washington, 1986).

Quandt, William B., *Peace Process. American Diplomacy and the Arab–Israeli Conflict since 1967* (Washington and Berkeley, 1993).

Rabe, S., *Eisenhower and Latin America* (Chapel Hill, 1988).

Rabe, S., *The Most Dangerous Area in the World* (Chapel Hill, 1999).

Randall, B. and Woods, J., *J. William Fulbright, Vietnam and the Search for a Cold War Foreign Policy* (Cambridge, 1998).

Reagan, Ronald, *An American Life* (New York, 1990).

Reeves, R., *President Kennedy: Profile of Power* (New York, 1994).

Reich, Robert, *Locked in the Cabinet* (New York, 1997).

Roosevelt, Kermit, *Countercoup* (New York, 1979).

Rostow, W., *The Diffusion of Power* (New York, 1972).

Rubinstein, A. Z., Shayevich, A. and Zlotnikov, B. (eds), *The Clinton Foreign Policy Reader* (New York, 2000).

Rusk, Dean, with Rusk, R. and Papp, D. S., *As I Saw It* (New York, 1990).

Saikal, Amin, *The Rise and Fall of the Shah* (Princeton, 1980).

Salinger, P., *With Kennedy* (New York, 1966).

Schlesinger, Arthur M., *A Thousand Days: John F. Kennedy in the White House* (Boston, 1965).

Schlesinger, Arthur M., *The Imperial Presidency* (New York, 1974).

Schmertz, Eric J., Datlof, Natalie and Ugrinsky, Alexej (eds), *President Reagan and the World* (Westport, 1997).

Schoenbaum, Thomas J., *Waging Peace and War. Dean Rusk in the Truman, Kennedy and Johnson Years* (New York, 1988).

Schrecker, E., *Many Are the Crimes: McCarthyism in America* (Toronto, 1998).

Schultz, Richard H., *The Secret War Against Hanoi* (New York, 1999).

Schwarzkopf, H. Norman, *It Doesn't Take a Hero* (New York, 1992).

Shacochis, B., *The Immaculate Invasion* (London, 1999).

Shamir, Yitzhak, *Summing Up* (London, 1994).

Shawcross, William, *Sideshow. Kissinger, Nixon and the Destruction of Cambodia* (New York, 1979).

Shawcross, William, *Deliver Us From Evil: Warlords and Peacekeepers in a World of Endless Conflict* (London, 2001).

Sheehan, M., *A Bright Shining Lie* (London, 1976).

Shultz, George P., *Turmoil and Triumph* (New York, 1993).

Sick, Gary, *All Fall Down. America's Fateful Encounter with Iran* (London, 1985).

Smith, Dennis B., *Japan since 1945. The Rise of an Economic Superpower* (Basingstoke, 1995).

Snead, D. L., *The Gaither Committee: Eisenhower and the Cold War* (Columbus, 1999).

Sorenson, T., *Kennedy* (London, 1965).

Spanier, John, *American Foreign Policy since World War II* (New York, 1985).

Spanier, John and Uslaner, Eric M., *How American Foreign Policy Is Made* (New York, 1975).

Stebbins, Richard P. and Adam, Elaine P., *American Foreign Relations 1971. A Documentary Record* (New York, 1976a).

Stebbins, Richard P. and Adam, Elaine P., *American Foreign Relations 1972. A Documentary Record* (New York, 1976b).

Stebbins, Richard P. and Adam, Elaine P., *American Foreign Relations 1973. A Documentary Record* (New York, 1976c).

Stebbins, Richard P. and Adam, Elaine P., *American Foreign Relations 1974. A Documentary Record* (New York, 1977a).

Bibliography

Stebbins, Richard P. and Adam, Elaine P., *American Foreign Relations 1975. A Documentary Record* (New York, 1977b).

Stephanopoulos, G., *All Too Human: A Political Education* (Boston, 2000).

Sullivan, William H., *Mission to Iran* (New York, 1981).

Thatcher, Margaret, *The Downing Street Years* (London, 1993).

Truman, Harry S., *Memoirs*, Vol. 1, *Year of Decisions* (New York, 1955).

Truman, Harry S., *Memoirs*, Vol. 2, *Years of Trial and Hope* (New York, 1956).

Vance, Cyrus, *Hard Choices* (New York, 1983).

Vandiver, Frank E., *Shadows of Vietnam* (College Station, 1997).

Volkogonov, D. A., *Stalin: Triumph and Tragedy* (London, 1991).

Weinberger, Caspar, *Fighting for Peace* (New York, 1990).

White, Mark J., *The Cuban Missile Crisis* (Basingstoke, 1996).

White, Mark J., *Kennedy: The New Frontier Revisited* (Basingstoke, 1998).

White, Mark J., *The Kennedys and Cuba: The Declassified Documentary History* (Chicago, 1999).

Wicker, Tom., *J.F.K. and L.B.J.: The Influence of Personality upon Politics* (Chicago, 1991).

Wilson, A. J., *Irish America and the Ulster Conflict, 1968–1995* (Belfast, 1995).

Winand, P., *Eisenhower, Kennedy and the United States of Europe* (London, 1993).

Woods, Randall B., *J. William Fulbright, Vietnam and the Search for a Cold War Foreign Policy* (Cambridge, 1998).

Woodward, Bob, *The Commanders* (London, 1991).

Wyden, P., *The Bay of Pigs: The Untold Story* (New York, 1979).

INDEX

Index

Bush, George W., 305–6
  administration, 294–5
  'axis of evil' speech, 299
  terrorist attacks on New York
      and Washington and,
      297–8
  unilateralism, 295–6
Byrnes, James, 9, 18–19, 23

Cabral, Donald Reid y, 130
Cambodia, 151–2, 147–60, 183
Camp David summit (1978),
    196–8, 211, 217–18
Camp David summit (2000), 291
Canada, 271
Carroll, Paul T., 53
Carter, Jimmy, 6, 212, 217, 245,
    267
  administration, 187–8
  Afghanistan, 207–9, 211
  arms limitation, 200–3
  Carter Doctrine, 208
  China policy, 198–200
  human rights, 189, 201, 214
  Iranian crisis, 203–7, 209–11
  Panama negotiations, 192–4,
      199, 202
  Camp David agreements,
      194–8, 211
  relations with USSR, 190–2
Casey, William, 214
Castro, Fidel, 82–3, 88, 91–4, 107,
    111
Ceausescu, Nicolai, 195, 244
Cedras, Raul, 266–7.
Central Intelligence Agency, 30,
    66–7, 72–3, 83–4, 88, 91–4,
    107–9, 134, 135–6, 146, 156,
    189, 203, 209, 214, 222, 232,
    260–1, 283–4, 301
Chamberlain, Neville, 19, 120, 172
Chechnya, 278–9
Cheney, Dick, 295
Chernenko, Konstantin, 215, 228,
    240
Chernobyl disaster, 230
Chiang Kai-shek, 3, 32–3, 49, 64–6
Chile, 156, 273

China, 2–3, 32–4, 38, 43, 47–50,
    56, 60–1, 64–6, 81, 113, 145,
    160–3, 190, 198–200, 241–2,
    273–5, 281, 296–7, 302
Chou En-lai, 63, 160–3, 199
Christopher, Warren, 260, 267–8,
    288
Churchill, Winston S., 2, 10, 14,
    16, 21
Clayton, William L., 25, 27.
Clifford, Clark, 23, 36, 137
Clinton, Hillary Rodham, 258
Clinton, William J., 4, 6–7, 256,
    304–5
  administration, 257–62
  Asian policies, 273–6
  Bosnia, 267–71
  Haiti, 266–7
  Kosovo, 284–7
  Middle East peace process,
      287–91
  Northern Ireland peace
      process, 291–3
  relations with Russia, 276–80
  Rwandan crisis, 264–5
  trade expansion, 271–3
  weapons of mass destruction,
      280–4
Cold War, 4, 6, 29–31, 52, 55, 57,
    68, 70, 89, 107, 114, 118,
    228, 237, 241, 259, 267, 278,
    286, 295, 302–3
Cominform, 29, 41
Commonwealth of Independent
    States, 255
Conference on Security and
    Cooperation in Europe, 186,
    278
Congo, 106
containment, 27–8, 44–5, 50, 56,
    58, 184, 215
Croatia, 268–70
Cronkite, Walter, 140–1
Cuba, 12, 82–3, 88, 91, 107–112,
    202, 227–8, 302
Cuban Missile Crisis, 5, 107–112,
    146, 156, 302–3
Cutler, Robert, 53

318

Index

Czech Republic, 279–80
Czechoslovakia, 39, 73, 142, 146, 150, 243–4

Dayton agreement, 270–1
De Gaulle, Charles, 101, 150–1
Deng Xiaoping, 199–200, 242
DeSoto missions, 123–4, 127
détente, 148–51, 163–5, 181, 208, 213
Diem Ngo Dinh, 63–4, 115–17, 121
Dominican Republic, 107, 130–2
Dukakis, Michael, 238
Dulles, Allen, 53, 58–9, 83, 88, 93
Dulles, John Foster, 52–3, 65, 73, 79, 86, 162

Eden, Anthony, 74
Egypt, 73–5, 80, 138, 147, 174–9, 184–5, 195–8, 218, 248, 251, 253
Eisenhower, Dwight D., 7, 87, 91, 112, 147, 150, 184, 303
 administration, 51–4
 Berlin crisis, 82
 Cuba, 82–3
 disarmament, 70–1, 76–7, 84–6
 Eisenhower Doctrine, 75
 intelligence and covert operations, 66–70
 Korean War, 60–1
 Lebanese crisis,79–81
 missile development, 77–9
 Polish and Hungarian crises, 71–2
 Project Solarium and New Look, 56–8
 South-east Asia, 61–4
 Suez Crisis, 72–5
 Taiwan crises, 64–6, 81
 Third World, 75–6
Elsey, George, 23
European Defence Community, 58

Ford, Gerald, 187, 190, 192–3, 211
 administration, 180–1
 Helsinki conference, 186

Middle East, 184–5
Vietnam, 182–4
Vladivostok summit, 182
Formosa Doctrine, 65
Forrestal, James, 29
France, 9–10, 42, 50, 58–60, 61–3, 69, 101–2, 106, 113, 147, 150–1, 167, 182, 220, 223, 251, 254, 281, 300
Fulbright, J. William, 135, 149

Gaddafi, Muammar, 234–5
Gaither Report, 78
Gates, Robert, 236–7, 238
Gemayel, Bashir, 221
Geneva agreement (1954), 63
Geneva summit (1985), 229
Germany, 10, 16–17, 26, 28, 39–42, 58, 70, 94–5, 98–101, 150, 224, 228, 243–8, 251, 300
Gilpatrick, Roswell, 114
Giuliani, Rudolph, 298
Glaspie, April, 248–9
Goldwater, Barry, 126–7
Gomulka, Wladyslaw, 71
Goodpaster, Andrew J., 53
Gorbachev, Mikhail, 229–31, 233–4, 236–7, 239–40, 243–5, 246–7, 251, 254–6, 303
Gottwald, Klement, 39
Greece, 24–5, 217, 267
Grenada, 227–8
Gromyko, Andrei, 150, 192, 227–9
Guatemala, 68–70, 91
Guzman, Jacobo Arbenz, 68–9

Habib, Philip, 218, 220
Haig, Alexander, 214–5, 218–9
Haiti, 258, 266–7
Helsinki conference, 186
Henderson, Loy W., 36
Hiss, Alger, 52
Ho Chi Minh, 9, 50, 135, 154, 302
Holbrooke, Richard, 270–1, 285–6
Honecker, Erich, 243–4
Hua Guofeng, 199–200
Hull, Cordell, 3

Index

McGovern, George, 170
McMahon Act, 11
Macmillan, Harold, 74, 101–2
McNamara, Robert, 88, 117, 121, 123, 125–6, 134, 147
Madrid conference, 256
Malta summit, 244–5
Mao Tse-tung, 32–3, 42, 162–3, 199–200
Marshall, George C., 23, 25–7, 29, 32
Marshall Plan, 25–7, 51, 300
Masaryk, Jan, 39
Mexico, 271–3
Milosevic, Slobodan, 270, 284–7
missiles, 76–7, 85–5, 112–14, 146–7, 163–7, 181–2, 190–2, 200–3, 213, 224–31, 233–4, 278
Mitchell, George, 292, 300
Molotov, V. M., 15, 18, 26
Monroe Doctrine, 12
Mossadegh, Mohammed, 67
Mujahedin, 209, 215, 233, 303
Munich Agreement, 19, 47, 300

Nagy, Imre, 71–2, 240
Nasser, Gamal Abdul, 73–5, 80, 104, 137–8, 155–6
National Liberation Front, 64
National Security Act, 29, 300–1
National Security Agency, 30, 124
National Security Council, 29, 43–5, 53, 94, 205, 232, 301
Netanyahu, Benjamin, 289–90
New Look, 56–7, 66.
Nicaragua, 232
Niles, David, 36
Nitze, Paul, 179–80, 225, 230
Nixon, Richard, M., 6, 50, 52, 87, 143, 144, 182, 187–8, 190, 192, 203, 211
  administration, 147–8
  Cambodia, 151–2, 157–60
  Chile, 156
  China, 160–3, 19.9
  détente, 148–51, 163–5, 172–3

Middle East crises, 154–6, 174–9
Nixon Doctrine, 153, 203
relations with USSR, 146–7, 163–7
Vietnam War, 144–6, 150–4, 157–60, 168–72
Watergate, 144, 172–3, 174–5, 179–80
North American Free Trade Agreement, 271–3
North Atlantic Treaty Organization, 30, 41–2, 44, 51, 54, 58–9, 70, 101–2, 146, 150, 164, 217, 224, 238, 247, 269, 271, 277–80, 284–7, 298, 300
Noriega, Manuel, 245–6
Northern Ireland, 291–3
Norway, 288
'NSC 68', 43–5, 301
'NSC 162', 57

Okinawa, 35, 49
Oppenheimer, J. Robert, 43
Organization for Security and Cooperation in Europe, 285
Organization of American States, 68, 131–2
Oslo accords, 288–9

Pahlavi, Mohammed Reza, 67, 203–7, 210
Pakistan, 165
Palestine, 23, 35–8
Palestine Liberation Organization, 185, 218–21, 235–6, 288
Palestinian Authority, 290
Palestinians, 194–7, 219, 235–6, 288–91
Panama, 12, 192–4, 199, 202, 245–6
Paris Agreement, 171–2, 182–3
Peace Corps, 105
Peres, Shimon, 288–9
Pham Van Dong, 154
Philippines, 34, 37, 50
Pinochet, Augusto, 156

321

Index

Index

CPSIA information can be obtained
at www.ICGtesting.com
Printed in the USA
LVOW03s2354231217
560660LV00003BA/288/P